A SOCIAL HISTORY

CASS SERIES: BRITISH POLITICS AND SOCIETY
Series Editor: Peter Catterall
ISSN: 1467-1441

Social change impacts not just upon voting behaviour and party identity but also the formulation of policy. But how do social changes and political developments interact? Which shapes which? Reflecting a belief that social and political structures cannot be understood either in isolation from each other or from the historical processes which form them, this series will examine the forces that have shaped British society. Cross-disciplinary approaches will be encouraged. In the process, the series will aim to make a contribution to existing fields, such as politics, sociology and media studies, as well as opening out new and hitherto-neglected fields.

Peter Catterall (ed.), *The Making of Channel 4*

Brock Millman, *Managing Domestic Dissent in First World War Britain*

Peter Catterall, Wolfram Kaiser and Ulrike Walton-Jordan (eds), *Reforming the Constitution: Debates in Twenty-Century Britain*

Brock Millman, *Pessimism and British War Policy, 1916–1918*

Adrian Smith and Dilwyn Porter (eds), *Amateurs and Professionals in Post-war British Sport*

Archie Hunter, *A Life of Sir John Eldon Gorst: Disraeli's Awkward Disciple*

Harry Defries, *Conservative Party Attitudes to Jews, 1900–1950*

Virginia Berridge and Stuart Blume (eds), *Poor Health: Social Inequality before and after the Black Report*

Stuart Ball and Ian Holliday (eds), *Mass Conservatism: The Conservatives and the Public since the 1880s*

Rieko Karatani, *Defining British Citizenship: Empire, Commonwealth and Modern Britain*

Des Freedman, *Television Policies of the Labour Party, 1951–2001*

Marvin Rintala, *Creating the National Health Service: Aneurin Bevan and the Medical Lords*

Mark Clapson, *A Social History of Milton Keynes: Middle England/Edge City*

A SOCIAL HISTORY OF MILTON KEYNES

Middle England/Edge City

MARK CLAPSON

Foreword by
JEFF ROOKER, MP

FRANK CASS
LONDON • PORTLAND, OR

First published in 2004 in Great Britain by
FRANK CASS PUBLISHERS
Crown House, 47 Chase Side
London N14 5BP

and in the United States of America by
FRANK CASS PUBLISHERS
c/o ISBS, 920 NE 58th Avenue
Portland, Oregon, 97213-3786

Website: www.frankcass.com

British Library Cataloguing in Publication Data

Clapson, Mark
  A social history of Milton Keynes: Middle England/edge
  city. – (Cass series. British politics and society)
  1. Sociology, Urban – England – Milton Keynes   2. City
  planning – England – Milton Keynes   3. Milton Keynes
  (England) – Social conditions
  I. Title
  307.7′6′0942591

ISBN 0-7146-5524-4 (cloth)
ISBN 0-7146-8417-1 (paper)
ISSN 1467-1441

Library of Congress Cataloging-in-Publication Data

Clapson, Mark.
  A social history of Milton Keynes: middle England/edge city / Mark Clapson.
    p.   cm. – (Cass series – British politics and society, ISSN 1467-1441)
  Includes bibliographical references and index.
  ISBN 0-7146-5524-4 (cloth) – ISBN 0-7146-8417-1 (paper)
  1. Milton Keynes (England) – History. 2. Milton Keynes (England) – Social
life and customs. 3. Milton Keynes (England) – Social conditions. I. Title.   II.
Series.

DA670.M66C65 2003
942.5′91–dc22   2003060309

Typeset by Servis Filmsetting Ltd, Manchester
Printed in Great Britain by MPG Books Ltd, Bodmin, Cornwall

Contents

Illustrations

The author acknowledges the permission of English Partnerships
to reproduce figures 1, 2, 3, 4, 5, 11, 12, 13, 14.

Tables

Foreword

The building of new communities is a major challenge for any society, in which a wide range of values and interests need to find expression. Experience from history shows that it can take many forms, from our own industrial communities such as Bournville or Port Sunlight to the Japanese 'science cities'.

The post-Second World War British new towns were a bold attempt to provide decent homes, jobs and facilities such as schools, hospitals, parks, shops and leisure centres for a growing population. They were sponsored by a Labour government, but found continued favour with later Conservative governments. They had new legislation to provide the necessary funding and powers to support their delivery. The New Towns Act is still on the statute books, and gave rise, in amended form, to the Act under which the Urban Development Corporations were formed in the 1980s.

Government provided the framework, the initiative, and the pump-priming investment, but relied on individual people and private-sector firms to provide the personal and financial commitments that brought the towns to life.

Milton Keynes was the last and the most ambitious new town. Designated in 1967, its planning and delivery learnt much from earlier models, and the experience of its development has much to inform us in our new efforts to promote sustainable communities.

All of the new towns were delivered through the use of purpose-designed locally based Development Corporations. These were accountable to government, but by the time that Milton Keynes was designated there was a clear understanding that local accountability was also essential. This was achieved through various means; about half the Board members were from Local Authorities, and several more were from local business and voluntary organisations. There were also regular formal liaison meetings with the Local Authorities, who were consulted on all planning and development proposals.

The result was a vibrant, socially mixed and economically suc-cessful new community, one that has seen the fasted growth rate in England over the past 35 years. The fact that Milton Keynes is now embarking with confidence on a new phase of growth, likely to double its population over the next 30 years, is clear evidence that successful integrated development can produce an appetite for change and a belief that growth, properly managed, can produce real benefits for local communities.

Much of this experience is still relevant today. Though the cir-cumstances have changed, and some of our aspirations are dif-ferent, the lessons are there to be learnt and used. I commend this book to all who seek to understand what can be achieved by consistent, focused and inspired direction, taken forward in partnership.

JEFF ROOKER MP
Minister of State for Regeneration and Regional Development
September 2003

Series Editor's Preface

I was in a café in the sprawling and fast-growing Missouri town of Columbia in 2000, when I noticed a group of men huddled around a map. As it turned out, they were inspecting a plan for a system of cycle routes they intended to put up to the local authorities. When I observed that their plan looked a lot like Milton Keynes, they responded that it was based on Milton Keynes.

It might seem odd that Milton Keynes, so often vilified for inflicting a slice of North America on England's rural idyll, should in turn be imitated as a way of bringing some order to the largely unplanned chaos that characterises too many American towns. But then, of course, there is much about Milton Keynes that is not American. It does not have the seedy strip developments, the profligate use of land, or the impossibility, all too often, of even crossing the road without recourse to an automobile. The size and scale of some of the initial architecture in Milton Keynes, particularly because of the deliberate eschewing of vernacular styles, may have suggested a North American aspect. The road system certainly did, and so Milton Keynes has been termed 'the Little Los Angeles in North Buckinghamshire'. The comparison can be stretched too far, however. Anyone who has driven along the leafy main roads in Milton Keynes, with the surrounding urban developments all carefully screened off, and thinks that this reminds them of Los Angeles has obviously never been to Los Angeles.

Milton Keynes is not an English homage to the American dream. Its roots, as Mark Clapson rightly reminds us in this book, lie in indigenous soil. In contrast to the amorphous autopia of Los Angeles – or indeed, on a smaller scale, Columbia – Milton Keynes was carefully planned and controlled. It drew upon native ideas, not least that of the garden city. And it sought to incorporate, rather than subsume, the existing communities in its corner of North Buckinghamshire. To these were added new communities of in-migrants, though here again attempts were made to foster a sense of local identity. A degree of dispersal could also minimise the bane of commuting. At the same time, the fast main roads linking the various parts of the new city reduced traffic jams, and therefore pollution, and tried to take on board the considerations of Colin Buchanan's very influential 1963 *Traffic in Towns* report. Meanwhile, the linear parks were to prevent the kind of seamless suburban vistas of semi-detached properties that grew to ring London during the 1930s. It might be claimed that some aspects of these parks owed something to North America. However, the tree cathedral, for instance, is far more redolent of the utopian community of New Harmony, Indiana, than anything to be found in Los Angeles.

Milton Keynes, as Clapson points out, has been the victim of too many facile judgements over the years by visitors whose views seem to have been formed before they stepped out of Milton Keynes Central station. Unable to locate it conveniently within their simplistic schema of urban, suburban or rural, commentators found it easier to sneer than try to analyse the new city, still less to understand its success. For success it has been. Milton Keynes is not without its social problems, as Clapson makes clear. But one of the many strengths of this book is his careful analysis of the social life of the new city and the reactions of the inhabitants to its development. All, of course, has not gone according to plan. Clapson shows how earlier, architecturally driven plans gave way to more multi-textured development by the 1980s, a process which also coincided with a shift towards more suburban vernacular styles. But in the process Milton Keynes arguably moved from being an architectural vision towards a city for the people living in it, towards a compromise between planning and usage.

Milton Keynes was virtually the last, and undoubtedly the greatest development to emerge from the postwar new towns development in Britain. Planning on the grand scale was already going out of fashion as the first turfs were cut. Economic planning was dealt a mortal blow by the failure of the 1965 National Plan. System-built architecture was similarly laid low by the collapse of Ronan Point a couple of years later. At the same time, in the late 1960s, attention began to turn in Britain from the creating of new towns to the problems left behind in the old, in the decaying inner cities. Though different remedies and techniques have been used, three decades later urban policy in Britain remains focused on such sites. Urban means metropolitan for the principal policymakers, and a location like Milton Keynes doesn't seem to fit any of their conceptions. There is talk of cramming an additional population at least equivalent to that of Milton Keynes into London, even if it means building on remaining greenfield sites, whilst adding to the housing density of the capital and the problems of its creaking transport infrastructure. At the start of the twenty-first century these ideas seem to run the risk of replicating the problems which led to the new towns movement in the last century in the first place.

But development outside London across the south-east is now also being planned, not least for Milton Keynes itself. If these developments are to avoid becoming exercises in suburban sprawl, then there is much that can be learnt from the unique experiment of Milton Keynes in attempting to locate a planned city within an existing rural landscape. Milton Keynes may not have always got the balance between planning and social usage right but, as Clapson shows, it has been far more successful than its detractors claim. In the process, I would suggest that not only the would-be developers of south-east England, but urban communities across North America – not just in Columbia, Missouri – should have much to glean from this book about the experience of Milton Keynes.

Peter Catterall
London

Acknowledgements

Part of my ageing process is forgetting what other people have done for me. I should have said thanks to many people, earlier. In particular, I'm very grateful to Jagiro Goodwin and Jerry Goodwin for being such kind and stimulating and effective sixth-form teachers at Ashmead School, in Reading, all those years ago.

In Milton Keynes, Mike Synott the Director of the City Discovery Centre has always been helpful and erudite, and some of his many words of wisdom over the years have been synthesised and included as my own in this book. Thanks too to the various archivists at the CDC over the years. I am also grateful to the staff at the Milton Keynes Library, and the Jennie Lee Library at the Open University.

Many thanks are also extended to the International Planning History Society, particularly Steve Ward, Anthony Sutcliffe and Rob Freestone, for their support and good counsel over recent years.

Peter Catterall at Queen Mary, University of London, made many constructive criticisms of an earlier draft of this book, and supported its publication, and I am particularly grateful to him. Robert Bruegmann at the University of Chicago read some of the manuscript in an earlier form, and made some very helpful suggestions. Warm thanks also go to Martin Doherty and Tony Gorst at the University of Westminster for making this year at the Regent Campus such an enjoyable one.

English Partnerships kindly permitted the use of relevant illustrations and provided financial assistance for the use of colour illustrations. I am also very grateful to Heavenly Records, St Etienne and Julie Burchill, for permission to quote from *Too Young to Die*.

Finally, I would like to dedicate this book to the students and the staff of the History Department at the University of Luton, 1993–2001. Of the historians, particular thanks go to Ian Beckett, Steve Bunker, Jackie Burton, Larry Butler, Harriet Jones, Peter Neville, Nick Tiratsoo and Kier Thorpe.

Chronology of Events

1965   Second New Towns Act passed in Parliament.

1966   Centre for Environmental Studies established by Richard Crossman, the Labour Minister for Housing and Local Government, and Lord Llewelyn-Davies, an architect and a Labour peer.

1966   Frederick Pooley, Chief Architect and Planner of Buckinghamshire County Council, published *North Bucks New City* with Bucks County Council.

1967   9,000 hectares of North Buckinghamshire designated for a new town in North Bucks in January 1967.

1967   Lord Jock Campbell appointed as Head of Milton Keynes Development Corporation by Richard Crossman, Minister of Housing and Local Government.

1967   Planning consultancy firm of Llewelyn-Davies, Weeks, Forestier-Walker and Bor appointed to draw up the *Plan for Milton Keynes*.

1968   Milton Keynes Development Corporation published its *Interim Report*.

1969   The Open University at Walton Hall begins operations.

1970   Milton Keynes Development Corporation published its two-volume *Plan for Milton Keynes*.

1973   Hospital Action Group formed early in the new city's life.

1979   Civic Offices completed in Central Milton Keynes.

1979   Shopping Building opened in Central Milton Keynes.

1980   The Bowl Venue opened near site for Furzton Lake.

1981   Construction of Milton Keynes Hospital begun.

1983   Henry Chilver replaced Lord Campbell as Head of Milton Keynes Development Corporation.

1992   Christ the Cornerstone Ecumenical Church opened in Central Milton Keynes.

1992   Milton Keynes Development Corporation wound up; replaced by Commission for New Towns.

1995   City Discovery Centre at Bradwell Abbey, Milton Keynes,

hosts 'Witness Seminar' in which some of the original
planners talked about their role, and their current
impressions of Milton Keynes.

1997   Milton Keynes Council becomes a unitary authority.

1999   Commission for New Towns replaced by English
Partnerships.

1999   Theatre District opened in Central Milton Keynes.

2000   Xscape opened in Central Milton Keynes.

2000   Midsummer Arcade opened in Central Milton Keynes.

Abbreviations

BTAG	Beanhill Tenants Action Group
CCPR	Central Council for Physical Recreation
CES	Centre for Environmental Studies
CMK	Central Milton Keynes
CNT	Commission for New Towns
DNS	Direct Nominations Scheme
DoE	Department of the Environment
GLC	Greater London Council
HMSO	Her Majesty's Stationery Office
HP	Hire Purchase (credit)
ISS	Industrial Selection Scheme
KWIET	Keep Willen Ever Tranquil
LCC	London County Council
MHLG	Ministry of Housing and Local Government
MK	Milton Keynes
MKBC	Milton Keynes Borough Council
MKDC	Milton Keynes Development Corporation
MKEP	Milton Keynes Economic Partnership
NETS	New and Expanded Towns Scheme
NFU	National Farmers Union
OU	Open University
TCPA	Town and Country Planning Association
YIS	Youth Information Service

Welcome to Milton Keynes

In 1967, the Beatles recorded the legendary *Sergeant Pepper's Lonely Hearts Club Band*; the ground-breaking film *The Graduate* turned Dustin Hoffman into an instant star; Israeli and Arab forces battled in the six day war; Britain was hit by foot and mouth disease; and Milton Keynes was designated a new town.

Janet Haslam, 'Finding a pulse', *Guardian*, 20 June 2001

Milton Keynes, in Buckinghamshire, is England's largest new town. It was designated in 1967, with an intended target population of 250,000. Between 1967 and 1970, the key planning principles and the overall framework for the new urban area were worked out, and published, by Milton Keynes Development Corporation (hereafter MKDC). Construction of the new city began in 1970, and people started to move in very soon after the first homes had been built. Since 1970, it has been England's fastest growing city.

The new town was generously allocated 22,000 acres (9,000 hectares) of North Buckinghamshire to house the incomers who would make up the population of the city. Whilst the target population of Milton Keynes had been revised downwards to 200,000 by 1992, nonetheless, with the current predictions of household growth, it is likely that sometime during the first quarter of the twenty-first century Milton Keynes will expand beyond the current target population of 206,000 that is intended for the new town by 2008.[1] In fact, by the year 1999, Milton Keynes numbered over 170,000 people, and was still growing.[2]

Because of its size, the original planners of Milton Keynes wanted it to become a city. It was and remains bigger than all the

other postwar new towns. And most people living in Milton
Keynes since have been happy to view it as a new city, rather than
a new town. 'City' sounds more impressive. This writer is one of
the many people who have moved to the new city of Milton
Keynes, and one of over one million people who live in the British
postwar new towns. But to a degree never enjoyed, or endured, by
the other new towns, Milton Keynes has become both the most
famous and infamous of the postwar experiments in new town
living.

One of the joys of living in Milton Keynes is the awareness of
what it is like to be treated as some sort of unique specimen. Milton
Keynes is visited by many people who feel the need to pass some
sort of critical judgement upon it. Accordingly, people who live in
the city are peered at, sneered at, puzzled over, laughed at, misunderstood and often subjected to the tyranny of being judged by
first impressions. Rock stars, including the late Kirsty MacColl,
and Paul Weller of the Style Council, have even sung songs about
it.[3] Many observers, to be fair, have been quite favourable in their
judgements of Milton Keynes, whilst some others have been more
nuanced and objective, finding things to both praise and criticise
in this new city.

What is it about Milton Keynes that has attracted so much attention? The answer lies in a number of reasons, and the first reason
is the road grid. The whole framework of the new city is based
upon a huge American-style grid of fast roads, many of them dual
carriageways. These roads were essential to the vision of the planners, a vision discussed in detail in the next chapter, who felt that
in the future people would enjoy, and would want to enjoy, a
wealthier lifestyle based upon motorised transport and telecommunications. Hence Milton Keynes came to be called 'the Little Los
Angeles in Buckinghamshire'. The road grid of Milton Keynes
would facilitate mobility and choice: it would enable people to
move freely across the city. No other town in England was provided with such an extensive and dominant road system.
Alongside the roads on this grid, moreover, but buried in the earth,
a cabling system was laid, to enable Milton Keynes to become, and
here is another American term, a 'wired city', a computerised new
town within the global village.[4] Instant contact with people, near
and far, was also essential to the vision of the planners.

Within the grid roads lay the 'gridsquares'. Some of the gridsquares are residential estates. Others are made up of employment
and retail parks. Like most planned new places, Milton Keynes is

zoned: employment and residence are kept largely separate. People do'not have to live cheek by jowl with huge distribution warehouses, noisy workshops, and busy offices and shops.

Some of those residential gridsquares, though, were prime examples of architects leading the new city by its chin into the world of media scrutiny. Right from its outset, people had to live with some unpopular experimental domestic architecture, and that helped to shape early images of Milton Keynes. A number of the less prepossessing homes built during the 1970s looked unlike anything a house traditionally looks like. They have not weathered very well, either, as will be discussed in a later chapter, and critics of new towns were quick to fasten upon some of the early housing and to use it to denigrate Milton Keynes.

A further reason for the critical gaze upon Milton Keynes is the fact that Central Milton Keynes saw the opening, in 1979, of the first really 1980s-style shopping mall. Unlike the poorly lit and down-at-heel Arndale Centres and their like that have blighted some of the town centres of England during and since the 1970s, the mall in Central Milton Keynes is a glitzy affair, all marble and glass, and light and spacious. It is also over a kilometre in length, an impressively large late-modern public building. But many people in England hate shopping malls, no matter how good they are. The ostensibly artificial and commercially driven shopping environment appears to symbolise, for its critics, something artificial and empty about the consumers who move around it.

Perhaps the most risible reason for Milton Keynes' notoriety, however, was the gift in 1978 of its first artist in residence, a Californian named Liz Leyh. It was a gift of concrete cows, inanimate bovines non-grazing in a linear park near the West Coast railway line. Those cows, it will be seen, have rarely failed to elicit comment from visitors to Milton Keynes.

WRITERS WHO HAVE VISITED MILTON KEYNES

The first person to be mentioned may well be unknown to some readers of this book. He is also unique amongst the writers discussed here because he actually lived in Milton Keynes from the late 1970s until his death in 1991. Jack Trevor Story became recognised during the 1950s for his novel *The Trouble With Harry*, which was made into a film of the same name by Alfred Hitchcock, and released in 1955. Story wrote other, less successful novels, a number of television screenplays and many newspaper and magazine columns and articles. He had lived in the posh Hertfordshire town of Harpenden during the 1950s, and also in the new town of Welwyn Garden City. He also lived in Hampstead in North London during the 'swinging sixties'. In January 1977, at the behest of Milton Keynes Development Corporation, he became the city's first 'writer in residence', and was given a flat to live in.

The development corporation probably regretted Story's presence, at least sometimes. For example, Story angered a number of people in Milton Keynes in August 1977 after he appeared on television and gave a rather grim account of life in 'the midden heap city'. Letters to the local press attacked his rather opinionated views.[5] Yet a few months later he stated that basically he was 'all right' in Milton Keynes, and had a certain regard for the place.[6]

Subsequently, however, Story was often miserable in Milton Keynes. For a number of years he lived with a much younger woman than he, whose pet name was 'Dwarf', and after she left him for Oxford University he went to pieces. He wrote of his 'fragmenting mind' and his misery at being 'sixty miles from anywhere'. His passing references to the landscape or buildings of Milton Keynes in his autobiographical *Dwarf Goes to Oxford* (1987) were economical at best, and sometimes hostile, but indicative of the gaping chasm he felt inside: empty heart, empty cityscape. Yet he also tried to make the best of living in the new city by becoming involved in its social and cultural life. His time in the new city and the cumulative impressions and views of it that we can see in his writings describe a man who lived an emotionally complex and even self-obsessed life, yet someone who wanted also to be a part of the new city, for better or worse, once he had moved from London.[7] Yet at least he lived in Milton Keynes. Many other writers who ventured into the new city came to rapid and half-formed opinionated judgements about it, and then left.

The journalist and writer Christopher Booker visited the 'brave new world of Milton Keynes' in July 1974. That year was not a good one in the annals of the 'sad little island' about which Booker was writing. The country as a whole was suffering from the effects of the Oil Crisis, and from the industrial strife which pockmarked the 1970s. Yet 1974 was an early and critical formative year for the new city, with all its difficulties, and Booker laid into that easiest of targets, 'the planners'. They had purported, he argued, to know how the future was going to evolve, but they had failed to anticipate large-scale unemployment. They had thus begun a task that they could not properly finish.

Booker's 'brave new world' reference was of course to Aldous Huxley's novel about a future urban dystopia in England, a world of leisured and pleasured, drugged and bugged and hierarchically graded human automata. Here in Milton Keynes, pronounced Booker, was 'the utterly depersonalised nightmare which haunted Aldous Huxley just forty short years ago'. Booker, instead of revelling in the preservation of much of the existing countryside in the form of linear parks, or instead of acknowledging the planners for their vision of motorised easy living, viewed all this in negative Huxleyesque terms. So much for planning for leisure, he wrote, when the country was in the grip of unemployment.

In a postscript, written in 1980, Booker congratulated himself on the partial realisation of some of his predictions about the demise of Milton Keynes. Milton Keynes was a mistake for the reasons just noted, he argued, but a further error had been the estimates of population growth in South East England which had justified Milton Keynes as a new town. These estimates, argued Booker, had hardly been fulfilled. Planners had extrapolated from statistics about demographic growth, now the statistics had been proved wrong and so mechanical diggers stood motionless in the muddy undeveloped wastes of North Bucks.

Or so Booker thought. In fact he made the same mistake of which he accused the planners, for any slowdown in population growth and migration to the region was a short-term trend. The population of South East England continued to rise, as migration to the region hastened during the 1980s and 1990s. And a sizeable chunk of that population would move to Milton Keynes. More than that, despite the evidence during the 1970s of growing divorce rates and increasing numbers of single person households, or of couples without children, Booker, unlike 'the planners', failed to anticipate the growing number of homes that would be needed in the final two decades of the twentieth century, and thereafter, in order to cope with the proliferation of smaller households.

Booker made other statements about Milton Keynes which were equally myopic. He lambasted the housing, the 'hundreds of grim little misshapen boxes, in brick or corrugated metal, turned out by machine', which people had to live in. But some other housing developments were under construction from the early 1970s which did not fit Booker's description. He also expressed sympathy for those Londoners who had been almost forced to move to Milton Keynes from their old cosy capital city. It appeared that they had moved to Milton Keynes, only to find their earlier council tenancies relinquished, so that they were now stuck in the new city. Such sympathy was, however, pathetically misplaced. Most people who moved to Milton Keynes during the 1970s liked their new housing, and did not want to move back. This is the subject matter for a later chapter.

Booker's views of Milton Keynes were extremely limited, because they were tailored to fit into his embittered retrospective on recent Britain, *The Seventies: Portrait of a Decade*. Few contemporary historians have since quoted from that book as having anything definitive to say about that decade. And his main prediction about Milton Keynes, that its development would soon grind to a halt in a sea of mud and rusting tractors, was very wide of the mark.[8]

Other writers were to visit Milton Keynes after 1980. In the early 1980s, self-consciously emulating the *English Journey* taken by the playwright J. B. Priestley during the 1930s, the novelist Beryl Bainbridge took her own *English Journey, or, The Road to Milton Keynes*. In that name-dropping style beloved of *auteurs*, she describes how she enjoyed dinner and wine with the novelist Malcolm Bradbury, in Norwich, the night before she left for Milton Keynes. They talked about books, and worried about the bomb, understandable subjects for discussion given their vocations, and the late Cold War paranoia of the time. But whilst Bradbury went 'up to London' the next day to attend the Booker Prize ceremony, poor Miss Bainbridge travelled across East Anglia to the final destination in her tour, Milton Keynes.

She despised it. She went to Beanhill, one of the experimental housing estates of the type decried by Christopher Booker, and felt so alienated by it that she says she forgot the time of the day: 'In that out-of-the-way place time had left home.' In a typically superior comment, she felt like asking a dog coming out of the off-licence what it thought of 'the bomb'. She went to bed that night thinking that, if Milton Keynes had been in existence in the 1930s, Priestley would probably have detoured around it.

Bainbridge was wrong about that. Priestley was as interested in the emergence of the new suburban England of the 1930s as he was in the older industrial and rural areas of the country. Priestley wrote evocatively of the mass-produced motor cars, Woolworths, cocktail bars, dance halls, cinemas, factories that looked like exhibition buildings 'and where the smooth wide road' passed between miles of semi-detached homes. He observed that this new England belonged perhaps 'more to the age itself' than to the island of Britain, and remarked rather negatively on the Americanisation of England in the new world of cars and cinemas. Nonetheless, as he pointed out, 'Care is necessary, for you can easily approve or disapprove of it too hastily.'[9]

Following her visit to Beanhill, Bainbridge called into the shopping centre, which she erroneously referred to as 'the precinct'. It made her despise Milton Keynes 'all over again'. She met some Japanese Buddhists near the new Peace Pagoda, and then she went back to London.

Bainbridge's observations in *English Journey* were described as 'vivacious and immediate' by the *Sunday Times*, and as 'most flavoursome and poignant' by the novelist Anthony Burgess.[10] Yet she failed to provide anything other than an extremely narrow and self-serving impression of Milton Keynes and its people.[11]

More famous than Bainbridge and Booker (and Malcolm Bradbury for that matter) is Bill Bryson, the Anglophile American travel writer, who lived in Yorkshire for some years, and eventually went back to the USA. Visiting Milton Keynes during the early 1990s, Bryson was guilty of some of the worst judgements-by-appearance about the new city. But then so many travel writers do just that: they take a surface reading and get to work on it, showing off their apparently unique insights and literary prowess.

Milton Keynes simply did not measure up to the notion of a quaint, winsome Englishness beloved by Bryson. He arrived at Milton Keynes Central rail station on the train from London, walked into the plaza at the front of the station and tried to find his way to the city centre. He reckons he met hardly anybody, and when he finally got to the shopping mall, via the allegedly soulless roads and walkways, and the 'endless Bovisville' of housing estates, he could not have been ruder. He thought that the mall was a dark and gruesome place with inadequate public toilets and containing no seats. He was factually wrong on the last two counts, and his impressions of the shopping centre, as of all the other 'featureless buildings' of the city centre, revealed the rather narrow theme he was pursuing: Milton Keynes 'looked anything but English . . .'[12]

This is the same Bill Bryson who turned up in October 2000 at Ottakars bookshop in the large and recently opened extension to Milton Keynes' shopping centre. He was promoting his latest book. He was politely asked by a local reporter why he had written such negative things about Milton Keynes. He protested that he could not quite remember what he had written, and then went on to sign many copies of his latest book. He also described the new shopping building extension as 'fabulous' and expressed his admiration for its curved ceiling. This was indeed an 'amazing U turn', as the reporter Wayne Coles emphasised.[13]

A broadly favourable account of Milton Keynes was provided by the travel writer and broadcaster Susan Marling, in her book *American Affair: The Americanisation of Britain* (1993). She observed that, unlike most other new towns in England, Milton Keynes was promoted by an American-style corporate publicity – called 'place marketing' by academics – since the plans were first drawn up back in 1967 to 1970. Beautiful models of how the new city would look were displayed to the press and public in the later 1960s, and glossy brochures and an innovative advertising campaign during the 1970s and 1980s continued to provide a slick image of this innovative new city.

As Marling knew, Milton Keynes was a suburban, Californian-style city. But it was also a city whose planners drew with some sensitivity from the long-standing English garden city tradition of town planning influenced by Ebenezer Howard. Howard was a Victorian man, but his vision of combining town and country, of giving people the advantages and amenities of a sophisticated urban life, whilst encouraging access to the attractive and health-giving countryside, was one shared by many key town planners during the course of the twentieth century. Thus Milton Keynes was and remains a fusion of English and American ideas, all road grid, parks and lakes, Californian trim trails, a swanky shopping mall, bright new office parks, and housing areas zoned into grid-squares between the main roads. And into these gridsquares went quite a variety of housing. For, as Marling pointed out, MKDC had offered private developers the opportunity to design these grid-squares to their own blueprints. The planners of Milton Keynes, she says, '"pulled it off": the thing is that Milton Keynes does feel like a place that's very American'. She was writing at a time when many other new housing estates had sprung up in Milton Keynes that looked nothing like the starker experiments of the 1970s.

To be sure, there were damning touches of faint praise in Marling's descriptions of Milton Keynes. She described it as a 'reasonable city'; in other words, it appeared fine and clean but it perhaps lacked the buzz of a supposedly real thriving city. Moreover, she seemed to lament the lack of litter in the new city.[14]

Most people who go to London, where Marling lived at the time of writing, know just how litter-strewn and filthy many parts of the capital city can be. As a London-dweller, Marling probably shared a *de rigueur* disrespect for civic cleanliness as some sort of perverted measure of urbanity. Perhaps she thought a bit of litter was an essential element of town life. At her time of writing, Milton Keynes was cleaner than it is today. Unfortunately, it has since fallen foul of more litter dropping, and car dumping, too. Perhaps it has become more of a 'real' city as a consequence.

Finally, it must be pointed out that Marling seemed to think that the then Conservative Member of Parliament for Milton Keynes, William Benyon, was basically right when he described its people as 'classless' and 'apolitical'. But one of the great myths about the USA – and of Milton Keynes – is that it is classless. Marling felt that the planners had intended the barbecue smoke of both workers and bosses to mingle on Sunday lunch-times. Any such mingling, however, owes more to a strong breeze than to any residential mixing of socio-economic groups. This theme, the social tone and class composition of different parts of Milton Keynes, is also discussed in this book.

Academic and professional judgements of Milton Keynes have found plenty to dislike about the new city. John Stevenson, for example, a prolific and much respected social historian, writing of 'the Jerusalem that failed', namely the rebuilding of postwar Britain, placed Milton Keynes squarely within that failure. Stevenson argued that a city where home and work were consciously separated by planners through zoning policies, and which was designed for the motor car, had developed 'an inevitable anonymity'. Hence for Stevenson it had become 'a town which seemed more like a series of linked roundabouts than a living community'.[15]

One of Prince Charles's favourite architects, Leon Krier, has also picked on the fact that Milton Keynes is a zoned city. He wrote in the 1980s that Milton Keynes resembled a concentration camp because people lived away from their work, in quiet residential areas. Milton Keynes was a 'corpse' when compared to the 'true city', argued this eminent Luxembourger.[16] If the present book serves no other purpose than to confront such vacuous and distasteful judgements, then hopefully that alone justifies its existence.

But such highbrow disdain was not shared by every writer who visited the new city. Right at the end of the 1990s, and hence at the end of the twentieth century, some well-known writers ventured up to Milton Keynes from London. The new city was but one stop on a longer journey. As the end of the century approached, a spate of books appeared in England that were mixtures of travel writing with rumination about the *fin de siècle* 'state of the nation'. Yet these books were also personal voyages of middle-aged men, as much concerned with themselves and their shortening futures as with their country. In his journey *London to Loweswater*, the popular writer Hunter Davies provided an entertaining chapter on Milton Keynes. For someone who was privileged enough to have homes in both London and the Lake District – hence the title of his book – he could easily have succumbed to the usual prejudices about the new city in North Bucks, but he refrained.

For Davies, Milton Keynes was big enough, and bright enough, to look and feel like a city. He visited the shopping mall, which he described as 'one of the wonders of the late twentieth century'. He noted that the city centre church, the first purpose-built ecumenical new church in a new town, opened in the early 1990s, was busy and thriving. And significantly, Davies emphasised that the economy of Milton Keynes was a dynamic one, based heavily upon services such as banking and finance, retail and computing. This he saw as symbolic of a New Britain that the Prime Minister Tony Blair and the New Labour government were beginning to construct: smart, clean and well-paid workplaces where people felt they had a future because they were part of an expanding sector of the economy. The declining segments of the old industrial economy are absent from Milton Keynes. There is no coal mining, iron and steel production, textile or motor car manufacturing.

Yet Davies was also aware that, in the ostensibly 'post-industrial' economy of Milton Keynes, there was a new Fordism at work. He interviewed two young women who worked in a 'call centre', one of the huge high-tech warehouses in which people sit at a telephone and take down orders onto a computer. As Davies put it, 'a new factory system is springing up':

> Where once people were herded into industrial plants, textile works or shipyards, they are now herded into modern open-plan office blocks, treated nicely enough, given clean surroundings – but made to sit cheek by jowl and spend each day staring at a computer screen, talking to customers they will never meet.

Yet that did not mean the dawn of a new dehumanised workforce. The two young women that Davies interviewed had an active, even vibrant, social life. And they also liked the money they earned, and what it could buy.[17]

Davies was also aware of the other important sectors in the local economy. The local borough council, which had become a unitary authority in 1997, was the largest employer. And the second largest was the Open University, based in the gridsquare of Walton Hall. The public sector was still, therefore, a major presence in the occupational structure of the new city by the end of the twentieth century. Working in offices and shops rather than in factories was and remains a major characteristic of life in Milton Keynes.

The broadcaster and journalist David Aaronovitch was the next important writer to turn up in the new city. An ex-President of the National Union of Students, and by then a broadcaster and journalist, Aaronovitch got into his canoe and went in for some explorations of himself and his feelings about his country. His book *Paddling to Jerusalem: An Aquatic Tour of Our Small Country* was, like Davies's, written at the end of the twentieth century.

As the title suggests, Aaronovitch entered Milton Keynes not via the railway station or the M1, but by the much navigated Grand Union Canal. He moored his craft, and headed uphill in the direction of the city centre. In common with Bill Bryson, he met few people on his way to the shopping mall, but, as he entered the building 'by a modest door', all that changed.

Like Davies before him, Aaronovitch was impressed by the shopping building. He also understood, in a way that Beryl Bainbridge and other critics did not, that the mall was not simply a site of consumption, but a place to meet people. One could be both a sociable person, and a selective, evaluating, self-empowering consumer. As he sat in the small outdoor square in the shopping building, Aaronovitch was seized by what he called 'the heretical thought that all this was just fine':

> The food halls were full, not of ersatz rubbish but of desirable breads, of organic honey, of home-made pasta sauce, of coffees and teas from all over the world. For the first time that I had even seen, there were baby-changing facilities in the gent's toilet. The gents!
>
> [And] most of the folk I saw here were happy. Despite the temptations and the occasional silly shop, they didn't creep around in a zombie-like state of shopaholism, of gift-addiction. They gabbled, and scrutinised, and smiled and wheeled their kids to and fro, and met their lovers in John Lewis's cafeteria.[18]

Aaronovitch had experienced a sort of shopping mall epiphany. But this was a realisation that came about not just because he was impressed by the shopping building. Rather, Aaronovitch had been a left-wing activist in his student days, and he had long held a residual neo-Marxist suspicion of consumerism as a signifier of false consciousness in a capitalist society. In other words, instead of buying fancy goods, the workers should be fomenting revolution. Now, it seemed, they were more interested in designer gear and a wide range of British and continental breads, and were the happier for it.

Aaronovitch and Davies were not inclined to be immediately rude about Milton Keynes. They did not succumb to the temptation of easy journalism, or knocking-copy. And if we move beyond knocking-copy, the more serious newspapers indicate a changing, and sometimes even improving, image of Milton Keynes as the new city became more firmly established both in North Bucks and in the newsprint media.

MILTON KEYNES IN THE NATIONAL NEWSPAPERS AND MAGAZINES

The following throwaway statement reflects a common assumption about Milton Keynes that is frequently found in British broadsheets. Writing of her attendance in 1998 at a pop concert by singer Chris Rea, a journalist described the 'I'm sorry, rather *déclassé* crowd: imagine Milton Keynes on a Saturday night: I have never seen so many cheap clothes and male perms in one place'.[19] Alongside the persistence of such vacuous knocking-copy, however, other more open-minded and knowledgeable accounts have been kinder to Milton Keynes. Such accounts became more common during the 1980s and the 1990s, as the new city became more established, and as a greater variety of domestic architecture – housing – began to mushroom across the virgin areas of the city. In 1990 the journalist Simon Hoggart noted that the newly constructed traditional brick-built housing blended with the older brick-built houses, and that this was housing that was popular with its inhabitants. The association of Milton Keynes with those metal-clad experiments of the 1970s was always one-sided, and Hoggart's article was a long-overdue reminder of that.[20]

Thus during the 1980s, Milton Keynes' housing became more populist, in that there was a marked return to the suburban styles of semi-detached and detached housing for sale. The 'rationalist'

1970s gave way to the reassertion of traditional housing. However, for those who favoured modern housing, such traditional or 'vernacular' domestic styles were also derided as something that evidenced the vacuous and shallow nature of the new city. In a sense, Milton Keynes could not win: its modern housing met with disapprobation, and so did its more popular styles. This is discussed further in a later chapter.

Nonetheless, whilst prejudice against Milton Keynes has continued until the present day, a varied and even sympathetic range of articles on the new city can be found in the national newspapers since 1970. Many pieces were more objective and balanced because they were not based upon simple impressionism. Rather, they assessed Milton Keynes not only from surface readings, but also socially and economically. Hence in 1992, on the 25th anniversary of its designation, the city enjoyed a great deal of attention for its rapid establishment in the years since 1967. Also in that same year, MKDC was wound up, and the combined forces of the Commission for New Towns and the local council took over. Some of the comments on the new city in *The Times* and the *Guardian* were unfavourable, but the anniversary offered an opportunity for a more serious evaluation of MKDC's performance, and the city's first generation. The *Financial Times*, a newspaper that has, for the most part, taken a supportive position towards Milton Keynes, pointed to the 'successes on many fronts'. It was viewed as the largest and most dynamic experiment of the postwar new towns programme. Its economic achievements, and the fact that it was the fastest-growing urban place in England in terms of population and job creation, were focused upon, and acknowledged as a considerable success. And the green and clean environment was, more than twice, singled out for recognition. The rapid formation of new town communities, something that had occurred with no riots or major conflicts, was also a subject of praise.[21] In other words, Milton Keynes had its critics, but it had also earned some favourable assessments.

THE ENIGMA OF MILTON KEYNES

No pun is intended in the use of the term 'enigma', despite the fact that Bletchley Park was included within the area allocated for the new city. The Park, with its re-created wartime atmosphere of austerity and decoding machines, is now a tourist destination within the new city. A little flurry of literature during the 1990s, notably Robert Harris's popular novel *Enigma*, and a variety of 'expert' books on Bletchley Park, helped to ensure that this, at first glance unprepossessing military-camp of a place, is now widely respected.[22] The mathematician Alan Turing and his colleagues successfully broke some deliberately complex and ambiguous Nazi military codes, thus hastening the end of the Second World War. And for those who try to understand or define Milton Keynes, the task of deciphering the new city is almost as complicated.

Milton Keynes has been viewed so ambiguously, because, in less than two generations, it became a thoroughly nuanced place. This was evident in many ways. It was a brand new city with an emphasis upon mostly traditional housing. It was both very English and very American. It gained a '1980s' shopping mall during the 1970s, an 'out-of-town' mall that was, moreover, placed in the centre of the city. It was planned as an urban development pervaded by a rural ethos, a new town that certainly spread the paraphernalia of urbanisation across North Bucks, yet which is now recognised for its outstanding countrified parklands and outdoor spaces. Milton Keynes has been viewed as a greedy young place full of crass materialism, yet it is home to the Open University and to a growing range of serious and high-quality cultural facilities. And it is a city that is not even, technically, a city: the Queen has yet to grant Milton Keynes city status.

There is, however, a more profound reason, for the new city reveals a huge and evolving contradiction. Milton Keynes, this ostensibly unique place, tells us more about the nature of both urban and social change in late-twentieth-century England than almost any other provincial city. It reveals a great deal about the English and what they wanted in the latter years of the twentieth century. It has been a Buckinghamshire test-bed for the 'new' economic, technological and social forces shaping England in the late twentieth century. In other words, Milton Keynes managed to achieve the feat of being both an utterly unique new city and a city that was typical of the changes that swept through England after 1970. Because, for all those people in England who wanted to move into a bright new residential estate, to break free from older housing, to enjoy a cleaner and greener environment, to gain more secure and better-paid employment, and also to enjoy a mobile lifestyle based around the motor car, then 'Milton Keynes is Us'. As the writer Blake Morrison has argued, 'You can go to any medium-sized town anywhere in the country':

And find much the same: the pedestrianised high street, the out-of-town shopping or leisure centre, the light-industrial estates with corrugated sheds. This is where most of us live now, in a place vaguely resembling Milton Keynes.[23]

IN THE MIDDLE . . . BUT ON THE EDGE

There is certainly much that is 'middling' about Milton Keynes, a new town named after a village in North Buckinghamshire. One half of that village name, 'Milton', is given by the Oxford *Dictionary of English Place Names'* as 'a very common name, usually "middle farmstead or estate"'. The village was recorded in the Domesday Book of 1086 as Middletone, and during the mediaeval period as Middletone Kaynes. The Keynes is a bastardisation of the Norman 'de Cahaignes', a family that settled in North Bucks during the twelfth century.[24]

The term 'middle estate' in a city of new estates has a coincidental but charming resonance in a city with a predominance of households headed by those in administrative, 'intermediate' and professional and managerial occupations. This is discussed in later chapters.

The term 'Middle England', however, is highly resonant in another way. During the 1990s, much was made of the *political* significance of Middle England. This did not really refer to the geographical heart of the country, but to the middle classes, and to those aspiring and comfortably-off sections of the working classes. And millions of this huge constituency resided not in the countryside or in the hearts of the cities, but on housing estates built during the twentieth century. It was here, in the appeal or lack of appeal to this broad heterogeneous mass located between the poor and the wealthiest sections of society, and between the urban cores and the countryside, that general elections were won or lost. This was the party-political lesson of the 1980s and 1990s.

Thus in 1991, after 12 years of Conservative government, Labour activists and socialists were beginning to sense victory at the forthcoming general election of 1992. Until then, Milton Keynes had been represented by one MP, the Conservative William (Bill) Benyon, since 1970, when the area was still predominantly rural. However, 'because of the increasing numbers of escapees of the London fug', stated a book on 'the battle for the marginals', the Boundary Commission had, in 1989, divided the *borough* of Milton Keynes into two general election constituencies. These were Milton Keynes South West, the most urbanised section of the borough, comprising Bletchley and most of the southern and western parts of the new city. North East Milton Keynes incorporated a number of wards that made up the northern area of the new city, and also the comfortably-off small town of Newport Pagnell. However, unlike the South West seat it also comprised a sizeable rural hinterland that included many small and attractive villages from Woburn Sands to Sherington.[25] The Conservative dominance of this area had been long established in local and national elections, and the Conservatives were expected to win. Yet the impact of migrants to the area, particularly in the south east, had rendered it a more marginal constituency. And Wolverton, the largely working-class railway town, had recently returned a Labour county councillor in Buckinghamshire. 'Labour is much better placed than the Liberal Democrats in this seat', argued the book on the marginals, 'but will be unable to erode the Tory lead without substantial tactical voting, or a dramatic upsurge in Labour loyalism from the leafy glades of the new town.'[26]

The analysis was correct in the short term: the Conservatives won the 1992 election in Milton Keynes. Since then, however, those leafy glades of the new town became increasingly reddish in tint. There are always specific reasons of policy and performance why governments lose general elections, but there are also broader social trends. The years since 1994, with the instigation of Tony Blair as Labour leader following the death of John Smith, witnessed the coalescence of leafy-glade constituencies with the rise of 'New Labour' politics. This was in no small part because many leading politicians in the Labour Party had looked to the triumph of the remodelled 'New Democrats' in the USA in 1992, following more than a decade of politics dominated by Ronald Reagan and George Bush. The Democrats had developed a more moderate language and ditched expensive reformist policies in order to successfully appeal to the 'aspirational classes of Middle America', many millions of whom lived in the suburbs. Similarly, Labour leaders such as Tony Blair, Gordon Brown and Peter Mandelson understood the need to appeal to the Conservatives' allegedly core constituency of the middle classes and the affluent working classes.[27]

New Labour began its hugely successful 'American-style' general election campaign of 1997 in Milton Keynes. Speaking at the smart new National Hockey Stadium, Tony Blair made his modest promises within a campaign whose policies and rhetoric were carefully calculated to appeal to Middle England. Labour won both Milton Keynes seats. Four years later, during the 2001 general election campaign, Blair was booked to the live debate of BBC television's 'Question Time', held at Bletchley Leisure Centre. Both Milton Keynes seats were still marginal constituencies in 2001, but Labour won them with increased majorities.[28] As more than one writer felt compelled to argue, 'If Tony Blair was a city, he'd be Milton Keynes.'[29] There was something fitting about this. After all, the new towns had been a Labour creation. Hence the writer Paul Barker dubbed Milton Keynes 'Labour's New Jerusalem', a year before New Labour swept to power.[30]

Milton Keynes was not only representative of 'Middle England' in these senses; it was and remains also on the edge in terms of its geographical location. It is on the upper fringes of the prosperous South East of England, just within a comfortable railway commuting time of London's Euston station, or about a 50-minute drive from London along the M1. If it is on the edge of one region, however, then it must be on the edge of another, or others. Milton Keynes is also on the cusp of the southern Midlands. It is about a 20-minute train ride from Northampton, or half an hour in the car, this time along the M1 in a northerly direction from MK. The new city is also only 20 miles from Bedford, on the fringes of East Anglia. Positioned as it is on the geographical outer reaches of these regions, the new city does not really belong to any of them.

Yet it is an edge city in more profound ways than this. In 1991 an influential appreciation of new suburban growth in the USA was published, entitled *Edge City: Life on the New Frontier*. Written by an American historian and journalist, Joel Garreau, *Edge City* was an enthusiastic endorsement of urban growth and sprawl at a time when many were fearful that suburban life in the USA was becoming too thinly spread and dissipated.

But what exactly was and is an edge city? For Garreau, it was the USA's latest manifestation of renewal, its newest 'frontier'. Unlike older suburbs, where there were often large tracts of housing and little else, edge cities were not only about housing: wherever they were built, usually on the fringes of existing cities or metropolitan areas, new edge cities brought shopping malls and golf courses and a wider range of commercial and cultural facilities. This was almost 'post-suburban', a new direction in low-density urban expansion. As Garreau describes American edge cities, their characteristic buildings are a large opulent shopping mall, smaller shopping plazas, glassy office blocks with

tree-lined atria, fitness centres and suburban housing surrounded by gardens. In terms of transport and communications
they are held together by fast roads and rooftop satellite dishes,
rather than by subway trains or tram lines. This in itself is a quite
accurate description of Milton Keynes, although the cable also
serves the city and its television and computing needs: the new
city remains ahead of most of the UK in cable television provision
and usage, and in the under-grounding of telecommunications in
general.[31]

For Garreau, there are five major defining characteristics of
edge cities, which can be transposed onto other countries.[32] The
geographer Julie Charlesworth and the sociologist Allan Cochrane, in a number of fine articles and chapters on Milton Keynes as
an edge city, have done just that. They argue that 'Milton Keynes
has one of the greatest claims to fitting the edge city paradigm outlined by Garreau'.[33] Much of the following argument is derived
from their example:[34]

- *An edge city must have five millions of square feet of leasable office space
  – 'the workplace of the information age'. It should also contain at least
  600,000 square feet of leasable retail space, or at least the equivalent of 'a
  fair-sized mall'.* Milton Keynes never exactly fitted this profile, but
  its economy has become, nonetheless, dominated by offices and
  shops, and also by the huge edifices required for the distributive
  industry. By December 2001 there was over 3,367,470 million
  square feet of floorspace in the new city, comprised largely of
  offices, warehouses, shops and also education and training facilities.[35] As noted above, Milton Keynes has a very large mall, in
  addition to local shopping centres, some small and some quite
  large.

- *It must have more jobs than bedrooms: 'When the workday starts, people
  head toward this place, not away from it. Like all urban places, the population increases at 9 am.'* Milton Keynes today certainly employs
  many people from outside the city. As the Strategic Director for
  Environment at Milton Keynes Council argued in 2001, 'New jobs
  outnumber new workers, producing a 7 per cent net daily commuting inflow.'[36]

- *It is perceived by the population as one place. It is 'a regional destination
  for mixed use [that] "has it all" from jobs, to shopping, to entertainment'.*
  This was the major rationale for placing Milton Keynes in North
  Buckinghamshire, and today the new city has a wide catchment
  area for its shops, entertainments and jobs.

- *An edge city 'was nothing like a "city" as recently as thirty years ago, when it was mostly countryside'.* This is certainly true of Milton Keynes: even though there were a number of small towns and villages within the designated area of the new city, that area was indeed mostly green fields and woodlands. (The erosion of the North Bucks countryside, and the impact on those who worked on it, is discussed in a later chapter.)

Garreau also notes that settlers in edge cities came from older urban areas, often 'downtown'. Further, he shows throughout his book that these big new rapid-growth places were the visions of businessmen and property speculators who bought up the land for their edge cities in order to profit handsomely from it.

Here, some care is required. Certainly, many migrants to Milton Keynes came from older, sometimes declining urban areas, notably inner London boroughs, whilst others have come from suburbs and other towns which were by no means 'downtown' in terms of characteristics and location. This is illustrated in later chapters. More starkly different to the US configuration, however, is the issue of land ownership. Unlike American edge cities, Milton Keynes was no glint in the eye of a wealthy real-estate speculator. Rather, it was a collective and corporate vision, and one that was carefully planned and phased into existence by Milton Keynes Development Corporation, which itself was established by the Ministry of Housing and Local Government under the 1960s Labour government's new towns legislation. Milton Keynes certainly grew quite rapidly across the North Bucks countryside over 30 years, but it was not the unplanned (sub)urban explosion of American edge developments.

Milton Keynes is an edge city in other important ways. For Garreau argued that, of all the American suburban explosions that most merited the term, it was Los Angeles, the sprawling, low-rise Californian metropolis. Garreau called LA 'the great granddaddy' of all edge cities. During the later 1960s, when Milton Keynes was being planned, Los Angeles was a cult city among many town planners and architects. That road-grid, designed to facilitate fast-moving motorised traffic, and the low-rise nature of most of Milton Keynes' architecture, is a conscious reference to the notion of a laid-back city of easy living. Thus has Milton Keynes been dubbed the 'Little Los Angeles in Bucks'.[37] This is discussed more fully in the next chapter.

Milton Keynes should not, however, be viewed as an isolated

example of edge city development. For it is part of a pattern of suburban growth that stretches from the 'silicon fens' around
Cambridge in East Anglia, south and westwards through the
'silicon valley' of the Thames Valley and beyond. This includes
Reading, Slough and Swindon, towns that have expanded greatly
since 1970. Although much of Milton Keynes' expansion was
unique, in that it was led by a public sector 'urban entrepreneur-
ial' development corporation with considerable power and
resources to attract inward investment, the new city did nonetheless share in post-industrial growth since 1980.[38]

SOURCES, AND THE IMPORTANCE OF SYNTHESIS

Finally, it must be emphasised that little serious *history* has been
written about Milton Keynes. Here too, there is an important point
to be made. For the years in which Milton Keynes was born, the
later 1960s, were also years that witnessed the maturation of three
important disciplines within the canon of historical studies: social
history, urban history and planning history. Social history and
urban history have become increasingly popular on both under-
graduate and postgraduate courses in British universities since the
late 1960s. They were, both of them, wide-ranging and exciting
disciplines that sometimes intersected, for example, in the study of
the social life of great cities. Urban history, for example, looks at
the causes of urbanisation, and at the changing nature of towns
and cities. Social history is concerned with lived experience in the
past, and with the evolution of society and culture.

Planning history is a more focused discipline. It owes a great
deal of its existence to the work of the late Gordon Cherry and to
Professor Anthony Sutcliffe, both founders of the International
Planning History Society. Its major concerns are with the evolution
of town planning over the centuries, especially since the later
Victorian years, and with the personnel and influence of the town
planning profession.

The little serious history that has already been written about
Milton Keynes falls largely within the profession of planning
history. Terence Bendixson and John Platt's *Milton Keynes: Image
and Reality*, published in 1992, remains the most significant
example. As its dust jacket states, however, the book was 'not so
much about the people of the city as the creators of the place they
live in'. And Bendixson and Platt wrote a largely favourable 'top-

down' account of the planning of the new city, and its construction. They were even allowed to use 'confidential MKDC board minutes', minutes that are denied to mere academics under the 30-year rule. This fact in itself explains the warmth of the book towards MKDC and its key figures. Whilst there is much that is useful to subsequent historians in the book, the lack of an attempt to synthesise the planning history of Milton Keynes with its social evolution has created an opportunity for just such a project. This present book hopes to meet that opportunity.

In addition to Bendixson and Platt, architectural historians and critics have made many judgements on the built environment of the new city. And there are a number of shorter anecdotal and anti-quarian histories, and also oral histories, of Milton Keynes. Furthermore, a number of writers within the professions of sociology and social anthropology have made investigations into aspects of Milton Keynes. Other academics who have researched the new city come from the discipline of urban geography, and also those interested in agricultural and estate management. And of course, as a planned new city, Milton Keynes has been the subject of a number of assessments in town planning journals. There is thus a diverse range of studies on Milton Keynes that can be used by contemporary historians.

Probably the most useful sources of information about the new city, however, were generated by the Milton Keynes Development Corporation itself. In addition to the two-volume *Plan for Milton Keynes* and its accompanying documentation, MKDC undertook regular household surveys, economic and employers surveys and a host of other specially commissioned reports. These surveys and reports amount to a uniquely invaluable archive for the historian of this new city. After the development corporation was wound up in 1992, Milton Keynes Borough Council and then the unitary authority of Milton Keynes Council from 1997 also undertook regular annual surveys of the new city.

And finally, where would any historian of local and national social history be without newspapers? The interest of national newspapers in Milton Keynes has already been noted, and later chapters of the book include a number of articles and features on the new city. The local newspapers, however, have been a more important primary source. During the late 1960s, the local press was largely composed of the free *Bletchley Gazette*, the more stentorian *North Bucks Times* and a few small-scale free local papers in Wolverton and Newport Pagnell. The arrival and growth of Milton

Keynes soon converted the *Bletchley Gazette* into the *Milton Keynes Gazette*, and it also generated a number of new newspapers in addition to these. They were free weekly sheets; no regular daily local newspaper had taken root in Milton Keynes by 2000. Nonetheless, these weekly newspapers add up to an important source of reports and current perspectives on issues affecting the formative years of Milton Keynes. Taken together, all of these sources have been invaluable in exploring the relationship between the rapidly evolving urban fabric and the social life of the planned new city.

So Milton Keynes, so often referred to as the city of the future, deserves an early historical analysis of its recent past, an analysis that synthesises social change with urban growth and town planning. This city is of infant heritage, but its heritage is rich enough to provide an understanding both of the new city itself and, more widely, of the social evolution of England since the 1960s.

STRUCTURE OF THE BOOK

The book is organised in the following way. Chapter 2 discusses the origins of Milton Keynes, and the long-established as well as the more recent forces that led to the designation of the new city during the 1960s. It necessarily discusses the formulation of the *Plan for Milton Keynes* by Milton Keynes Development Corporation between 1967 and 1970, and some of its key principles. These were, after all, intended to shape the future growth of the new city.

Chapter 3 provides an overview of the development of the physical fabric of the city from 1970, and it highlights the fact that the built environment of Milton Keynes, so often termed a 'suburban city', did not evolve quite like some of the original main planners had hoped or anticipated.

The fourth chapter discusses the reaction of the existing population of North Buckinghamshire to the early designation of the new city, and their responses to the *Plan for Milton Keynes* between 1967 and the early 1970s. It also assesses the impact of urbanisation on the farmers and farm workers. Not surprisingly, they were amongst the most vociferous opponents of a city that would remove most of the agricultural land in the area. So this is not only a chapter about Milton Keynes *per se*. It can also be viewed as one experience among many in the oftentimes unhappy story of postwar farming in Britain.

Chapter 5 asks who moved to Milton Keynes, and the following chapter evaluates the experiences of settling down in the new city. Together, these chapters demonstrate that the general description of Milton Keynes as 'Middle England', a largely affluent and increasingly middle-class population, is and remains broadly legitimate. Chapter 7, however, looks at those who were on the margins of Middle England in Milton Keynes, the poor and the unsettled of the new city who struggled, often unsuccessfully, to make a life there.

Chapter 8 discusses the lively and diverse social life that evolved in the new city between 1970 and 2000. It emphasises that the many levels of social interaction, both formal and informal, were proof of the ideas in the *Plan for Milton Keynes*: locality would remain as a base for community, but the growing range of interests in people's lives would draw people together on a voluntary basis as and when they felt the need to enjoy a shared enthusiasm, fight for a cause or take up an issue. Milton Keynes, it becomes clear, was never a dormitory city or a sleepy satellite of London.

Finally, Chapter 9 observes the negative attention that Milton Keynes continued to attract into the early years of the twenty-first century. It also notes that the lessons of Milton Keynes since 1967 have been ignored by some of the most important figures in the debate about England's so-called 'urban renaissance' during the 1990s and since. The chapter argues that, by ignoring Milton Keynes, many leading architects and planners displayed an indifference to a sizeable and demonstrably popular experiment in urban living.

NOTES

1 Nick Nuttall, 'Prescott bids to cut urban sprawl', *The Times*, 8 March 2000; Helen Johnstone, 'Villagers fear being engulfed as Milton Keynes expands', *The Times*, 8 March 2000; Commission for New Towns, *Milton Keynes: 2001 Official City Atlas* (Reading: GEOProjects, 2001), p. iv.
2 Milton Keynes Council, *Facts and Figures, 1999–2000* (Milton Keynes: Milton Keynes Council, 1999), p. 4.
3 Kirsty MacColl, *Still Life*, on *What Do Pretty Girls Do?* CD (Hux Records, 1998); The Style Council, *Come to Milton Keynes*, on *Our Favourite Shop* CD (Polydor, 1985).
4 Mark Clapson, 'Technology, social change, and the planning of a post-industrial city: a case study of Milton Keynes', in David Goodman and Colin Chant (eds), *European Cities and Technology: Industrial to Post-Industrial City* (London: Routledge, 1999), pp. 279–300.
5 Letters, *Milton Keynes Express*, 26 August 1977. See also Jack Trevor Story, 'Story of my life', *Milton Keynes Express*, 2 September 1977.
6 Muriel Cato, '"I'm all right here" says Jack', *Milton Keynes Express*, 18 November 1977.

7   Jack Trevor Story, *Dwarf Goes to Oxford* (Milton Keynes: Leveret Press, 1987).
8   Christopher Booker, *The Seventies: Portrait of a Decade* (Harmondsworth: Penguin, 1980), pp. 145–8.
9   J. B. Priestley, *English Journey* (London: Heinemann, 1934), p. 401
10 Beryl Bainbridge, *English Journey, or, The Road to Milton Keynes* (New York: Carroll and Graf, 1997), front and back covers.
11 Bainbridge, *English Journey*, pp. 153–7.
12 Bill Bryson, *Notes From a Small Island* (London: Black Swan, 1996), pp. 175–9.
13 Wayne Coles, 'Now Bill loves the city', *Milton Keynes Citizen*, 19 October 2000.
14 Susan Marling, *American Affair: The Americanisation of Britain* (London: Boxtree, 1993), pp. 55–66.
15 John Stevenson, 'The Jerusalem that failed? The rebuilding of postwar Britain', in Terence Gourvish and Alan O'Day (eds) *Britain since 1945* (London: Macmillan, 1991), p. 102.
16 Leon Krier, *Houses, Palaces, Cities* (London: Architectural Design Editions, 1984), pp. 48, 104.
17 Hunter Davies, *London to Loweswater: A Journey through England at the End of the Twentieth Century* (Edinburgh: Mainstream Publishing, 1999), pp. 36–51.
18 David Aaronovitch, *Paddling to Jerusalem: An Aquatic Tour of Our Small Country* (London: Fourth Estate, 2000), pp. 63–9.
19 Barbara Ellen, 'Dire Rea', *Observer*, 1 February 1998.
20 Simon Hoggart, 'Forever England', *Observer Magazine*, 10 June 1990.
21 See special reports on Milton Keynes and the new towns in *Financial Times*, 1 October 1992; The Milton Keynes Survey, *Financial Times*, 3 April 1992. Other reports in other newspapers include David Young, 'Urban revolution in full bloom after 25 years of growth', *The Times*, 26 April 1991; Charles Nevin, 'Myth and Milton Keynes', *Guardian*, 29–30 July 1989.
22 Robert Harris, *Enigma* (London: Hutchinson, 1995); Ted Enever, *Britain's Best Kept Secret: Ultra's Base at Bletchley Park* (Trowbridge, Wiltshire: Sutton Publishing, 1999); Michael Smith, *Station X: The Codebreakers of Bletchley Park* (London: Channel 4 Books, 1998), Milton Keynes Library holds a sizeable collection of materials on Bletchley Park.
23 Blake Morrison, 'How the other half lives', *Independent on Sunday Magazine*, 15 June 1997.
24 A. D. Mills, *Oxford Dictionary of English Place Names* (Oxford: Oxford University Press, 1998), p. 243.
25 Milton Keynes Council, *Facts and Figures, 1999–2000*, p. 20.
26 Gareth Smyth (ed.), *Can the Tories Lose? The Battle for the Marginals* (London: Lawrence & Wishart, 1991), p. 132.
27 Mark Clapson, 'Suburbia and party politics', *History Today*, September 2001, pp. 16–18.
28 Steve Larner and Nick Hammond, 'D-Ream comes true', *Milton Keynes Citizen*, 8 May 1997; Richard Cooper, 'Blair set for city TV debate', *Milton Keynes Sunday Citizen*, 13 May 2001.
29 Ralph Rugoff, 'Inside the virtual city', *The Business, Financial Times Weekend Magazine*, 22 January 2000.
30 Paul Barker, 'Though un-English and much sneered at, Milton Keynes is a success' [etc.], *New Statesman*, 4 October, 1996.
31 David Firnberg and David West, 'Milton Keynes: creating an information technology environment', in William H. Dutton, J. G. Blumler and K. L. Kraemer (eds), *Wired Cities: Shaping the Future of Communications* (London: Cassell, 1997), pp. 392–408.
32 Joel Garreau, *Edge City: Life on the New Frontier* (New York: Doubleday, 1992). pp. 6–7.
33 Julie Charlesworth and Allan Cochrane, 'Anglicising the American Dream: tragedy, farce and the "post-modern" city'; draft of conference paper presented to the British Sociological Association Conference 1995: 'Contested Cities', University of Leicester, 10–13 April 1995, pp. 9–10.
34 Charlesworth and Cochrane, 'Anglicising the American Dream', p. 17; see also Julie Charlesworth and Allan Cochrane, 'American Dreams and English Utopias', in Mark Clapson, Mervyn Dobbin and Peter Waterman (eds), *The Best Laid Plans: Milton Keynes since 1967* (Luton: Luton University Press, 1998) pp. 109–15; Julie Charlesworth and Allan Cochrane, 'Tales of the suburbs: the local politics of growth in the South-East of England', *Urban Studies*, 31, 10 (1994), pp. 1723–38.

35 Milton Keynes Council, *Geographical Information Services, information dated 'Stock at 31/12/2001'*. I am grateful to Julie-Ann Hammond of GIS at Milton Keynes Council for this information.
36 John Best, 'Milton Keynes: maturing new town or regional adolescent', *Town and Country Planning*, February 2001, pp. 54–5.
37 Tim Mars, 'Little Los Angeles in Bucks', *Architects' Journal*, 15 April 1992, pp. 22–6.
38 Charlesworth and Cochrane, 'Tales of the suburbs', pp. 1727–30.

— 2 —

Where Did Milton Keynes Come From?

On a sunny day you'd think you were driving through California.
John Grigsby, *Daily Telegraph*, 23 January 1992

New towns have been built for centuries. Some of the forces which brought the new city of Milton Keynes into existence began in ancient times, for example the growth and movement of population, and the need for commerce, communication and social interaction. As this chapter will show, during the 1960s the planners of the new city were attempting to harness these long-established antecedents to the demands of an increasingly affluent, and an increasingly mobile, population. The 1960s were an exciting time, and not simply in the realms of sexuality, permissiveness, radical politics and rock and roll. The decade also witnessed some stimulating debates about urban change, and a great deal of speculation about the 'city of the future'. More than most cities, Milton Keynes deserves to be viewed as the outcome of some dynamic new thinking about the nature of urban life.

THE PROLOGUE

New towns and cities are an ancient idea. The Minoans on the Aegean island of Crete appear to have been the first civilisation to have developed planned new settlements. As Minoan civilisation spread across the island, some 1,900 years before the birth of Christ, new cities appeared to be the most rational and controllable way of directing population growth and of maintaining the rule of law. Knossos is the most famous example of these Minoan cities. According to classical historians, it was not a forbidding place. It was an unwalled settlement, unused, as far as we can tell, to the wars to which later fortified Mediterranean cities would become victim. It was also a low-rise settlement, with most buildings of a geometric shape, and of just one, two or three storeys. An impressive palace and a temple, and a number of busy streets and corners were at the centre of Knossos. Elegant town houses were to be found at the centre of that city, and also in other Minoan settlements. As one Cretan authority on his island has written of Minoan civilisation, 'We even seem to discern traces of town planning in the settlements of the time.'[1] Yet this does not appear to have been an oppressive project of town planning. It did not attempt to tie everything into the centre. A large part of the residential area of Knossos spread out from its symbolic and practical heart, suggesting a gradual merging of town and countryside the further one travelled from the centre. Many houses enjoyed gardens and cultivated spaces.

The wealthiest inhabitants possessed comfortable homes, some of which even had running water and flushing toilets. Minoan cities also benefited from economic expansion for many years which, according to the great urban historian Lewis Mumford, 'permitted life to flower during the earlier phases of Minoan culture'. That life, as Minoan art reveals, was heavily influenced by hedonism and a respect for the beauty of the natural world.[2]

Today, Knossos is a busy tourist attraction, but walkers in Crete who care to move off the tourist trails can discover the age-old ruins of smaller Minoan settlements that were built over two centuries before the birth of Christ. They occupy, in common with Central Milton Keynes, well-positioned sites, with good views of the surrounding countryside.[3]

In a conscious reference to Knossos, Milton Keynes took as its initial symbol the Minoan double-headed axe. This symbol can still be seen carved into the ruins of those ancient Cretan settlements. It can also be seen on the early records and documents created by Milton Keynes Development Corporation, and can be identified on the first place signs erected in the new city. This icon is a monogram comprising the letters M and K: **M**inoan-**K**nossos; **M**ilton **K**eynes.

There are other and more compelling similarities between Ancient Greece and contemporary Milton Keynes. Pre-classical

Greeks colonised large swathes of Aegean and Mediterranean lands, and as they settled they sometimes laid out their new cities along gridsquare lines. The grid was a rational and regular design that facilitated easy direction and orientation. These gridsquare-based cities have been described as 'the first fabricated neigh-bourhoods'. For example, Thurium, founded in 443 BC, was a geometric city, divided by four horizontal and three vertical arter-ies. Within these arteries, 10 'neighbourhoods' provided a territ-orial base for the local tribes.[4] Over subsequent centuries, many new communities were built within gridsquares. The Classical Greeks went on to do so, and so did the Romans. Within the modern and contemporary era, American cities are obvious exam-ples of such cities. Today, Milton Keynes is famous for being one of very few cities in England based upon a grid.

More references between Ancient Greece and contemporary Milton Keynes may be contrived. In classical Greek mythology, the new town of Thebes owed its origins to Cadmus, the son of the King of Tyre. The story goes that Cadmus arrived at Delphi where he had been told to erect a settlement on the spot where a cow lay down once she had left the temple. A cow was duly seen trotting out of a temple, and Cadmus built his citadel, or Cadmea, at Thebes, where she eventually lay down.

It was very hot on the site, and Cadmus needed water. Blocking his way to the river was a dragon. Cadmus killed it. Unfortunately, the dragon was a son of the God of War, Ares, who forced Cadmus into servitude. Luckily for Cadmus, however, the attractive goddess Athena visited him and told him to sow the dragon's teeth in the earth in order to make himself a little army. This he did, and a clutch of armed and irritable warlike men sprang up, whom Cadmus dealt with by setting them to fight against each other. The survivors of this incident became allies of Cadmus, and estab-lished themselves as the ancestors of Thebes, the 'sown men' or 'Spartoi'.

This is the stuff of legend: Milton Keynes was founded by a man whose initial was also a C, Lord Campbell of Eskan, the head of Milton Keynes Development Corporation. The new city was built on fields where many cows once grazed, but it is now associated forever with those concrete cows. The personnel of Milton Keynes Development Corporation were sown into place by the Ministry of Housing and Local Government. Those early founders have also left their mark: streets, buildings and parts of the new city bear their names, just as the surviving areas of ancient metropolises bear the names of earlier, more powerful, men. And although the King of Tyre is long dead, the tyre is king in Milton Keynes: without motorised transportation, the new city would cease to function. For the grid roads and the vehicles upon them are the products of the evolving human need of mobility and connection.

LONG-TERM FORCES: INDIVIDUALISM, TRANSPORTATION AND MOBILITY

In 1949, the professional journal *Town Planning Review* carried two articles on the growth of a small country town in Buckinghamshire from the thirteenth century to the nineteenth, that is, from the late mediaeval period to the modern era. The town was Stony Stratford, and it had developed and expanded as a continuing historical consequence of two profound forces. One was the growth of economic individualism, and the other was the rise in transportation and communications networks.

As people broke free from feudal and manorial ties during the mediaeval period and became independent labourers, rural employers, tradesmen and landowners, Stony Stratford became a relatively prosperous place. Along with North Buckinghamshire more generally, the town was known for its large numbers of free tenant farmers relative to villeins, that is, to those ostensibly bound to the manor by social obligation and economic dependence. This explains why North Buckinghamshire enjoyed high levels of private wealth accumulation over the centuries, and that in turn led to higher levels of land purchase, and a system of small tenants renting from landowners. Others were independent small farmers in their own right.

The privatisation of the countryside expanded during the enclosure movements of the eighteenth and nineteenth centuries, as wealthy landowners and some small farmers with surplus capital competed to buy land for more intensive and mechanised farming. A growing population in England necessitated rationalised and more productive food and clothing production. In common with thousands of other market towns, Stony Stratford became an essential place to trade foods and clothes, and to make the social and economic connections essential to the local rural economy.[5] Moreover, the old Watling Street ran straight through Stony Stratford, and as a principal coaching route it had brought into being a number of well-known and prosperous local inns, notably the Cock Inn and the Bull Inn. Stony Stratford was just seven miles north along Watling Street from another centre of coaching inns, Fenny Stratford, whose Swan Inn, Saracen's Head and Red Lion were also popular local hostelries and resting places for weary travellers, and also for the horses which drew along their coaches. Travellers from Fenny to Stony, moreover, had to pay a toll at the gate by Two Mile Ash, a small collection of farms alongside Watling Street.[6] This is because that section of Watling Street, which was originally built as a Roman road, had been made into a turnpike road between the Bedfordshire village of Hockliffe and the Buckinghamshire hamlet of Two Mile Ash, following an Act of Parliament in 1706.

Yet the roads were about to lose their monopoly as the means of conveyance for people and goods. During the course of the later eighteenth century, the revolution in transportation began. Canals, also called navigations, were cut across England as the industrial revolution gathered pace. The Grand Junction Canal Act of 1795 brought the canal of the same name into North Bucks, and it was followed by many shorter canals linking Fenny and Stony Stratford to local points north, south, east and west. And the canals, in their turn, brought into the area a variety of changes. Many hundreds of navigation workers dossed down in the cheapest rooms available in the area for the duration of the construction work, bringing coarse language, heavy drinking and thus welcome earnings for innkeepers. The canals also lent an interest and a man-made beauty to the landscape, because they brought locks, and also rustic brick-built bridges, a number of which still grace the canal where it flows through the new city. Water transport also produced the impressive iron trunk aqueduct across the River Great Ouse near Old Wolverton. The canals also brought prosperity, carrying the goods of the country more cheaply than roads.

The canals were brought into existence by private companies. These companies often included landed capitalists. They, and also smaller landowners, stood to make a fortune, or at least a tidy sum, from the sale of part of their land to a canal company, and from charges for use of the waterway. Yet the great era of the canal was relatively short-lived: it lasted from the 1790s to the 1830s. For during that latter decade, newer money-making opportunities became apparent in the form of a new elongated metal beast. A number of unsuspecting people were killed by them, and contemporaries often claimed that they were dirty noisy things, but the trains were on their way. The first major railway line through

North Buckinghamshire was built by the London and Birmingham Railway Company during the 1830s. It would become a key artery of the national railway network.

The London and Birmingham Railway Company decided that Wolverton, a village in North Bucks, about halfway between London and Birmingham, would be a suitable site for a central engine works where locomotives could be serviced and repaired. Construction was begun on the Wolverton Works in 1837, and, in addition to the engine shed and the workshops, a station was also constructed on the main line between London and the Midlands. Furthermore a residential area of closely packed terraced houses was built nearby. The illustration of this development in Sir Frank Markham's *History of Milton Keynes and District* reveals what town planners call a rectilinear layout: the main streets are dead straight, and the little streets off them are also very straight, like a little grid. As a local historian has argued, 'The settlement at Wolverton station was a consciously founded new town.'[7]

The terraced houses were built for the obvious reason that the Wolverton Works required workers. The most numerous groups were skilled, semi-skilled and unskilled manual workers and labourers, and engineers, train drivers and administrators. From 1837 to 1861, as Wolverton grew and was consolidated, it became a 'magnet for migrants' who were looking for regular work and improved housing. Many newcomers to Wolverton came from the local and adjacent towns and villages in Buckinghamshire, Bedfordshire and Northamptonshire. Yet others came from much further afield, and from most English counties. Middlesex and London in the South East of England, Lancashire and Yorkshire in the North, and Warwickshire in the Midlands, for example, were quite well represented in Wolverton. There were also Scots, Irish and Welsh workers, and even an engineer from America.[8] Thus did a new town of the nineteenth century provide a sort of historical dress rehearsal for the later new city in North Bucks. It also became an ageing part of Milton Keynes post-1967. Today, the tidily built and partially ornamented red-brick Victorian houses of Wolverton provide an interesting alternative, within the new city as a whole, to the newer housing developments of recent decades.

The town of Bletchley also became quite dependent on the train. Denbigh Hall Junction Bridge, opened in the early Victorian years, symbolised the significance of the train both in Bletchley's purview and in its local economy.[9] It was the most elegant part of a highly visible viaduct of lines rising above Bletchley, but the smoke and soot belching into the air above this architecturally nondescript town gave Bletchley a down-at-heel image which it has had difficulty in living down. George Orwell, for example, in his 1938 novel *Coming Up for Air* depicted the drab grey suburban town of 'West Bletchley'. And as we will see in a later chapter, Milton Keynes Development Corporation also did little to improve Bletchley's image, despite its early promises.

The local and national railway network continued to grow throughout the nineteenth century. And well into the twentieth century, moreover, the railways were extensive. An iron lattice of branch and local lines spread across so much of the Home Counties, including as far as Verney Junction, at Winslow near Buckingham. Yet the Verney Junction to London connection was axed in the same decade that the new city of Milton Keynes was born, the 1960s. And the reason for both of these seemingly unconnected developments was also based upon transportation, notably, the rise and rise of the motor car.

This is why Dr Beeching, Head of the British Railways Board, felt during the 1960s that the railway system was perhaps too extensive and costly for the country at a time when the motor car was in the ascendant. He is now remembered as the man responsible for cutting back on the railway network during the early 1960s. Yet Beeching was not the only one who felt that a new future of motorisation raised questions for the railways. During the 1950s, the Conservative government had begun the motorway system. The M1 had been opened in 1958 as the main new road from London to the North, and it ran through North Buckinghamshire, on its way to Northamptonshire and, ultimately, to Yorkshire. At a time when the British motor industry still seemed to have a future, many in the town planning professions understood that the growing ownership and popularity of the motor car was probably unstoppable, at least for the time being.

In 1961, therefore, the Ministry of Transport appointed Colin Buchanan, an expert on urban planning and transport, to study the effects of motor cars on the urban environment. Buchanan's report, *Traffic in Towns*, was published in 1963, and it has been described as 'one of the major planning documents of the postwar era' because of its understanding about the huge impacts of motorisation on English towns in the near future. The report argued that new urban designs were required to accommodate and minimise the worst effects of mass motor car use.[10]

Other reports emphasised an increasingly motorised future.

The Ministry of Housing and Local Government, in its *South East Study*, published in 1964, argued that the population shift to the South East of England from the declining industrial areas, in alliance with the growing demands for roads and for space for motorised transport, required the consideration of planned new urban developments in the region.[11] The *South East Study* had accepted the principle of the planned urban expansion of nearby Northampton in the southern region of Northamptonshire, and also of a potential new town in North Bucks. Planned growth, unlike sporadic urban expansion, would enable population, transport and employment to be channelled into specific areas of the region.[12] This, among other things, would help to conserve the countryside. Brand new towns, then, would be the product of the motor age, just as Wolverton had been a product of the railway age.

There is an irony here. For at much the same time as the railway system was being modified, a man working in Buckinghamshire County Council was dreaming Corbusian dreams of a city of apartment blocks, rising up beside lakes, and whose principal form of transportation would be, not cars, but the train. The man was Frederick Pooley, Chief Architect and Planner of Buckinghamshire. He wanted Bucks County Council, in the form of its County Development plans, to take advantage of the possibilities for the planned urban expansion in the northern area of the county. Development in North Bucks would also help to preserve the green belt in the southern half of the county from further encroachment.[13]

Pooley's dreams for North Bucks were very different to what would subsequently grow there. As noted, the train was essential to Pooley's ideas, just as it had been essential to the economy of North Bucks towns since the Victorian years. Yet this was not to be an old steam train or even a new-generation diesel-powered engine. Instead, it was to be an upside-down train, to wit, a monorail. As Tim Mars, a writer and consultant on urban affairs, argued in 1995, 'it is difficult to decide why monorails are so special':

> Railways we know are old-fashioned, but monorails somehow are gee-whiz technology. They are the future. Somehow, getting a train to run on one rail and hanging it upside down fundamentally transforms it from a boring old train. The interesting thing about monorails is that they have been built; and where are they built successfully? Disney Land. But they don't lead anywhere, [they] take you around Disney Land . . .[14]

Pooley's monorail would not have led anywhere except 'Pooley-ville' itself. It was to have been a huge figure of eight. Within it, people would live in blocks of flats and town houses, and travel to work and places of leisure by monorail. For Pooley's design was a modernist one: a space-age city which was intended to reflect the totalitarian urbanism of the Swiss architect Le Corbusier.[15] The way people lived their lives was subordinated to the public functioning of the city.

Pooley's ideas were supported by a number of key personnel on Bucks County Council, notably the County Clerk and various members of the council housing planning committee. And they were bold enough to attract the attention of Ian Nairn. Writing in his 'Architecture' column in the *Observer* newspaper's *Weekend Review* in 1964, Nairn described Pooley's potential town as 'the most adventurous and imaginative scheme in Britain' and 'a city of the future which isn't just an abstract diagram or intellectual firework'.[16]

Unfortunately for Pooley, his city would never be realised. In a classic containment manoeuvre, he was invited onto the Board of Milton Keynes Development Corporation from 1967 as a 'special advisor', and, as Walter Bor has since recalled, 'we started to assemble our arguments against [Pooley's plan]':

> and eventually, in Pooley's presence, we had to demolish the plan, and Pooley eventually, gracefully, agreed that his plan was not implementable. So that was the story about Pooley.[17]

Pooley's personal vision, with its emphasis upon closely built, high-density housing in order to support a monorail, was thus firmly rejected by Llewelyn-Davies *et al.*, the company formulating the Plan on behalf of MKDC. They deplored its limited conception of movement, and instead plumped for that road-grid to facilitate motorised traffic and movement across the future new town.[18]

Ultimately, however, Pooley was marginalised for yet another reason: he was a provincial operator in the 1960s, and so he was not permanently at the heart of the influential network of planners, politicians and academics based in London.[19] There were some ironies in this situation. Pooley was a Londoner by birth. Milton Keynes, moreover, was to be a new city which drew heavily upon London as a source of population from 1970. Moreover, as we saw in Chapter 1, it has been often derided by London journalists. Yet it was largely the product of a group of elite architects, planners and social scientists based in the bookish heart of the capital city, in Bloomsbury. The man in the middle of this network was the Labour peer, Richard Llewelyn-Davies. He was Professor of Architecture and Planning at University College, London and of course the head of the consultancy that drew up the *Plan for Milton Keynes* on behalf of Milton Keynes Development Corporation.

At this juncture, two important forces combined to bring about Milton Keynes. One was that network of elite professionals, so many of whom worked in London, at the Centre for Environmental Studies. The CES was established in 1966 and based at University College, London. And the second force was the new towns programme, first begun in 1946, but which was revived during the mid-1960s. Both deserve to be discussed in turn.

THE NEW TOWNS PROGRAMME

The new towns were a Labour creation. The first New Towns Act was passed in 1946, and it was a central part of the Reconstruction of Britain following the Second World War. Aerial bombardment had left hundreds of thousands of homes damaged and destroyed, and many of these lay in the industrial areas of England's great cities and towns. London had been particularly badly hit, as a third of its homes had been partially or completely ruined by German bombs. Many Londoners were forced to live with relatives or friends. More than that, there was already a housing shortage in England before the war. During the 1930s, governments had cut back on local authority house-building projects to save money during the Great Depression.

There was thus a housing crisis in early postwar Britain, and the New Towns Act was one solution to it. In England, 11 new towns were built from 1946 in order to relieve pressure on the old city and town centres. This was to be accomplished by the planned dispersal of the population of those centres to bright new communities built in the countryside. Eight of the 11 original new towns were built in the South East of England, in order to relieve bomb-damaged, overcrowded and smog-filled London. These were Basildon, Bracknell, Crawley, Harlow, Hatfield, Hemel Hempstead, Stevenage and Welwyn Garden City. Welwyn was a symbolic reminder of the garden city heritage of most of the postwar new towns. It had been built in Hertfordshire, nearby to the

Edwardian garden city of Letchworth, during the 1920s and 1930s.

Both Letchworth and Welwyn Garden City were established by Ebenezer Howard, whose book *Garden Cities of Tomorrow*, first published in 1898, was probably the most important single influence on the modern garden city movement. He was also central to the establishment of the Town and Country Planning Association (TCPA) in Britain. For Howard and the TCPA, a major solution to the social and environmental ills of the Victorian city was the small-scale garden city in the nearby countryside. Garden cities would not be densely packed industrial places, but offer low-density residential areas of cottages and flats within close and convenient employment. The garden city was to be economically self-sufficient, in that most people would be employed by local employers, but industry was to be zoned separately from residences into distinct areas. Howard also hoped and anticipated that local people would bring about a lively and urbane civic culture: regardless of income and class, people would engage socially with each other, and they would take an interest in their town, and work to keep it sociable, and environmentally healthy and secure.[20]

By 1939, Letchworth and Welwyn stood as interesting and influential exemplars of what gentle but inspired town planning could achieve. They had become known across the world to those interested in urban problems and in new communities as a solution to them.[21] The impact of the Second World War, moreover, further elevated the status of the town planning profession. The destroyed areas of England's industrial towns and cities would require radical environmental surgery once the war was over. And the slums had continued to undermine English towns throughout the 1930s and since. The formation of the Ministry of Town and Country Planning in 1943 allowed town planners such as Raymond Unwin and Frederick Osborn to argue for a large-scale programme of new towns in order to solve the imminent and pressing urban problems facing Britain. Slum clearance and council housing was also part of this grand solution. The New Towns Act, and the new communities that it produced, remains a major achievement of the first postwar Labour government.

The Conservative governments from 1951 to 1964 were less directly engaged with the TCPA, for many reasons, but the election of a Labour government in 1964, with Harold Wilson as Prime Minister, more fully renewed acquaintances between politicians and planners. In the following year the second New Towns Act was passed. Along with Milton Keynes, other new towns, for example at Northampton, the county town of Northamptonshire, at Peterborough in Cambridgeshire, and Telford in Shropshire, were enabled by the Act of 1965.

There were a number of reasons for this revival of new towns legislation during the mid-1960s. One has to do with the reforming zeal of the recently elected Labour government. The Conservatives had been in power for 13 years until 1964, and, although they had continued to invest in new towns and although the existing new towns had continued to be built, there was something of a 'retreat from planning' during the 1950s.[22] Only one new town was constructed, namely Cumbernauld in Scotland. By the mid-1960s, many Labour politicians and sympathetic professionals concerned with urban issues wanted a new lease of life for planned new towns. This was in no small part because they felt that the planning of a further phase of new towns could learn lessons from the previous generation. They also felt that social change, notably greater mobility due to the increasing use of the motor car, and the growing use of telephones and other forms of telecommunications, held important lessons for the 'city of the future'. Some academics, for example, were arguing that the idea of the 'local' as a basis for community was becoming redundant. Finally, as noted above, there was considerable population movement across Britain. This meant that planning for the physical environment, in all its complexity, required fuller and more imaginative research and debate.

THE CENTRE FOR ENVIRONMENTAL STUDIES

Lord Llewelyn-Davies and his wife Patricia were very much part of the Labour Party 'establishment' of the 1960s. Both Llewelyn-Davies and Richard Crossman, the Minister for Housing and London Government, were proactive in the formation of the Centre for Environmental Studies (CES). They sought substantial funding from the Ford Foundation, a philanthropic organisation established by Henry Ford between the wars, and based in New York. It was clear that the new towns were a major justification for the CES bid. In the USA, many town planners and civil rights activists were in favour of a programme of planned new racially integrated communities, model alternatives to the white suburb/ black inner city pattern that dominated and demoralised so many of America's larger urban centres. The British new towns programme, the largest of its kind in postwar Europe, was something that could be learned from.

The first phase of British new towns, however, was viewed by many commentators on town planning as a largely successful, if flawed, experiment. There had been something missing in the new town programme, a lacuna derived from a wider problem in British town planning. Crossman, Llewelyn-Davies and others in their respective professions shared the common view that British town planning lacked systematic and policy-directed research into the social and economic implications and consequences of planning the physical environment.[23]

This was a long-term failure. Under the years of the Conservative government, throughout the 1950s and early 1960s, many independent micro-sociologies had been published on the social consequences of town planning. Unfortunately, so much of this research had occurred in a vacuum, within a space which seemed divorced from housing and town planning policies. British sociological journals of the 1950s contained many articles on urbanisation and social problems, yet they went unread by most town planners. The development corporations that built and managed most new and expanded towns, furthermore, had not really commissioned any detailed and systematic qualitative research on the needs and experiences of their residents. These issues surfaced during Crossman's ministry from 1964, and it was fundamental to his and Llewelyn-Davies's appeal to the Ford Foundation.

Crossman drafted the terms of the early draft request to the Foundation. He played to the important lessons that could be learned from the British experience of physical planning, but noted its pragmatic character and what he viewed, accurately or inaccurately, as the national insularity of British town planners. Significantly, the minister highlighted the failure of town planners in Britain to incorporate the work of social scientists and economic geographers in their approaches to urban problems.[24] Hence the 'mission' of the CES was 'to serve as an intellectual stimulus for more effective attacks on urban regional problems, particularly through the marshalling of experience and through the financing of systematic research':

> The Centre is concerned mainly with bringing together progressive thinkers, practitioners and experts from universities, research centres, government bodies, private planning and contracting concerns and similar bodies abroad to consider together the most prac-

ticable approaches toward the solution of various urbanisation problems . . . [Research] will emphasise medium-range problems, with a view toward the next fifteen years.[25]

The grant makers at Ford felt that 'Foundation participation in the initiation and financing of the London Centre would represent a substantial contribution toward improving the quality of British efforts to solve serious urban problems, and toward linking Britain with the urban experience and research of other countries.' They also emphasised that 'foreign experts have been helpful in confronting urban problems in the United States and US experience has been profitably studied abroad'. There was also a desire to assist British town planners and politicians in confronting current problems of urban growth, its new phase of new towns and its slum clearance programme.[26]

Once it was established, the Board of the CES was headed by Llewelyn-Davies, whom Crossman more or less ordered into place. The Centre included some of the leading academic and public professionals of the 1960s and early 1970s, including David Donnison, a Professor of Social Administration at the London School of Economics. Its first Director was Sir Henry Chilver, an engineer, who was replaced in 1969 as Director by Donnison. The reasons for including these details are because the CES, Llewelyn-Davies, Donnison and Chilver would all be associated with the planning of Milton Keynes. Various key aspects of the rationale of the CES, furthermore, notably the importance of introducing more sociological and social thinking into town planning, would become directly incorporated into the formulation of the new city. And Milton Keynes was also the product of an Anglo-American network of town planners, some of whom were associated with the CES.

THE PLANNING OF MILTON KEYNES

Between 1967 and 1970 members of the CES, and visiting academics and researchers, worked on the *Plan for Milton Keynes*. David Donnison was a long-standing advocate of the importance of informing planning and housing policies through social investigation and responsive decision-making. In this, Donnison was part of an Anglo-American network of sociologists, including R. E. Pahl in Britain, and Herbert J. Gans and Melvin Webber from the

USA. Each of these men also had an interest in the formation of new communities.

Each of these sociologists was involved in the CES in some way. Gans, for example, had given a conference paper at the Centre in 1968 entitled 'Planning for people, not buildings'.[27] But of particular note was the invitation to Melvin Webber of the University of California, Berkeley, a visiting academic at the CES, to delineate for the Milton Keynes planning team the nature of 'the urban society of the future'. Donnison was keen on Webber's inclusion, and in a series of seminars Webber emphasised the need for town planning to encompass a holistic approach which included technological developments and their impact upon social and economic action. Webber's views had a clear affinity with the work of Alfred J. Kahn at Columbia University. The Russell Sage Foundation was instrumental in promoting such work. Kahn emphasised 'social planning'. This was largely an American innovation. It emphasised the need for planners and government officials to identify and provide for often only barely visible social and cultural trends.[28]

Derek Walker, who was the Chief Architect at MKDC from 1970 to 1976, has argued that Webber deserves the accolade of 'the father of Milton Keynes'.[29] This is because Webber's writings during the 1960s were influential upon many town planners who were trying to reformulate their ideas about what towns should look like, and about how towns and cities were functioning, in an era of rapid technological change. Webber's ideas and arguments were complex, and are summarised in the following paragraphs.

Webber took Los Angeles, and also San Francisco and other fast-growing urban areas of California, as a model for his interpretation of the changing nature of towns and cities in relation to technological advances. California revealed much about the social and technological forces which were endemic to postwar towns and cities as they moved 'beyond the industrial age', that is, as their economies became less dependent on manufacturing and increasingly so upon services. People and employment were dispersing away from town and city centres. Service sector places of employment, composed of shops, offices, distribution warehouses and leisure parks, were lighter and easier to move to cheaper sites than heavy industrial plant or such fixed industries as ship-building and coal mining. As a consequence, towns were continuing to expand, but their spatial spread did not unravel or disintegrate social and economic relationships: these were held together by the car and by instant communications via the telephone. In addition, news and information was passed on through screens, the television screen and increasingly the computer. In tandem, these developments widened and stretched personal relationships and business networks spatially, far beyond the small scale implied by the term 'local'. People still bonded and interacted with each other, but they did not necessarily have to live next door or just up the road any more. This was 'community without propinquity'.

Webber argued strongly, therefore, that town planners should liberate themselves from the restrictive idea that a town centre with high-density developments close to it was the ideal form of town life. He argued against any notion that people were solely dependent upon nearby nodal centres. Instead, in affluent societies, increased opportunities of mobility through speedy travel enabled a greater range of residential and locational choices. The impact of global communications in advanced societies, furthermore, notably the television and the telephone, which were fast becoming items of mass consumption, were providing people with instant access to news and information no matter where they might be.

His insights can be most sharply comprehended through the key words and terms which he used to portray his interpretation of the dynamic and changing relationship of urban form to social change in postwar Los Angeles. His key words were 'plurality', 'diversity', 'individualism', 'mobility' and 'affluence'. His key terms were 'interest communities', the aforementioned 'community without propinquity', 'the nonplace urban realm', 'disparate spatial dispersion', 'the knowledge explosion', and the culmination of all these forces in the 'post-city age' and the 'post-industrial era'.

Care is needed when using the term 'post-industrial'. Anyone who argues that Britain still has a significant industrial base, and therefore cannot be 'post-industrial', clearly has not read Daniel Bell, one of the first academics to use the term 'post-industrial' in the 1950s. For Bell, a conservative American sociologist, there was still a considerable industrial component to the American economy, but it was no longer the dominant sector. Bell also argued that, as countries moved away from goods production to an increasingly services-based economy, certain things would occur. For example, he predicted the fairly obvious growth in service-based employment. He also anticipated the growth of 'intellectual technologies' and the ascendancy of a more information-based society as communications became more sophisticated, but accessible.[30] Webber, without ever saying so, shared much of Bell's analysis, but he related it specifically to urban theory and town planning.

Webber's work was cogent, but conjectural. He made no focused or limited predictions about the future of urban societies. Instead, he saw himself as 'trying to foresee latent qualitative consequences before they become manifest'.[31] In this spirit, Webber argued that town planners needed to embrace the spread of urban dispersal as a spatial expression of social forces which were working in harness with technical and economic forces.

Webber, then, stood against those pessimists who saw dispersal and suburbanisation in negative terms. Many American and British writers had argued in the 1950s that the suburbs were essentially bland areas of mass-produced houses providing accommodation for millions of atomised and privatised people whose status consciousness and cult of domesticity meant that they were forgetting how to be truly communal. The 'suburban malaise' or the 'suburban sadness' were seen to result from the alleged isolation of suburbia.[32] For example, a number of sociologists compared the older, supposedly more vital, urban communities of close and extended kinship networks, with the fate of allegedly bored and lonely suburbanites in their ostensibly nice but spiritually desolate new home. Peter Willmott and Michael Young's *Family and Kinship in East London*, first published in 1957, notably discussed Londoners who had moved from the cockney vitality of Bethnal Green to the dormitory suburbs of Essex.[33] Here, they huddled round the television set, became pathetically competitive with their neighbours, and communicated with relatives and old friends down the telephone wires, whereas once they had 'popped in' for a chat. Willmott and Young castigated planners for bringing about this alleged social degradation through planned dispersal policies.

Webber was altogether more optimistic than this. People were 'realising ever expanding opportunities for learning new ways, participating in more diverse activities, cultivating a wider variety of interests and tastes, developing greater capacities for understanding, and savouring richer experiences'. In this scenario, the role of place as a basis for stimulating social interaction required reconsideration. It was only one of many variables which brought people together, and an increasingly less important one.[34] Hence the significance, then, of phrases such as 'interest communities' and 'taste communities'. The planners of Milton Keynes broadly shared this view of the nature of social interaction, and they set about devising an urban framework which would facilitate it. To this end, a grid system was adopted, comprising fast roads which served a pattern of dispersed but easily accessible residential settlements.

The grid system, therefore, reflected planners' interpretations of the impact of technological developments upon social change. The idea that community was only stimulated by proximity was jettisoned. As Derek Walker of MKDC argued in 1982, 'The scale of society has changed':

> A village or a neighbourhood in a city had a social relevance at a time when physical nearness was the only basis for social contact. Today, we organise our social lives through the telephone, post box, private cars and public transport. Our lives are more influenced and informed by TV, radio and newspapers than by meetings in the street or chats over the garden fence.[35]

And as Walker went on to say, this meant that the physical nature of the city had to be planned to reflect freedom of movement and of choice, and to provide the means whereby people could make and take their opportunities. Hence, he described the grid as 'an open matrix for selection' for the individual citizens of the new city. This conception of mobile and increasingly flexible living patterns would find its physical expression in the gridiron of roads which would be spread, like a net, over the designated area of North Bucks.

This interpretation of spatially complex patterns of mobility and interaction had further consequences. Significantly, the *Plan for Milton Keynes* did not use the concept and language of 'neighbourhood'. Lord Llewelyn-Davies, writing in the planner's journal the *Town Planning Review*, in 1966, had argued that some of the planning principles that had informed the older new towns were 'under question'.[36] And one concept that was being heavily interrogated was that of the 'neighbourhood unit'. Many of the early postwar new towns had been designed to neighbourhood unit principles. This had been a mode of arranging residential family housing around the nearby school or schools, and shops and other amenities. It had assumed that most people would live most of their lives within the immediate locality.[37] Yet as sociologists had found, people rarely concentrated all or even most of their lives in their immediate neighbourhood.[38] Such findings were well known within the Centre for Environmental Studies and MKDC by the later 1960s.

Nevertheless, whilst localism was relegated as the mainstay of community, it was not rejected outright. The physical planning of the city was to operate in synthesis with a programme of social development. In her 1969 paper on 'Social development', Suzanne Beauchamp of MKDC outlined the view of the programme at that time. It was to consist of arrivals workers, officials who would meet and greet newcomers, and encourage them to do the same to other newcomers. They were also sources of information for people who were not used to the new city. The longer-term programme of social development, however, was to promote community development by encouraging people who wanted to be 'doers' on behalf of others. In addition, whilst MKDC was to build schools, sports and leisure facilities, it also saw itself as a catalyst in the provision of other facilities should there be an identifiable collective demand. They would make available space and other resources.[39]

Social development was also to be underpinned by a programme of research into the social needs and aspirations of the people of the new city. This was termed 'monitoring and evaluation'. David Donnison, along with others at the Centre for Environmental Studies, notably the sociologist Michael Harloe, assisted in the preparation of the programme for MKDC. It broke new ground in British town planning. A series of criteria were devised in the identification of goals, the resource requirements to meet them and the measurement of success. For example, housing policy was to be measured not simply in terms of numbers of houses built, nor solely in terms of the right houses for the right income groups, but how far the housing provided would meet the demands of various types of household and their lifestyles. Another major aim of monitoring and evaluation was to provide research to enable inter-agency cooperation between MKDC, the local and county councils, and various voluntary and philanthropic bodies. Here, again, the aims were both responsiveness and flexibility when catering for the needs and desires of local people.[40]

It is somewhat disappointing to report, then, that this innovative monitoring and evaluation programme did not really happen. Peter Waterman, who worked as manager of social development in MKDC from 1972 to 1988 has since recalled that the monitoring and evaluation programme fell foul of professional rivalries and short-term considerations: 'It was a victim of inter-professional rivalry in the MKDC, opt-out by statutory agencies, and the general manager's view of its secondary importance in 1972.'[41] The general manager of MKDC, Fred Lloyd Roche, appears to have not put his weight behind it, thus hastening the demise of a programme that would have provided a uniquely rich and detailed social audit of the new city in its first 25 years. Such information would have been based upon the input of many significant institutions and associations working with the people of the new city. MKDC did commission regular social and economic surveys, however, but these were limited in aim and scope. Nonetheless, they do at least provide some very useful data.

INFRASTRUCTURE AND ENVIRONMENT

Beyond social considerations there were, of course, more mundane factors. Land had to be cleared, pipes and cables set down, roads laid and buildings built. Anyone interested in the engineering and constructional history of Milton Keynes can usefully turn to *The Plan for Milton Keynes* or to the *Milton Keynes Planning Manual* (1992), both produced by the development corporation. These describe in both words and illustrations the rapid evolution of the city's infrastructure, and also the great care and imagination that informed the landscaping of the new city's wider environment.

Much of the landscaping was placed alongside the roads and inserted into gridsquares in the form of small or large parks. But the linear parks remain the city's greatest green achievement. They were intended to be attractive additions to the landscape and to provide people with pleasant walking environments: all of the parks are laced with combined walkways and cycleways. Hence the linear parks became an essential part of what is now known as the 'green grid', the system of walkways and cycle-paths called 'redways', that flowed from and into the residential gridsquares, through the linear parks and alongside the lakes and the waterways of the new town. These paths passed under or over the main arteries of through traffic, the grid roads. There was, furthermore, and in theory at least, to be no through-traffic whizzing through the gridsquares.[42] And it was also intended, and became reality, that horse riders could ride without interference from road traffic, on the bridleways that also lace the city.

Water was also envisaged as a major amenity and attraction. The rivers, streams and a canal run through the parks, and the corporation preserved and enhanced much of the existing green spaces alongside the river and canal banks. And a number of lakes were also landscaped into the city's parks. The lakes certainly had a run-off function for road water. The lakes, moreover, are quite small compared to most natural lakes. Nonetheless, a number of them, notably Willen Lake and Caldecotte Lake, are large enough for fishing, sailing and other water-based sports, and they provide a great visual interest to the city's built environment.

CONCLUSION

Milton Keynes, in common with all other cities, new and old, was a product of demographic, economic and social forces. It was also a unique outcome of those town planners, architects, sociologists and other professionals who came together at the Centre for Environmental Studies and in London, and in MKDC headquarters in Milton Keynes, to debate and formulate the framework of the new city. The scope of their collective approach was historical, contemporary and futuristic. Milton Keynes became effortlessly imbued with the light-touch city-centre-in-the-countryside that can be identified in Minoan cities. We can add to this some key planning principles of the English garden city movement, and a nuanced relationship to the suburban ethos. This was apparent in the rejection of Pooleyville, and in the adoption of its alternative, the Los Angeles-style road-grid with residential estates separated from employment gridsquares. The very fact of the grid recognised the greater role of mobility, motorisation and choice in most people's lives. The new city, then, was born from a complex synthesis of ideas, influences and intentions. Hence the Plan explicitly and implicitly recognised that there was room for both 'urban' and 'rural', and 'new' and 'old', and 'local' and 'non-place' connections, within the lives that people wanted to lead. And the Plan wished to create an attractive city, whose citizens would be able to make the most of life.

As the next chapter will show, these principles were given expression in the construction and development of the city from 1970.

NOTES

1 Theocaris E. Detorakis, *History of Crete* (Heraklion, Crete: Geronymaki, 1994), p. 11.
2 Colin Chant, 'Greece: urbanisation in the Aegean region', in Colin Chant and David Goodman (eds), *Pre-industrial Cities and Technology* (London: Routledge, 1999), pp. 50–2; Lewis Mumford, *The City in History* (Harmondsworth: Penguin, 1979), p. 144.

3 Gerald Cadogan, *Palaces of Minoan Crete* (Methuen: London and New York, 1980).
4 Mumford, *The City*, p. 225.
5 Francis E. Hyde, 'The growth of a town, part 2: a study of the economic forces control-ling the growth of Stony Stratford, Buckinghamshire', *Town Planning Review*, 20, 3 (1949), pp. 187–99.
6 This account of canals and railways is based upon Sir Frank Markham, *History of Milton Keynes and District;*, vol. 2, *From 1800 to about 1950* (Luton: White Crescent Press, 1986), pp. 1–106.
7 J. French, 'Wolverton: a magnet for migrants 1837–1861', *Records of Buckinghamshire*, 28 (1986), pp. 138–47.
8 French, 'Wolverton', p. 144.
9 Markham, *History*, vol. 2, pp. 67–9, and illustration of Denbigh Hall Bridge circa 1850, between pp. 150 and 151.
10 Gordon Cherry, *Town Planning in Britain since 1900* (Oxford: Blackwell, 1996), pp. 162–3.
11 Ministry of Housing and Local Government, *South East Study, 1964–1981* (London: HMSO, 1964).
12 Ministry of Housing and Local Government, *Northampton, Bedford and North Bucks Study: An Assessment of Inter-related Growth* (London: HMSO, 1965), Foreword.
13 Buckinghamshire County Council, *North Bucks New City: CDA and Designation; 1, – Written Statement* (Aylesbury: Buckinghamshire County Council, not dated); Buckinghamshire County Council, *North Bucks New City: CDA and Designation; 2, – Report* (Aylesbury: Buckinghamshire County Council, not dated).
14 Tim Mars, 'Milton Keynes: a view from exile', in Mark Clapson, Mervyn Dobbin and Peter Waterman (eds), The *Best Laid Plans: Milton Keynes since 1967* (Luton: Luton University Press, 1998), p. 119.
15 Fred Pooley, *North Bucks North City* (Aylesbury: Departments of Architecture and Planning, Buckinghamshire County Council, 1966); Fred Pooley, 'Buckinghamshire new city', *Ekistics*, 19, 114 (1965), pp. 281–3.
16 Ian Nairn, 'The best in Britain', *Observer Weekend Review*, 22 November 1964.
17 Bor, in Clapson, Dobbin and Waterman (eds), *Best Laid Plans*, p. 9.
18 Bor, in Clapson, Dobbin and Waterman (eds), *Best Laid Plans*, p. 9.
19 In 1974, however, Pooley became Head of Planning and Transportation of the Greater London Council, and went on to become its Chief Architect. Pooley died on 11 March 1998. See Obituaries by Andrew Saint and Illtyd Harrington in the *Guardian*.
20 Peter Hall and Colin Ward, *Sociable Cities: The Legacy of Ebenezer Howard* (Chichester: John Wiley, 1998).
21 A comprehensive collection of materials on Letchworth and Welwyn Garden City, and other garden cities that were influenced by them, is held at the Sir Frederick Osborn Archive, Welwyn Garden City public library, Hertfordshire, England.
22 D. V. Donnison, *The Government of Housing* (Harmondsworth: Penguin, 1967), pp. 306–7.
23 Richard Crossman, *The Diaries of a Cabinet Minister*, vol. 1, *Minister of Housing, 1964–1966* (London: Hamish Hamilton and Jonathan Cape, 1975), pp. 228, 233, 527.
24 Ford Foundation, New York, grant number 6700083, Centre of Environmental Studies: *Memorandum by the Minister of Housing and Local Government; Centre for Environmental Studies* (not dated), p. 1.
25 Ford Foundation, New York, grant number 6700083: Memo from F. Champion Ward via Joseph Daniel to McGeorge Bundy, *Grant Request, International Affairs*, 14 July 1966.
26 Ford Foundation, New York, grant number 6700083: Memo from F. Champion Ward via Joseph Daniel to McGeorge Bundy, *Grant Request, International Affairs*, 14 July 1966.
27 Herbert J. Gans, 'Planning for people, not buildings', *Environment and Planning*, 1 (1969), pp. 33–46.
28 Alfred J. Kahn, 'The social planner and the city: the task in perspective', in Alfred J. Kahn, *Studies in Social Policy and Planning* (New York: Russell Sage, 1969), pp. 157–93; see also Alfred J. Kahn, *Theory and Practice of Social Planning* (New York: Russell Sage, 1969).
29 Derek Walker, *The Architecture and Planning of Milton Keynes* (London: Architectural Press, 1982), p. 8.
30 Daniel Bell, 'The coming of the post-industrial society', in Charles Jencks (ed.), *The Post-Modern Reader* (London: Academy, 1992), pp. 250–1.
31 Melvin M. Webber, 'Planning in an environment of change, part 1: beyond the indus-trial age', *Town Planning Review*, 39 (1968–69), p. 181.

32 David Reisman, *The Lonely Crowd: A Study of the Changing American Character* (New Haven, CT and London: Yale University Press, 1950).
33 Michael Young and Peter Willmott, *Family and Kinship in East London* (London: Routledge & Kegan Paul, 1957).
34 Melvin M. Webber, 'Order in diversity: community without propinquity', in Lowdon Wingo (ed.), *Cities and Space: The Future Use of Urban Land* (Baltimore, MD: Johns Hopkins University Press, 1970), p. 28; Melvin M. Webber, 'The post-city age', in Larry S. Bourne (ed.), *Internal Structure of the City: Readings on Space and Environment* (New York: Oxford University Press, 1971), pp. 496–501.
35 Walker, *Architecture*, p. 8.
36 Richard Llewelyn-Davies, 'Town design', *Town Planning Review*, 37, 3 (1966), p. 157.
37 Andrew Homer, 'Administration and social change in the postwar British new towns: a case study of Stevenage and Hemel Hempstead' (Luton: University of Luton, unpublished Ph.D. thesis, 1999). An original study of the early postwar new towns, which contains an informed discussion on the problems of the neighbourhood unit.
38 See, for example, Norman Dennis, 'The popularity of the neighbourhood community idea', in R. E. Pahl, *Readings in Urban Sociology* (Oxford: Pergamon Press, 1968), pp. 74–94; Peter Willmott, 'Housing density and town design in a new town: a pilot study at Stevenage', *Town Planning Review*, 33, 2 (1962), p. 125.
39 Suzanne Beauchamp, 'Social development' (1969), reprinted in Clapson, Dobbin and Waterman (eds), *Best Laid Plans*, pp. 59–69.
40 Milton Keynes Development Corporation (hereafter MKDC), *The Plan for Milton Keynes*, vol. 1 (Milton Keynes: MKDC, 1970), p. 21; *The Plan for Milton Keynes*, vol. 2 (Milton Keynes: MKDC, 1970), pp. 129–31; MKDC, *The Plan for Milton Keynes: Technical Supplement No. 4: Notes on Monitoring and Evaluation* (Milton Keynes: MKDC, 1970).
41 Peter Waterman, 'Social development in action', in Clapson, Dobbin and Waterman (eds), *Best Laid Plans*, p. 82.
42 MKDC, *The Plan for Milton Keynes*, vol. 2, p. 325; MKDC, *Milton Keynes Planning Manual* (Milton Keynes: MKDC, 1992), pp. 52–5.

— 3 —

The Suburban City Takes Shape

The British like the idea of the country in the town and Milton Keynes has achieved this to an unusual degree. Although Milton Keynes has very good architecture – it has millions of very good trees. These make the town almost invisible from the roads – and perhaps it is true of almost all of the [new] towns that the landscaping puts the architecture in its place.

> Colin Amery, 'The rural fabric of domesticity', *Financial Times*, 1 October 1992

There are duck ponds, cricket greens, paddocks full of horses, and pubs surrounded by fields instead of car parks. Petrol stations are banished to the main roads and the new houses meld with the old, being in the same red-brown brick and tile.

> Simon Hoggart, 'Forever England', *Observer Magazine*, 10 June 1990

It was emphasised in Chapter 2 that the influence of Melvin Webber and the Los Angeles-style grid both contributed to a perceived suburbanity in the planning and design of Milton Keynes. In their 1992 book on Milton Keynes, Terence Bendixson and John Platt, both writers on urban matters, described the new city with much justification as a 'grand suburban design'.[1] Whilst all of that is true, however, the story is not particularly straightforward. For the suburban city that Milton Keynes was to become after 1970 was neither wanted nor anticipated by some of the key planners of Milton Keynes. As Tim Mars has argued, the planning of the physical environment of MK was ultimately a victory for suburban influences over the cooler modernist urbanism

envisaged during the later 1960s and the 1970s.[2] Commercial
forces and popular preferences, as well as a change in the management of Milton Keynes Development Corporation, contributed to
the demise of the more modernist vision for Milton Keynes. This
happened both to the city centre and also to the residential and
even the employment gridsquares beyond it.

CENTRAL MILTON KEYNES

The development of Central Milton Keynes (CMK) between the
publication of the Plan in 1970 and its implementation through
until the year 2000 owed much to the original Plan. But the planners themselves were not necessarily agreed upon the interpretation of the Plan.

Of the original planners, Walter Bor, for one, has since recalled
that he and other members of the planning team preferred a
clearly defined urban centre of low-rise squares surrounded by a
variety of commercial, recreational and residential buildings.
Originally he and his allies in MKDC were in favour of a modest
central area that would become *primus inter pares* with most of the
other gridsquares.[3] The idea was to disperse the activity centres
around the city so that much of what people wanted or needed
would be located within convenient distances at many small
nodal points. To some extent that did occur, as each gridsquare
was provided with its own shops, and a number of large decentralised 'district centres' were built, each containing a large super-
market and a range of other outlets, as well as burger and pizza
restaurants. Employment gridsquares, moreover, were also dispersed across the city. Employment areas were not to be dispro-
portionately located in the heart of the new town, as they were in
so many traditional towns. Hence the relationship of the city
centre to the rest of the city was a fundamental one. And the basic
question, during the mid-1970s, was simple but consequential:
should CMK become that *primus inter pares* type of place, or
should it turn into a big bristling dominant core for Milton
Keynes?

During the mid-1970s there was liaison between the development corporation and the public about what type of city centre,
and what type of shops, would be most popular and successful for
the city. As Bor, who was Czech by birth, has recalled, 'Derek
Walker and I took part in a public discussion':

We didn't want to be too prescriptive, but we did want to convey something which was a unique opportunity. And that was to avoid all the major contradictions of city centres as we know them, like the over-concentration of jobs, particularly offices, the central role it plays as a hub which attracts all the city's traffic. Because of the dispersal of employment, because of the general flexibility in the arrangements [outlined in the Plan], we felt here is a unique opportunity to create a city centre, traditional streets and squares, where people could meet, where there would be a feeling of common public realm. Because you can solve the major problems of congestion and of over-development, [we] suggested this idea simply as a concept to be developed further. And in that public meeting Derek Walker poured scorn on it, on me personally, for my continental background in trying to introduce something which is OK on the continent but of course completely un-British here. He said it was completely out of character with MK.[4]

Bor's and Walker's discussions with the public occurred within MKDC's survey of the local and regional population about potential 'shopping attractions' in the new city. It was an exercise designed to ascertain what type of shopping environment shoppers wanted, and their favourite outlets. The report of this survey, published in May 1976, makes fascinating reading, not only for its relationship to the subsequent plans for the shopping facilities in Milton Keynes, but also for what it reveals more generally about the aspirations and desires for shopping and spending during the mid-1970s, a period of consumer pessimism.[5]

The research was qualitative, and involved interviews with over 110 people from the nearby towns of Bedford, Bletchley, Dunstable, Luton and Northampton. The interviewees were subsectioned into 'teenagers', 'mixed adults', 'women' and 'men'. Most of the interviewees, however, were women. Both working-class and middle-class consumers were represented. The difference between the 'routine weekly shopping', which was largely considered a chore, and pleasurable shopping for luxuries and goodies was clearly apparent. Women were still most heavily burdened with routine shopping, and mothers with children found it particularly stressful. Shopping by car was preferred, but the expressed annoyance of finding parking spaces or jostling with other shoppers was noted by MKDC. A major worry 'was whether car parking would be adequate for peak demand'.[6]

There were clear preferences about what sort of shops people wanted: large department stores offered choice and cheapness, as well as the more expensive brands. Some women, however, presumably working-class, felt that John Lewis department stores were 'middle class'. And in towns where there was no Marks and Spencer the shop was clearly desired not for its inexpensiveness but for the quality and reliability of its products. Generally, shoppers wanted a wide range of clothes and luxury goods shops, as well as cafés and restaurants. Some also wanted a good market for the cheap variety and second-hand goods on sale because stall holders 'offer goods you don't get in the big stores'. Other words pertinent to shopping attractions were 'character', 'life', 'individuality', 'variety' and of course 'value'.[7]

There was, however, a clear divide between those who favoured covered shopping centres and those who did not. Those in favour pointed to the weather protection they offered, the traffic-free environment and their provision of convenient toilets. Those against thought that covered shopping centres were shabby and sometimes threatening places. A middle-class teenager from Luton, for example, referring to the town's Arndale Centre, commented that 'I find it a dirty place, and it sort of hasn't got any character either', while another stated that 'there are a lot more people just hanging about with nothing to do'. And the views of shoppers in Bletchley ranged from dislike to disgust at the Brunel Centre, a covered shopping area bequeathed to the town by Milton Keynes Development Corporation during the early 1970s. 'I'm not too keen on it; it's always too crowded,' stated one woman. 'Too dark,' stated another, and another agreed: 'That's right – I don't like that tunnel; it frightens me.' Its external features were also criticised: 'an eyesore'; 'ugly as anything'; 'sticks out like a sore thumb'.[8] (Pevsner's *The Buildings of Buckinghamshire* was equally scathing.[9])

Such popular criticism was also to be found in the responses to the designs for the proposed shopping building in Milton Keynes. The shoppers were shown beautifully drawn illustrations of the glassy exterior and the spacious light interiors. As the report found, 'responses were divided, but tended on balance toward the unfavourable'. Some women from Bletchley made the following points: 'I like my shopping to be more intimate than that.' 'It's cold.' 'Barren.' 'Unfriendly.' 'I'd like to see some nice brick.'[10]

Nonetheless, the decision was subsequently taken by Derek Walker and others in MKDC to build large strong modern buildings that would declare that the new city and its centre were 'here'. And in commissioning the huge shopping building, MKDC affirmed the original intention of the Plan to boldly grow Milton Keynes as an important regional magnet for retail, leisure and employment.[11] The shopping building, designed by Stuart Mosscrop, was mentioned in Chapter 1 for the strong reactions it produced from many people who had visited it as interested observers. Yet its large size and unrelenting functionality may be viewed as a successful experiment in mall design for a regional catchment area, and as an ultimate validation of Derek Walker's schema for the city centre. By 1981, over half the shoppers came from outside the designated area of the new city.[12] Even Walter Bor, whose intentions for CMK had been somewhat more modest, was obliged to acknowledge that the shopping building developed into a powerful economic generator, and also to admit that the mall was 'a very attractive alternative solution' to what he had had in mind.[13]

Others felt that the shopping centre was a fine building. The journalist Simon Hoggart, visiting Milton Keynes for the *Observer* newspaper in 1990, 'went to the vast, glassed-in, palm-infested shopping centre in the middle of the town'. To him the locals seemed more content and calmer than shoppers who lived in the 'vile city centres' full of 'loutish architecture' of traditional towns. The shopping building was spacious, jam-free and covered, and its users were 'spared many of the minor annoyances which plague the rest of us'.[14]

There were further issues, however, that directly stemmed from the building's undoubted success. First, its imposition may be said to have been authoritarian, given the generally unfavourable nature of the prior public responses towards it. Second, though, it was and remains a very popular building. The sheer volume of usage has proved that, and so did subsequent surveys of shopper attitudes. In 1988, for example, over 4 out of 5 (80 per cent) of people surveyed by MKDC were satisfied with the shopping in CMK, and only 1 in 10 (10 per cent) were dissatisfied.[15] This raises a tricky, perhaps even worrying, issue in an ostensible democracy: if the people reacted against something, but were provided with it anyway, and then actually liked it, is this a more generalised justification for promoting modern architecture in the face of popular suspicion?

There was, of course, also an outside realm to Central Milton Keynes. The surrounds of the shopping building were liberally provided with acres of safe and convenient car parking spaces. This of course was essential to the needs of a suburban city. People were driving in from elsewhere to the centre, and also commuting in from the hinterlands. An adequate number of car parking spaces eased the experience of motorists and through such convenience aided the economic success of the centre. And the concept of ease of mobility was not confined to motorists. It has also been noted that the one-level access to the building from the outside, with electrically operated doors, and no steps or stairs, made the centre extremely attractive to wheelchair users[16] (something which Beryl Bainbridge had failed to notice[17]).

Either side of the building, the city centre was also given wide boulevard roads, lined with London plane trees, from which shorter but equally straight streets and 'gates' were connected. The names of the boulevards and the gates, it has been pointed out many times, were folksy and suggested the ancientness of the area being concreted over: Secklow Gate, for example, was named after a Saxon meeting place, a mound now preserved near the council offices in the city centre. The shorter street names, however, were reminiscent of Manhattan: they were given such names as 'North Ninth Street', 'North Tenth Street' and 'South Seventh Street'. The railway station and the bus station were also built to be impressive functional structures. In common with the shopping building they were glassy, rectangular but impressively scaled buildings. Other avowedly modern buildings, however, were built of brick. The council offices were completed in 1979. The public library, completed and opened in 1981, was described in common with the shopping building as 'classically-inspired modernism', but the library was finished in red brick rather than glass.[18] The police station and law courts and other major public buildings were also located in Central Milton Keynes, between the main centre and the railway station.

The urbanity of Central Milton Keynes was widely celebrated, both by those who had been involved in its design and planning during the 1970s and by those who did not work for MKDC, but who were impressed with the modernity of CMK.[19] Yet from the early 1980s the heart of Milton Keynes was about to undergo some changes. The previous Chairman of MKDC, Lord Campbell, was replaced by the Conservative government in 1983 with Sir Henry Chilver, a businessman. Chilver had been involved with the Centre for Environmental Studies, but was also well known among planners for his Thatcherite sympathies.

The 1980s and 1990s witnessed less emphasis upon design as a _laissez-faire_ attitude increasingly held sway with MKDC's leadership. The proliferation of small to middling-sized buildings in Central Milton Keynes that filled the city between the station and the centre was proof of this. Many of the office blocks, cheaply built and not necessarily designed by architects, have been viewed as miserable little boxes, piecemeal intrusions into the cool rational cityscape that had been constructed prior to the years of Chilver–Thatcher.[20]

For Derek Walker and Stuart Mosscrop, this type of desecration was quite sharply symbolised in the impact of the deregulation of public transport – buses – on the bus station. A building dedicated to public service was converted, during the 1990s, into a Chicago restaurant, and a café for bus drivers so they could enjoy a cup of tea or coffee between shifts or journeys. It must also be emphasised that many fine buildings or environmental features that had been planned for CMK were, ultimately, never built. They were considered too expensive according to newer, more market-orientated considerations and were thus dropped.[21] Rather like Pooleyville, they were confined to the counter-factual realm, as Melvin Webber might have termed it: the realm of what-might-have-been.

Yet those small office blocks, along with much larger ones such as the Abbey National headquarters, were the product of an economic policy that was not just drummed up by Chilver. A commitment to grow Milton Keynes as a regional centre was expressed not simply in the commercial buildings of the 1980s, but also those of the previous decade. As Lee Shostak, a key planner in the development corporation for most of the 1970s and 1980s has stated, because of the Plan there was a clear aim to make MK one of the South East of England's premier office locations. This, he has claimed, contributed to the diversity and robustness of the local economy.[22]

Not everything going up in CMK was built for secular ends. In 1991 the dome was lowered by huge cranes onto the brick building that became, the following year, the first 'ecumenical cathedral' in England, namely the Church of Christ the Cornerstone, sited near to the civic offices and to the western wing of the shopping building. The church was built to resemble a minor version of St Paul's Cathedral in London, and architectural critics scoffed at its trimmed-down traditionalism. Within a very short time, however, it had established itself as a highly successful and popular place of worship for Anglicans, Roman Catholics, Baptists, Methodists and the United Reform Church. It has also acted as a meeting place for Buddhists and other non-Christian religions.[23]

In the eyes of some architectural critics, however, such diversity, allied to newness, did not make for a recognisably 'central'
city centre. Nikolaus Pevsner and Elizabeth Williamson's *The
Buildings of Buckinghamshire* volume concluded in 1994 that,
despite the assembly of public and commercial buildings, the city
centre looked like and functioned as 'an out-of-town shopping
centre and business park, unconventionally placed at the city's
hub'.[24] They were not alone. For Tim Mars, writing in 1997, the
jumble of office blocks and shopping buildings of CMK looked
and felt 'more like an out-of-town retail and business park [than]
a city centre'.[25] Yet even at that juncture, a new phase of buildings
was being planned. As Mars penned his impressions, Milton
Keynes was undergoing a change of governance. Milton Keynes
Borough Council became a unitary authority, Milton Keynes
Council, in 1997. This removed the influence of the Buckinghamshire County Council in local policy making, and gave a greater
level of self-determination to the council, in theory at least. And
soon afterwards, the Commission for New Towns corporately
morphed into 'English Partnerships' at the end of the 1990s.

In terms of land development, English Partnerships was, and
remains, a major influence on the development of CMK. It possessed considerable funds and powers in the selling-off of land to
developers. How far members of the new unitary Milton Keynes
Council agreed with some of the decisions about land use in the
centre is a mystery. But in the later 1990s a number of important
structures were soon added to Central Milton Keynes. The Xscape
building, opened in 2000, is a huge and dominant construction,
which contains Britain's first real snow ski slope, a 16-screen
cinema, and a variety of shops, restaurants and bars. It is situated
on the south eastern flank of the city centre, and at the time of
writing it was managed by Pierre-Yves Gerbeau, ex-Director of the
Millennium Dome in London. More architecturally stylish than
Xscape is the theatre and art gallery, opened in 1999, and designed
by the architectural company Blonski-Heard. These buildings and
the accompanying 'theatre district', situated between the ski slope
and the John Lewis end of the shopping building, have added both
cachet and diversity to Central Milton Keynes. Even Jonathan
Glancey, an eloquent enemy of suburban towns, wrote in favourable terms of the 'hip' architecture of the new theatre district and,
more generally, of the new city's 'special place in the architectural
firmament'.[26]

In addition, the new Midsummer Place was opened in time for

the new millennium. This was another glassy construction, an extension to the shopping building that brought with it more new shops and cafés, and added to the already considerable level of variety and choice that existed in the centre.

THE COUNTRIFIED CITY

Beyond the city centre, Milton Keynes became dominated by open space, housing estates and employment gridsquares. If we take the open spaces first, the ethos of 'the country in the city' was manifest in these recreational areas. They were generously provisioned with millions of new as well as the existing trees. A number of lakes were also constructed, the largest of which were at Willen, Furzton and Caldecotte. MKDC also preserved a number of sizeable ancient woodlands, for example Linford Wood and Shenley Wood. They are closely located between housing areas and employment gridsquares, and thus easily accessible by foot.

In addition, a number of linear parks flow throughout the city, providing an attractive and extensive network of walks. These recreational routes are lined with trees and shrubs, and in places they run alongside lakes, the canal and the River Ouzel.

As many editions of the *Bletchley Gazette* and the *North Bucks Times* illustrate, from 1968 to 1970 Milton Keynes Development Corporation had made much of the green and rustic aspects of the new city, and they also stressed the complementary conservation measures that were to be in the Plan.[27] These were ways of convincing the existing people in North Bucks of the city's future attractiveness, and thus of softening up public opinion. This corporate commitment was evident in the invitation by MKDC to Professor Sir Nikolaus Pevsner to provide a brief on 'Preservanda and Conservanda' in the designated area. An Anglophile with a detailed knowledge of provincial architecture drawn from his county surveys, Pevsner described the interesting and beautiful features of a number of churches and notable public buildings, some of which, such as old churches, are situated in parklands. In his *Technical Supplement* to *The Plan for Milton Keynes*, Pevsner emphasised that the new city would not 'absorb' these gems, but would aesthetically 'incorporate' them.[28]

The linear parks have proved to be an undoubted success. As noted above, these were largely intended for recreational and scenic purposes, but the range of activities embraced pedestrian and cyclist movement around the city. As Mars has argued, the lakes and the linear parks are to Milton Keynes what the beaches are to Los Angeles.[29] The paths that run from the parks pass under or over the main arteries of through-traffic, the grid roads, and thus connect the cyclist or pedestrian to housing areas with very little danger of collision with traffic.[30]

THE RESIDENTIAL GRIDSQUARES BEYOND THE CENTRE

It was noted above that the city centre was not intended to develop quite how it did. The same was true of the housing areas in Milton Keynes. As Elizabeth Williamson wrote in 1994, what Derek Walker originally 'had in mind [was] not a series of similar suburbs':

> but a variety ranging from the formal with urban streets in a rural setting – a humanised version of Corbusian ideas – to more picturesque layouts next to linear parks and incorporating existing villages.[31]

Hence, in his 1982 book *The Architecture and Planning of Milton Keynes*, Walker had asked 'will Milton Keynes feel urban in 1990?' He listed some of the components of 'urbanity': physical largeness and the large scale; a feeling of intensity of use and of people gathering together; a range of social, recreational, cultural and economic possibilities made possible by urban densities and scale; a positive contrast with the countryside; an enjoyment of these things as an end in themselves, that is, as an enjoyment and a celebration of urbanity.[32]

A suburban ethos and a more formal urban design for Milton Keynes were in a struggle with each other. This struggle, however, was functionally overlaid and in a sense tamed by the zoning policies in Milton Keynes. These policies kept employment and residential gridsquares separated, a classic 'suburban' preference. Each residential gridsquare was provided with retail facilities in discrete little parades of shops, a meeting place and outdoor recreational spaces. This spatial separation of residential gridsquares from each other, and most significantly from the economic life of the new city, was popular with the residents. A study of citizens' perceptions of the town, made for the development corporation during the early 1980s by Jeff Bishop of Bristol University's School of Advanced Urban Studies, found that such comments as 'Having spaces between estates doesn't cut you off' were common: 'I like it. I think MK's getting better but don't want to see things disappear, like green spaces and separation between the estates.'[33]

The quietness of the estates stemmed from their avowedly residential character. Apart from shopping and one pub on most grid-squares, there was no mixed use of the great majority of roads and streets for commercial, employment and leisure purposes. And by the 1980s most people were enthusiastic about this residential character: they liked the greenness, open space and cleanliness. Many were fearful that the low densities and the green and open aspects of many areas of Milton Keynes would be 'lost by over-crowding' and by 'filling-in'.[34]

However, differences in the environmental qualities of grid-squares became quite marked as the new city grew. These differences were partly a consequence of social class and income, and partly a consequence of MKDC housing policy. From the outset the development corporation aimed to build both private homes for ownership and rental housing. The development corporation was to be the major supplier of housing for rent. The provision of accommodation for both rent and purchase was a consequence of failures in earlier new towns, where housing for rent had dominated, and this had failed to attract the middle classes, with their desire for home ownership. So in Milton Keynes, the development corporation originally aimed to supply 50 per cent of the town's homes for rent, while home ownership made up the remaining 50 per cent. The 1970 *Plan for Milton Keynes* also made a clear commitment to mixing housing types, and thus to mixing tenure and occupational groups, across the city.[35]

The modern terraced housing on the gridsquares of Bradville, Beanhill, Fullers Slade and Netherfield, however, were mostly built for rent during the 1970s. They were, of course, the very antithesis of a suburban appearance. Architectural commentators praised the experimentalism of such housing, describing, for example, the aluminium-clad terraced houses and terraced bungalows of Netherfield as 'the most immediately impressive housing development in the city'.[36]

The housing was less popular with its inhabitants, however, most of whom were in manual working-class households.[37] Nevertheless, the operation of the planned dispersal policies within the British new towns programme, in addition to voluntary migration, ensured a continuing flow of migrants to Milton Keynes, from London and elsewhere. Its population continued to grow throughout the 1970s. Nonetheless, by 1980, the new town was tarnished by an image problem, as the first chapter made clear. The new city would continue to suffer, and much of the early housing was largely to blame.

In 1983, however, and as noted above, a change occurred at the top. During the so-called 'chill of Chilver'[38] commercial consider-ations came more fully to the forefront. Moreover, the Housing Act of 1980 brought to an end the building of public sector housing by both local councils and new town development corporations. The 'right to buy' a council or development corporation house also extended home ownership to those in this sector of housing, and demonstrated its popularity when compared to rental tenure.[39]

Milton Keynes reflected these new priorities. MKDC had begun consulting residents through its residential design feedback in the mid-1970s, and in the late 1970s it also commissioned the afore-mentioned study by Jeff Bishop to sound out the residents about the sort of city they wanted and the types of housing they pre-ferred. This study found a great deal of compelling evidence to support the view that most people loved the parklands and the countryside, but not the modern terraced housing. They wanted a low-rise, countrified, low-density city of traditional semi-detached or detached dwellings with gardens.[40] So MKDC was itself aware that its more experimental housing experiments had not proven successful, and that a fresh injection of housing was required.

This is what MKDC increasingly set out to deliver. Its housing became more responsive to popular tastes in domestic architec-ture. Under Chilver, and in the years leading to 1992, MKDC set about its task with some gusto. The 50 per cent rent and 50 per cent sales ratio was dropped in favour of more home ownership. More volume house builders were allowed to build in the mainstream suburban styles or what a recent study has called 'builder's ver-nacular'.[41] Housing thus became more traditional, something that the Pevsner and Williamson volume dismissed as 'post-modern medley'. So-called executive housing flourished.

In addition, the emphasis upon escape from the inner city to the city-in-the-country was re-packaged in the marketing of Milton Keynes. The famous 'red balloons' television campaign during the 1980s was perhaps the best example of this. MKDC deployed tele-vision advertisements that extolled the virtues of *rural* living in a city: the open parklands, lakes, fields and woods, and the villagey aspects of the housing areas. The advertisements certainly fea-tured the bright modern shopping building and some gleaming offices blocks, but they only hinted at what we might call the 'city-ness' of Milton Keynes.

The advertisements presented Milton Keynes as a place of opportunity and freedom, where individual aspirations could be more easily realised than in older urban centres. In one of the red balloons advertisements, for example, a generalised anti-urbanism is cleverly used against London. The capital city, with its frantic traffic jams, its faceless crowds and its rubbish, rubbish both on the streets and spilling out of a chute into a skip marked WASTE, is rejected by a young boy and his parents. Instead, this young boy is driven in a car by his masterful parent into a brave new world, a world that is young, innocent, knowable, green and clean. It could be anywhere; its red balloons could mean anything: they could even be fertility symbols.[42] But they float upwards; they are aspirational, and all this signifies perhaps that MKDC was attempting to move away from the association with the proletarian terraced gridsquare that had bedevilled MK's reputation.

Under Chilver, developers were given a freer rein in the design and layout of the gridsquares. Most building companies opted for more traditional suburban housing styles. This was more acceptable to more people. As Peter Waterman, a social development manager at MKDC since 1972, argued, 'the gridsquares with badly-designed terraces experienced an exodus' of people who could afford to move to more traditional or better-designed houses.[43]

Milton Keynes' housing thus became more mainstream following its early years. In their *Milton Keynes, Image and Reality*, Bendixson and Platt note that the town was 'taking on the housing market characteristics to be expected from its superb location. Buyers were even discovering that it had its share of houses such as might appear in *Country Life*'.[44] During the 1980s, the first new thatched cottage built in the area since the seventeenth century, in a particularly attractive gridsquare, was an unambiguous symbol of this. In fact, earlier research, undertaken during the mid-1970s, had found that most residents, regardless of class, preferred a 'traditional modern' house, built with bricks, situated in short streets, crescents and culs-de-sac.[45]

Hence the shift in direction from the early 1980s was both overdue and popular. It marked a transition from what the School of Advanced Urban Studies termed the 'rationalist' early years to the 'vernacular period'.[46] In estates such as Bradwell Common, for example, the changes led to increased variety in domestic architecture. Originally begun in the late 1970s, Bradwell Common Boulevard contained some fine architect-designed housing and layouts commissioned by MKDC. The 1980s had also witnessed the *Sunday Times* exhibition homes, and some radical and interesting designs for energy-efficient housing on Coleshill Place. But during the 1990s remaining land on Bradwell Common was filled with the more familiar designs offered by volume builders. The contrast between distinctive earlier housing and suburban-style dwellings was all too apparent. But nonetheless a considerable variety of housing had developed on the gridsquare. And in the newest gridsquares that were begun during the 1980s and 1990s, there was clear repudiation of rational designs for a wide variety of market-friendly styles, namely the square-paned windows and portico porches of mock-Georgian houses, or the exterior wooden beams and diamond-paned windows of the 'Tudorbethan' fashion, or the basic square box with a pitched roof and minimal ornamentation. Although some modernist private housing was built in twentieth-century Britain – for example the X models during the 1930s or Anglo-Scandinavian styling of the 1950s – most commercial volume house builders during the twentieth century, and most local authorities for that matter, ignored modern styling in mass low-rise housing. Milton Keynes, after a unique beginning, was no exception to this general rule.[47]

Any picture of bland uniformity, however, is misleading. Milton Keynes gained some of the more radical and 'different' experimental housing built in England during the latter twentieth century. Some smaller companies, and also individuals engaged in self-build, designed and constructed some high-quality modern housing, such as the experimental energy-efficient homes not only in Bradwell Common but also in Shenley Lodge and Kents Hill. These were built during the 1980s and 1990s.[48] More than most other cities in England, Milton Keynes possessed some truly innovative and environmentally friendly housing in a number of its residential areas.[49]

EMPLOYMENT AND INDUSTRIAL GRIDSQUARES

Finally, it is relevant to report that even employment gridsquares received a 'suburban' treatment: neat, low-rise office blocks and huge distribution warehouses were pictured near to attractive landscaping in MKDC publicity materials. These materials were full of beautiful photographs with nearby parklands, water courses and golf courses also emphasised.[50] This literature was aimed at company directors who were considering location in the new city. It emphasised the country-in-the-city aspects of Milton Keynes. The development corporation also used newspapers, notably the *Financial Times*, which was usually very favourable in its reporting of the economic development of Milton Keynes.

A special feature on MK in the *Financial Times*, for example, in October 1985, emphasised 'the advantages of living near to hi-tech offices' and 'the theory that high-technology companies thrive in rural surroundings . . .'. The feature quoted an MD from a company called Data and Research Services, which had moved from London to Milton Keynes in 1975. In his view, 'the major resource of science-based companies is people, and [they] are the kind of people who like outdoor life, pleasant surroundings, and easy access to their place of work'.[51] Thus, to companies and potential inward investors, MKDC could emphasise the attractive business parks within the industrial gridsquares. In its landscaping directives, MKDC had insisted that about 25 per cent of employment gridsquares were to be set aside for landscaping, to provide a green and pleasant setting for workers.[52] MKDC's advertising and marketing strategy was one aspect of its planning for employment within the new city, a planning supported by the government funding which enabled the corporation to subsidise land for sale or rent to potential employers. A relatively inexpensive and smart new working environment, full of high-tech workplaces and spacious and attractive surrounds, was of course an essential aspect of the 'economic development' strategy of the development corporation, and of the Commission for New Towns that replaced it from 1992.

Furthermore, MKDC and the CNT also played upon the locational advantages that the new city enjoyed. These were significant. The close proximity to the main roads of the M1 and the A5 gave the city enviable north–south motor links. And the new railway station in CMK, opened from 1982, with over 100 trains a day leaving to and from London, was another advantage. So too was the half-an-hour drive time from Luton Airport, and the hour's drive time to Heathrow Airport in West London.

By 2000, there were over 4,500 companies in the new city, and over 500 of those were foreign, 'with a high representation of European, American and Japanese companies'. The sizeable foreign firms included Alps Electric, a Coca-Cola canning plant,

Mobil, and Volkswagen. Of the largest UK operations, these included Abbey National, the bank, Argos, the discount retailer, Hays, a major distributor, the Open University, and of course the larger chain stores and supermarkets that located in the new city. Tesco, for example, had three supermarkets in Milton Keynes by 1995. However, it is important to note that, beyond these larger employers, the vast majority of workplaces in Milton Keynes were, and remain, small. They had fewer than 20 employees and, in many cases, fewer than 10.[53] This has implications for workplace unionisation, a point returned to in a later chapter.

Broadly, it is reasonable to argue that the *Plan for Milton Keynes'* advocacy of a diverse economy, largely but not solely services-based, was what came to pass. The planners had correctly identified the future decline of manufacturing in the country as a whole, and also within the North Bucks region. They had, nonetheless, also allowed for a proportion of industry and manufacturing in the local economy. They had further predicted that decentralisation of offices and other places of employment would continue, which it did.[54] The employment profile of Milton Keynes, dominated by services to the extent of about 70 per cent of jobs by 2000, and by white-collar work, was one local example of the growing 'post-industrial' economy of late-twentieth-century England.

CONCLUSION

In 1967, a horse breeder at Shenley Lodge Farm, a farm in the designated area, named a two-year-old brown mare 'Milton Keynes'. It was the daughter of 'Crystal Haven' out of the brood mare 'Tudor Jinks'. As the owner stated, 'I've a feeling we're going to be hearing a lot more about Milton Keynes.'[55] That little horse was anticipatory, furthermore, in a way that its owners probably never realised. Beyond the modernist crystal haven of the city centre, all glass and steely precision by 1980, the preferred direction towards an urban cityscape was almost certainly jinked by the commercial and popular preference for cheap-build, Tudorbethan and builder's vernacular.

This fact, moreover, went beyond domestic architecture. It exposed the implicit tension between 'urban' and 'rural' that was unwittingly programmed into the overall *Plan for Milton Keynes*. It left a great deal of space in between those two opposites, space that could be, and was, loosely described as 'suburban'. The generous provision of parks and trees reinforced the suburban mix. Yet the non-resolution of this local dialectic between urban intentions and suburban outcomes, certainly in the 30 years since 1970, was no bad thing for the residents of the town. The majority of residents gained a home in a suburban estate with easy access to nearby parklands, shops and other amenities. Furthermore, although the city centre was architecturally quite distinctive when compared to the hearts of older towns and cities, it was nonetheless *central*, a place to which people went for shopping and leisure, before returning home. This in itself was a classic pattern of suburban commuting; it was one of the main rhythms of life in Milton Keynes in addition to the weekly commute to the supermarkets, or the journey to and from work. To be sure, the possession of a car made access to these places easier, but is that not the case in older towns, too?

When MKDC was wound up in 1992, it had been through two managerial eras, that of Jock Campbell from 1967 to 1983, and of Henry Chilver from 1983 to the end of MKDC's life. Its economic legacy was impressive: Milton Keynes was the fastest-growing city in England throughout the 1980s, and this continued into the 1990s. The architectural legacy, however, was more mixed. Nonetheless, most of the designated area was developed by 2000, in terms of the physical and planned environment. The remainder of this book now looks at how the people experienced Milton Keynes. This includes not only the people who moved to the new city, but those already living in the designated area. It is to those already in the designated area that we turn in the next chapter.

NOTES

1   Terence Bendixson and John Platt, *Milton Keynes: Image and Reality* (Cambridge: Granta, 1992), pp. 167–80.
2   Tim Mars, 'The life in new towns', in Anthony Barnett and Roger Scruton (eds), *Town and Country* (London: Jonathan Cape, 1998).
3   On Bor, see Mark Clapson, Mervyn Dobbin and Peter Waterman (eds), *The Best Laid Plans: Milton Keynes since 1967* (Luton: University of Luton Press, 1998), pp. 16–20.
4   Bor, in Clapson, Dobbin and Waterman (eds), *Best Laid Plans*, p. 54.
5   Alan Hedges for MKDC, *Report on Research into Shopping Attractions* (Milton Keynes: MKDC, 1976). The following paragraphs on shopping are based on this report.
6   Hedges, *Shopping Attractions*, p. 31.
7   Hedges, *Shopping Attractions*, pp. 18–19.
8   Hedges, *Shopping Attractions*, pp. 21–4.
9   Nikolaus Pevsner and Elizabeth Williamson, *The Buildings of England: Buckinghamshire* (Harmondsworth: Penguin, 1994), p. 509.

10 Hedges, *Shopping Attractions*, pp. 74–5.
11 Stuart Mosscrop, 'Making sense of the centre', *Architectural Design Profile 111: New Towns* (London: Architectural Design, 1994), pp. 45–52.
12 Bendixson and Platt, *Milton Keynes*, pp. 145–50.
13 Bor, in Clapson, Dobbin and Waterman (eds), *Best Laid Plans*, p. 16.
14 Simon Hoggart, 'Forever England', *Observer Magazine*, 10 June 1990.
15 MKDC, *Milton Keynes Household Survey, 1988: Food and Grocery Shopping; Technical Report* (Milton Keynes: MKDC, 1989), p. 18.
16 Tim Mars, 'Milton Keynes: a view from exile', in Clapson, Dobbin and Waterman (eds), *Best Laid Plans*, p. 123.
17 See Chapter 1.
18 Pevsner and Williamson, *Buckinghamshire*, pp. 490–4.
19 Mosscrop, 'Making sense', p. 45.
20 Pevsner and Williamson, *Buckinghamshire*, pp. 488–94.
21 Derek Walker, 'Introduction', *Architectural Design Profile 111: New Towns* (London: Architectural Design, 1994), pp. 6–7; Derek Walker, 'Industrial and commercial buildings', *Architectural Design Profile 111: New Towns* (London: Architectural Design, 1994), pp. 53–7; Derek Walker, 'Unbuilt Milton Keynes', *Architectural Design Profile 111: New Towns* (London: Architectural Design, 1994), pp. 58–69.
22 Lee Shostak, in Clapson, Dobbin and Waterman (eds), *Best Laid Plans*, p. 55.
23 Damien Thompson, 'Churches unite to provide a central soul', *Daily Telegraph*, 23 January, 1992. See also Chapter 8.
24 Pevsner and Williamson, *Buckinghamshire*, p. 488.
25 Mars, 'The life', p. 272.
26 Jonathan Glancey, 'It's got plenty of roads. Now it's on the map', *Guardian*, 4 October 1999.
27 See, for example, Anon., 'Planners quizzed on new city proposals', *North Bucks Times*, 12 February 1969; Anon., 'City's assurances to the villages', *North Bucks Times*, 15 April 1970.
28 Professor Sir Nikolaus Pevsner, *The Plan for Milton Keynes: Technical Supplement No. 8: Preservanda and Conservanda in Milton Keynes* (Milton Keynes: MKDC, 1970) p. 1.
29 Mars, in Clapson, Dobbin and Waterman (eds), *Best Laid Plans*, pp. 111, 120.
30 MKDC, *Milton Keynes Planning Manual* (Milton Keynes: MKDC, 1992), pp. 52–5.
31 Pevsner and Williamson, *Buckinghamshire*, p. 498.
32 Derek Walker, *The Architecture and Planning of Milton Keynes* (London: Architectural Press, 1982), p. 8.
33 Jeff Bishop, *Milton Keynes; The Best of Both Worlds? Public and Professional Views of a New City* (Bristol: School of Advanced Urban Studies, 1986), p. 77.
34 Bishop, *Best of Both Worlds?*, pp. 75–7.
35 MKDC, *Plan for Milton Keynes*, vol. 1, p. 53.
36 Pevsner and Williamson, *Buckinghamshire*, p. 539; Ruth Owens, 'The great experiment', *Architects 'Journal*, 15 April 1992, pp. 30–2.
37 Mark Clapson, *Invincible Green Suburbs, Brave New Towns: Social Change and Urban Dispersal in Postwar England* (Manchester: Manchester University Press, 1998), pp. 104–5.
38 Mars, 'A view ', in Clapson, Dobbin and Waterman (eds), *Best Laid Plans*, p. 124.
39 Paul Hirst, 'Miracle or mirage? The Thatcher years', in Nick Tiratsoo (ed.), *From Blitz to Blair: A New History of Britain Since 1939* (London: Weidenfeld & Nicolson, 1997), p. 199.
40 Bishop, *Best of Both Worlds?*
41 J. W. R. Whitehand and C. M. H. Carr, *Twentieth Century Suburbs: A Morphological Approach* (London: Routledge, 2001).
42 One such advertisement is contained on the following video: City Discovery Centre, *Milton Keynes: The Development of a New City* (Milton Keynes: City Discovery Centre, 1993).
43 Peter Waterman, 'Social development in action', in Clapson, Dobbin and Waterman, *The Best Laid Plans*, p. 81; see also Bishop, *Best of Both Worlds*, p. 124.
44 Bendixson and Platt, *Milton Keynes*, p. 233.
45 Roger Kitchen, 'The silent majority speaks', *Architectural Design*, vol. 45, 1975, 754. See also MKDC materials for the *Residential Design Feedback*, 1975, held at the City Discovery Centre, Bradwell Abbey, Milton Keynes.

46 Bishop, *Best of Both Worlds?* p. 121.
47 Whitehand and Carr, *Twentieth Century Suburbs*, p. 53.
48 Pevsner and Williamson, *Buckinghamshire*, pp. 515, 548.
49 Andrew Bibby, 'Milton Keynes is twenty something', *Independent*, 18 January 1992; John Young, 'In the vanguard of social progress', *The Times*, 11 October 1996; Lesley Gillilan, 'Brave new town', *Observer Magazine*, 2 July 2000.
50 MKDC materials and, from 1992, Commission for New Town materials are held at the City Discovery Centre, Milton Keynes.
51 Financial Times Regional Report, 'Milton Keynes', *Financial Times*, 21 October 1985.
52 MKDC, *Milton Keynes Planning Manual*, p. 151.
53 This is based upon the following: Milton Keynes Council, *Geographical Information Systems, information*; Milton Keynes Economic Partnership, *Milton Keynes Insight*, 20 (2001); and also the writer's own knowledge of Milton Keynes. Further economic and marketing materials can be found in the City Discovery Centre, Bradwell Abbey, Milton Keynes.
54 MKDC, *Plan for Milton Keynes*, vol. 2, pp. 147–55; Milton Keynes Economic Partnership, *1998 Employment Survey* (Milton Keynes: MKEP, 1998), p. 6.
55 Anon., 'Milton Keynes is her name', *North Bucks Times*, 1 February 1967.

— 4 —

North Bucks and the New City

In the long run agriculture and a new city are mutually exclusive, but during the development period farm land will still
exist in the new city area and it will have to be farmed to the
highest standard possible in order to maintain the agricultural economic viability of the land and to preserve the visual
amenity of the new city.

MKDC, *The Plan for Milton Keynes: Technical Supplement
No. 9: Agriculture in Milton Keynes* (Milton Keynes:
MKDC, 1970)

Prior to their construction, most postwar new towns in Britain generated local opposition. The powers of compulsory land purchase
given to development corporations were of great concern to many
people living in the areas designated for the new towns.[1] Hence,
for example, a book about village life in Essex before and during
the construction of Basildon New Town in the 1940s was entitled
*From Country Life to the Brink of Despair: When the Bulldozers Take
Over.*[2]

At the beginning of the year of Milton Keynes' birth, over 40,000
people imhabited the designated area of North Buckinghamshire.
Of these, 23,000 were living in Bletchley, the largest local town.
Almost 10,000 lived in Wolverton and the nearby village of New
Bradwell. The small country town of Stony Stratford numbered
just 3,750 souls. The remaining population lived in a number of villages and small hamlets. Milton Keynes, for example, the village
which lent its name to the new city, was one such village, and it
was still relatively small and isolated.[3]

The employment profile of the designated area was broadly
similar to that of England and in Wales in general, argued Milton
Keynes Development Corporation (MKDC) from their sample of

heads of households and their occupations. They found that 81 per cent of heads of households were in work. Of these, 40 per cent held manufacturing occupations, and 32 per cent worked in the service sector, notably the public utilities and council work, and private companies. The remaining 9 per cent of workers were divided into two sectors, one declining and the other growing, namely agriculture and construction. The majority of heads of household, 55 per cent, were in non-professional, non-manual or skilled manual occupations, compared with a national average of 52 per cent.[4]

Spatially, that is, in terms of its land coverage, agriculture was still a significant sector in this area of North Bucks, as 17,700 of the designated 22,000 acres was farm land. A total of 225 farmers and farm workers, working on about 100 farms, earned a living there. Cereals, notably wheat and barley, were the mainstays of the fields, and, in terms of livestock farming, beef and dairy cattle amounted to almost one-third of grazing livestock per 100 acres, and ewes made up another third, the remaining fraction being accounted for by pigs and poultry.[5]

Looking beyond these rather dry agricultural statistics, we can view a very different area to the one that exists today. The suburban maw of Milton Keynes has spread across the fields of North Bucks in planned advances, obliterating the green vistas and rustic corners with residential gridsquares, industrial gridsquares and the road-grid itself. Much of the countryside remained as linear parks, and as interstitial 'wild areas' within the housing developments. But its character changed forever, as did the appearance and aspect of those irregular towns, villages and hamlets caught up and trapped within the rectangular netting of the new city. Within this environmental transformation, a human story of change and adaptation also unfolded. And it was, on balance, the rural population that felt the pain of change and adaptation most sharply. As Lord Campbell of Eskan, the Chairman of MKDC, pointed out, in 1968: 'The farmers are the worst hit, because farmers and new cities are mutually exclusive.'[6]

FEAR AND LOATHING OF 'LOS ANGELES' (IN BUCKS)

In 1968, Milton Keynes Development Corporation (MKDC) undertook the first of its regular household surveys, based upon a sample of the local population. The survey was a questionnaire, followed up with a series of public consultations in 1969. MKDC sampled just under 1,000 households, of which about 800 were located in the built-up parts of the designated area.[7] Such consultation was due partly to a genuine corporate desire to listen to the people of North Buckinghamshire and partly to a recognition that it had to be seen to be listening to that nebulous entity 'the public'. This was because MKDC was piecing together its plan at much the same time that the government's Skeffington Committee was working on its report *Planning and People*. Published in 1969, the report was a largely unsuccessful attempt to stimulate public participation in planning.

It must also be noted that the rationale of the Centre for Environmental Studies (CES), with which a number of key planners at Milton Keynes were associated, was also concerned to address the issue that urban research was increasingly needed to inform planning decisions. But there was a related concern that such research was marginalised into a technocratic ghetto. Hence during the earliest days of the CES, its instigator and Chairman, Lord Llewelyn-Davies, had made a strong case to the Ford Foundation that the CES itself would be the major generator of research into urban issues and town planning policies. He argued that research was often remote from the needs of communities and ought to more closely engage with those communities.[8] Milton Keynes Development Corporation clearly wished to connect its fact-finding missions to the *vox populi* of North Buckinghamshire and, in theory at least, to act upon the findings it had gained from its fieldwork.

The development corporation found that 'the greatest fear' of the locals was the destruction of their quality of life due to the impact of demolition to make way for urban development. In an area where over 50 per cent of the population owned or were buying their home, it was unsurprising that property prices were also of great concern.[9] And amongst those who rented from the local council, many tenants were worried that in-migrants would be given privileges in allocations to council housing. There was, however, nothing new in this: before the new city of Milton Keynes was built, an episode of local versus 'immigrant' feeling – terms used by MKDC – had occurred when the Lakes Estate was built during the mid-1960s. Begun by the London County Council (LCC) and completed by the Greater London Council following the abolition of the LCC in 1965, the Lakes Estates was constructed on the flat countryside at Water Eaton, or on Bletchley's 'south side'.

Today, everyone living in Milton Keynes has heard of the Lakes Estate. Originally a London overspill development, it consisted of 2,000 dwellings to house about 6,000 people. It was one of many dispersal schemes devised to 'decant' the excess population of the capital city into the Home Counties. It was designed to 'Radburn' principles. That is, following the famous example of Radburn, New Jersey in the 1920s, the Lakes Estate sought to separate pedestrians from cars by giving cars fast access roads, and walkers pedestrian-only walkways. Houses were not built along main roads, but along quiet little avenues or culs-de-sac, and garages and parking areas were provided nearby.[10]

But for many people living in Bletchley prior to or during the construction of the Lakes Estate, architectural matters were not the first thing on their minds. They were exercised by the perception that Londoners moving into the area were enjoying preferential housing allocations. Busloads of Londoners, moreover, turned up in Bletchley to look at the housing that they were to be given.[11] All of this prompted letters to the local newspapers, written by angry 'Bletchleyites':

> As a local couple waiting to be housed by Bletchley Council, we find it most infuriating to be confronted by our local paper showing younger couples who are happily housed: apparently because they are fortunate to be born in London. We fully appreciate the Greater London Council are sponsoring the building and upkeep of the premises for Londoners, but do we need the constant reminder that we are taking 'second place'? Yours etc., hopefully, Bletchleyites.

> After reading 'Bletchleyites' letter in this week's *Gazette* re. housing I feel I must write on the same lines. My eldest son has lived in Bletchley for twenty one of his twenty four years, yet when he went recently about housing [to the council] he was told that he and his wife would have to wait two years before there was any hope of accommodation. How about seeing to 'Bletchleyites' getting houses?[12]

During the 1960s, moreover, the concern about the impact of the Lakes Estate became linked up with widespread fears of the spectre of the new city. From 1962, both national and local newspapers carried a good number of articles about the various plans afoot for North Buckinghamshire. Before 1967, as we saw in a previous chapter, the spectre looming over the area was of a 'Pooleyville' dominating Bletchley and the nearby countryside.

But as the 'Little Los Angeles in Bucks' moved onto the planning agenda, popular local conceptions of the imminent new city responded. MKDC's version was just as threatening as Pooley-ville, because a suburban, spread-out, car-friendly city might undermine the differences between town and country, thus despoiling the countryside. For village and small-town folk, countryside and community were organically linked. To preserve the countryside was to keep the new city at bay, and the pervasive nature of suburbia threatened to dissolve village identity and community.

Thus the council of Woburn Sands, a village located near to the south eastern flank of the proposed city, warned of 'infill': of the gradual and remorseless spread of Milton Keynes across the countryside until it eventually engulfed Woburn Sands. The *North Bucks Times* report of a meeting of Woburn Sands Parish Council, in December 1968, reported fears of the 'terrible thing' facing the villagers, and one councillor forecast that within a few years there would be 'a suburbia covering and immersing' the whole of Woburn Sands and the nearby villages of Bow Brickhill and Little Brickhill:

> 'If you travel from London Airport', he said 'you go through villages, estates, where the only thing which identifies them is a signboard. Is this what we want for Woburn Sands?'[13]

The 'North Bucks Association', an alliance of villagers living in and near the designated area, also voiced their fears at the impact of urban development on the individual identity of their settlements.[14] In the face of such articulated fears, Labour ministers felt defensive enough to deny that Milton Keynes would be suburban. Anthony Greenwood, the Minister for Housing and Local Government, argued that the new city would not become the classic model based upon a major centre with suburban rings. Instead, it would 'break new ground' by becoming 'a series of well-spread-out developments linked by transport services, making it unnecessary to go into the centre, then out again'.[15]

The reference to transport services was made in an era when crises in public transport were not commonplace. It also exposed the centrality of transportation to the functioning of the new city, whether this was the much-hoped-for but ultimately disappointing public transport systems or the correct view that more and more people wanted cars to enable themselves to move about as freely as possible. More cars meant more roads, however, and as a columnist in *The Times* argued, in a piece entitled 'Battle in Bucks', the people of the designated area knew that 'you cannot have a modern town designed for the motor age unless there is something of a scorched earth policy'.[16] Those opposed to the new city found allies in other London publications that railed against this prospect. At the beginning of 1967, the popular sociological journal *New Society* drew attention to the looming threat of the 'North Bucks Monster', a beast to be invited in by official capitulation to the motor car. 'Milton Keynes', it lamented, 'promises to be the first English flirtation with planned urban decentralisation, Los Angeles-style.' The journal also warned that a consequent suburban sprawl of roads and houses might eventually result in a gross conurbation spreading all over North Bucks and South Northants. The expansion scheme at nearby Northampton appeared to make things worse.[17]

MKDC professed sensitivity to the concerns of local town dwellers and villagers. Explanatory 'condensed copies' of the plan, and of the 1968 interim report, were put through people's front doors. Regular public meetings and exhibitions were held. In each, the template for Milton Keynes was represented as one which would conserve the heart of each village, and preserve enough green space around them in order to prevent their disappearance into a suburban sprawl.[18] In February 1969, a *Daily Telegraph* report on the local consultation emphasised that a number of fears about dissolution and loss of local identity had been articulated to the development corporation. One fear was based on the idea that the basic framework of Milton Keynes, comprised of a gridiron of gridsquares of about one square kilometre, looked like a net thrown over the towns, with villages and farmlands lying within the site.[19] People appeared to feel a possible sense of entrapment within this urbanising net of fast roads.

As the design of Milton Keynes took early shape on the ground, opposition to the idea of a suburban new city was, again, not simply locally based. The metropolitan arts and listings magazine *Time Out* issued a 'dreadful warning' that Bletchley, 'already bulging with ex-Londoners', was to set the standard not for a 'super city' but for a 'super suburb' which would 'destroy the lush countryside of North Bucks', a countryside 'pocked with little villages destined to become the haunts of senior executives and doubtless the Mayor of Milton Keynes'.[20]

In 1971, the Architectural Press published *Civilia*, a blistering attack on what it termed the detestable 'semidetsia' of suburbia.

Civilia also tilted against the garden cities movement and its rationale of dispersing excess city populations to new communities in
the countryside. By the end of the 1960s, bemoaned the writers of
Civilia, British planners appeared to have lost sight of the notion of
compact modern cities [such as Pooleyville] and had succumbed
to the idea of the 'city region'. This was merely 'an exercise
designed to get the citizens to spread themselves over the surrounding countryside in "sectors of growth"':

> To a point ideally where all that remains of the city is its *centro*, while
> the population fans out in defined directions until suburb meets
> suburb meets suburb. Milton Keynes is the latest example of this
> new policy, the spearhead of an offensive which will, if the planners
> have their way, eventually link suburban London with suburban
> Birmingham, somewhere in the vicinity of twice-clobbered
> Cublington.[21]

This statement was factually incorrect. For one thing, it ignored
the efficacy of the Town and Country Planning Act of 1947, whose
greenbelt policy, namely the system of inviolable green belts
around towns and cities, had been a major force in counteracting
suburban sprawl across the South East. The Town and Country
Planning Association (TCPA) supported green belts, just as it also
supported the construction of Milton Keynes. Moreover, the reference to 'twice-clobbered Cublington' exposed the immaturity of so
much of the polemic in *Civilia*. Cublington had been discussed as
a possible future site for the third London airport. In fact, Milton
Keynes Development Corporation was a powerful ally to the local
lobby which persuaded the government to locate the airport elsewhere. A key argument of the campaigners, including MKDC, was
that this little area of Buckinghamshire would have been over-
pressured by the development accompanying an airport, in addition to the construction and growth of Milton Keynes.[22] The
development corporation itself, in 1968, was also worried that the
land-use demands and environmental impact of a nearby airport
might undermine the nature of the plans for the new city that were
then being formulated.[23] Finally, the polemical style of *Civilia* did
not allow for consideration of a key point: the spatial spread of
Milton Keynes was constrained by limits of development which
were specifically intended to, and subsequently did, define the
city's boundaries. Cublington and some other nearby villages lay
outside these limits. Ultimately, Milton Keynes was in fact an
obstacle to unplanned suburbanisation in North Bucks. Unlike Los

TABLE 1: CONCERNS OF PEOPLE LIVING IN THE DESIGNATED
AREA, 1968 (Questions put to the MKDC at public meetings)

Traffic, transportation, roads, monorail, dial-a-bus	97
Effect on existing settlements, property, demolition, disturbances	59
Finance, compensation, rates, rents, compulsory purchase	49
Phasing, provision of services apace with growth, planning blight	43
Industry and employment	28
Immigrants versus local people	24
Air pollution, brickworks	22
Character of new houses and buildings; landscape, gardens, population density	21
Leisure, recreation, linear parks	18
Water supply	18
Sewage	16
Flooding	14
Compensation for farmers, agricultural land	14
Vulnerability of city boundaries	14
Railway line, station	14
Education, schools, university	12
Shops, local traders	10

Angeles in California, the Little Los Angeles in Bucks was no unstoppable suburban devourer of land.

OTHER CONCERNS OF THOSE LIVING IN THE DESIGNATED AREA

MKDC's information-getting exercise through 1968 to 1969 has left us with a fascinating summary of the chief concerns and worries of those living in the designated area. They were a combination of material and financial considerations, and environmental issues, which cannot be helpfully separated off from each other. For example, fears about property values, whilst motivated by economic self-interest, were intrinsically connected with fears about the declining quality of rural and small-town life. MKDC themselves conflated categories in a rather mushy way, for example, 'effect on existing settlement, villages, property, demolition, disturbance', a broad catch-all which must have included many different sections of the local population. Nonetheless, the nature of popular misgivings is palpably in evidence in the development corporation's findings, as shown in Table 1 (see above).[24]

In addition to the obvious environmental concerns, conflated as they were within MKDC categories, it is possible to identify aspirations and needs. Interest was clearly expressed in what the new city might offer existing households, notably in terms of improved accommodation, education, shopping, transport and a range of local services. This point is returned to later in the chapter.

MKDC also made note of a feeling against Londoners within the 'immigrants versus local people' category, a feeling linked in part to the recent in-migration of Londoners into the Bletchley overspill estate. By 1968, thousands of people living in Bletchley had moved there since 1960. Anti-Londoner feeling was particularly high in the country town of Stony Stratford, on the western edge of the designated area. MKDC's 'attitudinal data' found that people living in the designated area rightly anticipated that most of the newcomers would hail from the capital city, as part of an oncoming human train of 'all sorts of ordinary people'. This prospect worried many in the designated area generally, but especially in Stony Stratford:

> Particularly high proportions of respondents in Stony Stratford and in the upper income groups (not mutually exclusive categories) mentioned Londoners, but Stony Stratford appeared to voice rather greater fears than others, in their expectations: 15 per cent specifically mentioned coloured people, 12 per cent rough people and hooligans, and 16 per cent working-class people and factory workers – all of which were much higher percentages than for the sample as a whole.[25]

In Wolverton, however, there was slightly less anti-newcomer feeling, but MKDC argued that the railway town, and nearby New Bradwell, were quite clannish communities and even felt some rivalry towards wealthier Stony Stratford. 'Because of a stable and high level of employment and the industrial background of the inhabitants', stated the development corporation's *Northern Towns Study* in 1970, 'Wolverton and New Bradwell have tended to become enclosed communities with less influence on, and attraction to, the population in surrounding towns and villages.'[26] As with Woburn Sands, Wolverton residents were worried at the loss of community and of the countryside that circumscribed the town and thus heightened its sense of internal cohesion. As one person argued, in 1975, although the Victorian railway town of Wolverton was often spoken of as 'ugly', it was nonetheless 'a clean town, a fairly small community where you knew everybody'. And another felt that Milton Keynes had begun to erode much of the nearby countryside: 'We've lost the rural aspect of life.'[27]

The expressed views of people living in the designated area, however, came from only a minority of the local population, notably activists and those confident enough to articulate strong opinions. Most people did not write to the local press. Significantly, MKDC itself expressed disappointment at the 'low response rate' to the meetings it held with local people. Yet such low response rates were typical of people living in the face of imminent urbanisation. In the late 1960s the Skeffington Committee found that public awareness of and participation in the town planning process was low. It had thus recommended public meetings as 'a valuable means of exchanging ideas as well as informing the public'. Yet MKDC estimated that less than 12 per cent of the total adult population in the designated area went to a meeting, of which it held 20, in a variety of locations.[28]

In order to maximise feedback from 'the people', MKDC also sent out 18,000 questionnaires, but unfortunately 'only 450 were returned':

> and of these only 370 could be analysed in any depth. So low a response rate was disappointing [and this] made it unwise to draw conclusions of less than a very general nature from the responses.[29]

MKDC attributed the low level of responses to the suggestions that most of the interested parties had attended meetings and perhaps felt that little more needed to be said. It admitted that the questionnaire itself was perhaps rather simplistic and uninviting in format, and also that postal questionnaires were subject to less of an involved response anyway than personal interviews or meetings.[30] In mitigation, however, the corporation argued that all towns and most villages in the designated area had returned a number of completed forms. Moreover, most age groups were represented in the total. Significantly, 'a majority of questionnaires were filled in by male heads of the population'. Was this an institutional paternalism projected into the homes of the respondents? It is an interesting question. MKDC added that this completion of the form by 'male heads of the population' did not appear to bias the results as most contributions had been prefaced by 'discussions between husband and wife' (and sometimes children) and a few carried more than one signature. This by itself, however, did not mean that household discussions were conducted on an equal footing, something which the gender of the signatures appeared to confirm.[31]

As for the educational and occupational backgrounds of those completing the questionnaire, these were 'diverse and included those of doctor, nurse, clergyman, railwayman, farmer, farm workers, school master, postmaster, shopkeeper and factory worker'.[32]

While most expressed various concerns about environmental impact – noted above – the shopkeepers, farmers and farm
workers were also motivated by strong economic misgivings. The
town shops felt that they faced a number of problems. Firstly, those
who ran small shops were fearful that the new shopping centres
planned for the new city would damage or destroy trade. In Stony
Stratford, for example, on the edge of the designated area, there
were already 16 empty shops by October 1968, according to the
local Chamber of Commerce. It also argued that MKDC was failing
to give the town's traders adequate information about where the
new centres of population, and thus markets, were most likely to
be situated. Secondly, the Labour government passed an industrial
training law which from August 1969 required businesses, no
matter how small, to allow for industrial and commercial training
for their staff. That meant additional costs. Following on from
these two issues, there was a widespread fear among local traders
that, when the new town was built, they would lose trainees to
larger stores. In sum, national and local forces seemed to be oper-
ating against small traders.[33]

Thus some members of Stony Stratford Chamber of Commerce
continued to oppose the new town, fearing it would damage the
'balanced economy' of a 'viable market town', a local economy
which the alternative expansion of nearby rural villages such as
Cosgrove or Deanshanger might have strengthened.[34] The meetings at which such views were aired were often held at the local
Conservative Club. However, whilst local traders found a sympathetic ear in the local Conservative MP, William Benyon, he was in
favour of the planned new town, because it would place a much-
needed economic engine in a relatively backward area of
Buckinghamshire. It was clear, moreover, to some in the local trade
organisations that there were potential advantages for small businesses in urban expansion, and the experience of initial development confirmed that for some businesses more people meant more
trade. By 1975, one small businessman was arguing that the new
city had provided 'an injection of life into a dying market town'.[35]
No such injection of life, however, was to await the farming sector.

FARMERS AND FARM WORKERS IN A 'DWINDLING AGRICULTURE'

The problems facing the agricultural sector in North Bucks were
not unique in either time or space. Urban growth in general, and

new towns in particular, had long spelt danger for farming interests, requiring, as they did, land to be built upon. And new town
development corporations possessed powers of compulsory purchase. The 1946 New Towns Act provided that corporations compensated only at existing use value, that is, current agricultural
value.[36]

In the winter of 1964 to 1965, as Fred Pooley and his vision
began to loom figuratively over the countryside, the Buckinghamshire branch of the National Farmers Union (NFU) began a campaign of protest to Bucks County Council. A leading figure in these
moves was W. G. Snook, chairman of the Bucks branch of the NFU,
and also a Bletchley-based member of its 'new town's steering
committee', a committee established by the farmers' union.[37]
Snook began by emphasising farmers' fear of the loss of good agricultural land. Yet he also argued angrily to the local press that the
county council was guilty of a lack of consultation with the NFU,
and was 'trying to rush through this project'.[38]

A further tactic adopted by the NFU was to argue that more
urban development in the South East of England would add to
congestion in an already overcrowded region of the country:

> In the opinion of the National Farmer's Union, before projects such
> as this are undertaken, more intensive use should be made of large
> areas of land where low density suburban development encroaches
> on farm land, and the congestion of South East England should be
> relieved, rather than aggravated by seeking to attract additional
> population.[39]

Thus did the agricultural lobby indirectly find common anti-
suburban cause with the urbanists of the architectural and town
planning professions. Furthermore, and also in common with the
outraged and outspoken opinion of metropolitan urbanists, the
NFU could do nothing to halt the progress of the designation of
Milton Keynes in January 1967. As soon as the designated 11,000
hectares was announced, Snook lamented that the plan for the new
city was 'a bitter blow to many farmers', especially tenant farmers,
whose chances of starting somewhere else, unlike the 'owner-
occupier' farmers, were very slim.[40]

Yet following designation, the NFU changed its tactics, and so
did individual farmers. The union engaged a soil expert, as well
as a leading barrister, to counter the claim of MKDC that the land
was of only second-rate agricultural quality.[41] Some farmers
stated their willingness to go to jail rather than move off their

land.[42] And at least one threatened to emigrate because he did not want his land to 'become one big exercise area for the new town people'. This man, along with his wife and children, applied for assisted passages to New Zealand: 'It is no use trying to carry out intensive farming', he argued, 'with a great city right on your doorstep.'[43]

Most farm workers perceived their interests to be with their employers. The National Union of Agricultural Workers (NUAW) worked with the steering committee of the NFU in order to oppose new town designation. In 1966, this liaison was presented to the public enquiry into the designation order as 'proof, not only of the unity of the agricultural cause', but also of the shared belief that 'the designation order before us is to be disastrous'. Neville Wallace of the NUAW argued that 'farmers and farm workers should not be expected to make a greater sacrifice in the interests of development than was required by other sections of industry . . .'.[44]

A series of studies by the Department of Agricultural Economics at the University of Reading, and partly financed by MKDC, were made into the conditions and morale of farmers and farm workers from 1967. Of almost 100 farms within or adjacent to the designated area, the surveys studied 90 which were to be most directly affected by the new city. The first study, undertaken in 1967, drew some important conclusions. First, the majority of farmers in the designated area wished to continue farming (70 per cent). Of the remaining 30 per cent, one half intended to retire, but the others were 'undecided about their future'.[45]

The second impression gleaned by the survey 'was one of extreme uncertainty about the future, and the depressing effect of this on morale and on farming practice generally'.[46] And a third observation noted by the survey was the anger and insecurity felt at the levels of compensation being offered. In 1967 this vital economic and psychological issue was far from being resolved. By December 1968, MKDC's first major planning document, the *Interim Report* on the *Plan for Milton Keynes* was only suggesting, rather than finalising, its plans for compensation, and was debating, rather than promising, whether to offer farmers improvement grants to offset some of the practical difficulties caused by the imminent development of the new city.[47] MKDC found that the insecurities of the farmers were felt most sharply by the 'less politically involved' tenant farmers and the least financially well-endowed smallholders: 38 per cent of the holdings in the designated area were under 100 acres, and the smaller the operation, the lesser the sum of compensation.[48]

MKDC had not simply alighted upon these facts as a result of their own enquiries. By Easter 1967, three months following the go-ahead given to the new city, agitation by the NFU for increased compensation had become a major tactic, and the NFU established a fighting fund in the spring of 1967 to this end. There were precedents for this. The parliamentary committee of the NFU had long negotiated with development corporations and local authorities to 'actively engage in helping farmers' whose land was affected by urban run-off and, especially, by new town designations.[49] Via the NFU, some Bucks tenant farmers argued angrily that their compensation would only be equivalent to a year's trading. Moreover, as the *North Bucks Times* reported on 10 July 1968, few farmers could expect to find other farms. Thus the NFU called for permanent liaison with MKDC in order to gain minimum disruption to agriculture and maximum recompense to those affected. It urged the larger farmers not to cooperate in the signing of the documentation to relinquish their land. Beyond these strategies, however, all the NFU could do was to advise farmers to 'sit tight' until their claims for compensation were met.[50] Some professed that they were prepared to go to jail unless their claims for compensation were met. Most landowners wanted more recompense, and most tenant farmers felt that a minimum of five years' rent was what they deserved.[51]

Once the planning and construction of the new city was under way, the University of Reading's survey was not surprised to find a sense of fatalism among many farmers. The survey found that the farming community was 'in danger of losing its sense of purpose'.[52] Farmers were using such phrases as 'farming in a vacuum' or 'farming to no end'. The prospect of only short-term survival for most farms, and the end of its working relationships, underpinned this sense of pointlessness. Twenty-six farmers stated that they would be 'especially sorry' to leave their farm, and they expressed regret that they would lose their employees.[53] Some of these employees were their offspring. The university team assessed the fortunes of 29 farmers' sons, 11 of whom were direct partners with their fathers and 18 of whom were wage earners.

Because inter-generational prospects for the farms were quite bleak, 13 of the 18 family wage earners found alternative employment. Nine of the partner sons, and one farmer's daughter, were still farming by 1973, but there was a big catch involved. Some of these had taken over the tenancy from their paternal parent, only to find themselves with a maximum of four years' occupation, and no hope of compensation 'for disturbance' once they had to move on.[54]

Despite such cases, however, most farmers' insecurities began to diminish as plans for the new city began to be implemented: the 'implementation plan' clarified the timing of development as it impacted on specific farms.[55] By 1973, the University of Reading team could conclude that, despite the farmers' earlier fears, the attrition of local agriculture has not by then affected most holdings as badly as had once been anticipated. The 1973 study, poignantly entitled *Case Studies in a Dwindling Agriculture*, found that over 50 of the original 90 businesses were still in existence. Forty-three farmers had quit the area, and many had found alternative farms elsewhere. Some had retired. Moreover, by 1975 'Many tenants [had] received compensation from their landlords, who [had] then sold advantageously to the development corporation with vacant possession.'[56] A number of the majority of farmers who had stayed on had taken advantage of MKDC's recommendations to increase cereal production and thus become entitled to improvement grants: gain for grain. Such production was of course a rational response to the increasingly interstitial nature of farmland in a rapidly urbanising area where livestock farming became more difficult as total acreage declined in the Milton Keynes area. It fell from 14,650 acres in 1967 to 9,530 by 1973.[57] Certainly, as cereal production increased so the proportion of dairy cows decreased from 7.9 per cent of livestock per 100 acres in 1967 to less than 3 per cent by 1971. Farmers found it difficult in such circumstances to justify long-term investment on milking equipment.[58] Nationally, moreover, the early 1970s were a time of high prices for cereal produce, following the slump which had beset British agriculture in the aftermath of the foot-and-mouth outbreak of 1967.[59]

Overall, although there were a number of ex-farmers who were resentful or indignant or both at the loss of their original livelihood, the university team concluded that 'in different circumstances the adjustment problems could easily have been far worse'.[60] And of those still farming in the designated area in 1974, most were by then more fully briefed of their future prospects, and they anticipated significant compensation from the development corporation. Yet the transition to this slightly happier state of affairs had been a painful one, as the academics also pointed out that 'This, of course, is not to say that [farmers] have welcomed what has happened.'[61] And as if to cruelly rub in the effects of urbanisation, 'the encroachment of people has meant a burnt-out barn, water put into petrol tanks, and sheep killed by dogs'.[62]

What became of the farm workers? They were ostensibly the most economically vulnerable group who worked the land, because they neither owned any property nor produced any goods that could become the basis of compensation. Most farm workers were generally agricultural labourers, taking work where they could get it. Such mobility and a concomitant lack of responsibility was, in fact, a distinct advantage when seeking other employment within or near to the growing city. By 1973, 60 of a sample of 79 farm workers (76 per cent), interviewed two years previously, had left their original site of work. To be sure, there were some cases of individual hardship to do with housing arrangements or the problems of developing 'alternative skills', but most ex-farm workers found other jobs. They became lorry drivers, general labourers (presumably on construction sites), factory workers or railway workers, or they retired. There was 'little or no reason to suggest' that for most ex-farm workers things had 'changed for the worse'.[63]

In 1985, looking back at the accelerated demise of agriculture in the designated area, two leading members of the original Reading University team, D. J. Ansell and A. K. Giles, reiterated their earlier findings: potential economic and personal disaster for most people involved with agriculture had not occurred. Yet they qualified this summation, pointing out that, as the new city had grown, people had experienced varying moods of irritation, insecurity and grudging resignation. By 1985, farming was largely 'clinging on' in the designated area. Ansell and Giles concluded by considering 'the personal fate of individuals who are asked to bear costs in the broader community interests'.[64]

By 1990, three-quarters of the original farms had gone, but 25 farms still remained. MKDC's *Employment Survey* for that year found that 151 people still worked in agriculture, a mere 0.2 per cent of the city's working population. That sum was based upon a standard industrial classification which did not include local gardening centres and greenhouses.[65] Hence it can be argued that Lord Campbell had been largely if not wholly correct: farming and the new city were for the most part mutually incompatible, and what had occurred in North Bucks was an accelerated and focused example of the wider postwar erosion of agricultural land by urbanisation. It was, furthermore, a local case of the national decline of agricultural employment. Agriculture employed 5.1 per cent of the British workforce in 1951, but that had more than halved to just 2.3 per cent by 1981.[66]

The figures produced by MKDC also indicate that 0.1 per cent of remaining agricultural workers in the designated area were female by 1990, compared to higher levels in other rural areas. This is the only real clue we have to the (negligible) presence of women workers on the land and in farming production in Milton Keynes during the last quarter of the twentieth century.[67]

THE ANTICIPATED BENEFITS OF THE NEW CITY

The prospect of a new city was not all bad news for existing locals; many people had no misgivings. MKDC found that 'half the respondents were pleased at the prospect of the new city and three-quarters felt it would bring advantages to the area in the form of better entertainment, shopping and employment prospects'.[68] To take the latter point first, many were pleased at the prospect of 'more choice of jobs'. Those who felt this way were school leavers and people already at work who wished for a career or job change. Others, working in London or some distance away, looked forward to jobs nearer to where they lived. Other comments requested 'plenty of heavy industry and large firms' because of the predominance of small businesses paying relatively lower wages.[69]

Most people go to work not simply for economic survival, but to earn the disposable income to enable them to go out and have fun. Hence, observed MKDC, the proposal for a new city generously provided with leisure facilities met with an overwhelmingly favourable response, a response which also exposed current levels of dissatisfaction at the paltry range of commercially or municipally provided entertainments then on offer: 'sports centres, a football stadium, ice rinks, bowling alleys, swimming pools, cinemas and dance halls all had several mentions' in MKDC surveys. Moreover, proposed lakes, the canal rehabilitation schemes, the linear parks and the wide variety of green spaces on offer met with, felt MKDC, 'enthusiastic and virtually unanimous support'. Anglers and those interested in other water-based activities had their own ideas and suggestions about how the new city might cater for their interests.[70]

People also wanted better shops. After all, most people then, as now, worked to buy things to render life less tiresome and more enjoyable. The type and availability of shops were important to people in the nearby towns, but this was the case even before the new city had brought with it new shops. Many people in the MKDC survey were also strongly in favour of the prospect of lots of new and bigger stores. In an era of growing affluence and increasingly complex levels of consumption, many local people perceived a lag between their own material expectations and desires, and the existing retail provision, which was bland and unexciting. The proposals for more shops were thus enthusiastically welcomed.[71]

New and better educational provision was another important aspect of the proposed city that locals felt would improve their lives and the life chances of their children. Thus a Mrs O'Reilly, 28 years old, 'married to a lorry driver and with two young daughters at school', was one of a number of locals quoted in the *Northampton Chronicle and Echo* on 19 January 1967. She welcomed the new town because there was 'nothing for the young ones at the moment'. As with shopping and leisure, a key reason was the inadequacy of existing levels of provision in secondary and, interestingly, further and higher education. MKDC found that more and improved higher and adult education facilities were in demand. Since the later 1960s, the further education system has seen the introduction of Milton Keynes College, based on a number of sites, providing technical and practical qualifications. And in terms of higher education, De Montfort University moved in during 1991, only to up sticks and move out 10 years later, because the university failed to meet local demand by providing only a limited range of courses. Most famously of all, of course, Milton Keynes has been identified, since 1969, with the 'university of the air', the Open University, following successful initiatives by leading members of MKDC to establish this government-funded new direction in higher education and distance learning. In terms of secondary education, Milton Keynes has also a unique recent heritage. The Plan provided for a series of American-style campus schools which incorporated sixth form colleges. The campuses were provided with sporting and cultural activity centres to encourage parents as well as children, and also people living nearby, to view the schools as centres for both education and community activities.[72]

It is revealing, furthermore, to note the responses of the locals to the proposed design and layout of Milton Keynes. The visual impact of the city and its general amenity were the unifying themes. Here, the road transport system, the design and appearance of buildings, and usable public spaces were areas of concern. Many felt that the gridiron pattern of the proposed road system might well be a monotonous one. Others felt that strangers would need reference points to be able to find their way around, and concern for pedestrian safety in the city of the car was a recurring one. As for housing, there was much criticism of the Lakes Estate in Bletchley, and a subsequent widespread aspiration that the new city should set new and higher standards of domestic architecture. However, as an MKDC social development worker found in the early 1970s, many of the views of the locals about the new housing styles were 'unprintable' but unambiguous: 'they hate them'.[73] Nonetheless, the fact of more housing was welcomed. More than that, the decision of MKDC to provide half of the new town's houses for rent and half for purchase was 'commended' for the greater availability it promised to a wide social mix of people. But traditional housing was preferred.[74]

Finally, and more generally, many of the public's responses and suggestions reveal a wider and complex menu of aspirations for the new city and its effects. There were a number of suggestions about the need for adequate car parking and for council-run inexpensive boarding kennels. Practical solutions for the avoidance of litter and graffiti were offered, and the idea of local or county-wide lottery schemes, with the first prize of a brand new house in Milton Keynes, was clearly favoured by many people. Not surprisingly, MKDC homed in on such comments as evidence of enthusiasm for the new city, and quoted a widow, aged over 70, who said 'I most sincerely hope I am alive to see the achievement and completion of the new city, and will do all in my power to assist to that end.'[75]

CONCLUSION

As MKDC had discovered by 1970, measuring the true nature and extent of local feeling about the idea of a new city was nigh-impossible. Apathy, and a consequent low turnout and response rate to the attempts of the development corporation to provide information, was a key reason for this. Nonetheless, the reaction of people living in or adjacent to the designated area, who did articulate their views, was not uniformly defensive or critical. Those with the most to lose, notably farmers and workers in the agricultural sector, were particularly apprehensive and fearful about the onset of the new city. Shopkeepers and small traders, too, were worried that large new retail facilities might marginalise and erode their livelihoods.

Moreover, the general reaction to the new city proposals revealed what some within the architectural and town planning professions might now see as a peculiarly English system of cultural confusion, whilst others might view it as an endearing contradiction. For it is clear that opposition to the death of much of rural North Bucks by suburbanisation was accompanied by a marked preference for the low-density cityscape, a preference which the 'grand suburban design' of Milton Keynes subsequently appeared to satisfy. This is discussed in the following chapters.

NOTES

1 Frank Schaffer, *The New Town Story* (London: Paladin, 1972), pp. 39–52.
2 George Ross, *Basildon 1915–1986: From Country Life to the Brink of Despair: When the Bulldozers Take Over* (Basildon: George Ross, 1986).
3 MKDC, *The Plan for Milton Keynes*, vol. 2 (Milton Keynes: MKDC, 1970), p. 96.
4 MKDC, *Plan for Milton Keynes*, vol. 2, p. 97.
5 University of Reading, Department of Agricultural Economics and Management, *Milton Keynes 1967: An Agricultural Inventory* (Reading: University of Reading, 1968), p. 13. MKDC, *Plan for Milton Keynes*, vol. 2, p. 98; University of Reading, Department of Agricultural Economics and Management, *Milton Keynes Revisited: 1971* (Reading: University of Reading, Miscellaneous Study No. 51, 1972), p. 7.
6 Llewelyn-Davies, Weeks, Forestier-Walker and Bor, *Milton Keynes Plan: Interim Report to the MKDC* (London: Llewelyn-Davies *et al.*, 1968), Foreword by Lord Campbell.
7 MKDC, *The Plan for Milton Keynes: Technical Supplement No. 2: Household Survey* (Milton Keynes: MKDC, 1970), pp. 25–8.
8 Lord Llewelyn-Davies, *Centre for Environment Studies: A Programme of Work for the Centre, Note by the Chairman for Discussion by the Governors* (New York: Ford Foundation; grant number 6700083, 1966, held on microfilm reel no. 2933 at the Ford Foundation Archives, New York).
9 MKDC, *Technical Supplement No. 2; Household Survey*, pp. 25–8.
10 Caroline Brooks, 'The Lakes Estate, Bletchley: a case study of a GLC overspill development built on Radburn principles' (Oxford: Oxford Brookes University, unpublished project, Diploma in Town Planning, 1991).
11 Anon., 'They look before they come', *North Bucks Times*, 12 June 1968.
12 Letters, *Bletchley Gazette*, 26 September 1969; 2 October 1969.
13 Anon., 'Anxiety about new city sprawl', *North Bucks Times*, 18 December 1968; Anon., 'Anxiety about new city sprawl', *Bletchley Gazette*, 20 December 1968.
14 *Buckinghamshire Standard*, 27 January 1967.
15 *Daily Mail*, 13 January 1967.
16 Anon., 'Battle in Bucks', *The Times*, 1 July 1966.
17 Anon., 'Planning: North Bucks Monster', *New Society*, 19 January 1967, p. 95.
18 Anon., 'Planners quizzed on new city proposals', *North Bucks Times*, 12 February 1969; Anon., 'City's assurances to the villages', *North Bucks Times*, 15 April 1970; Anon., 'A "pop" interim report to everyone', *North Bucks Times*, 22 January 1969; Anon., 'New city plan', *North Bucks Times*, 12 February 1969.
19 *Daily Telegraph*, 5 February 1969.
20 Anon., 'Milton Keynes: a dreadful warning', *Time Out*, 22–29 October 1972. See also

Ray Thomas, 'Impressions from Milton Keynes', *Town and Country Planning*, 40, 1 (1972), pp. 81–2 in response to the *Time Out* article.

21 Ivor de Wofle, with Ian Nairn, *Civilia: The End of Sub Urban Man* (London: Architectural Press, 1971), p. 25.

22 On the third London airport controversy, see David McKie, *A Sadly Mismanaged Affair* (London: Croom Helm, 1973).

23 MKDC, *Second Annual Report; Parliamentary Papers* 1968–69, vol. 43, p. 218.

24 Table drawn from MKDC, *The Plan for Milton Keynes: Technical Supplement No. 3: Public Reaction to the Interim Plan* (Milton Keynes: MKDC, 1970), pp. 9, 29.

25 MKDC, *The Plan for Milton Keynes: Technical Supplement No. 2: Household Survey* (Milton Keynes: MKDC, 1970), p. 125.

26 MKDC, *Northern Towns Study: Commercial Survey* (Milton Keynes: MKDC, 1970), p. 21.

27 Roger Kitchen, 'The silent majority speaks', *Architectural Design*, XLV (1975), p. 754.

28 MKDC, *Plan for Milton Keynes: Technical Supplement No. 3: Public Reaction to the Interim Plan*, p. 3.

29 MKDC, *Plan for Milton Keynes: Technical Supplement No. 3: Public Reaction to the Interim Plan*, pp. 22–3.

30 MKDC, *Plan for Milton Keynes: Technical Supplement No. 3: Public Reaction to the Interim Plan*, pp. 22–3.

31 MKDC, *Plan for Milton Keynes: Technical Supplement No. 3: Public Reaction to the Interim Plan*, p. 28.

32 MKDC, *Plan for Milton Keynes: Technical Supplement No. 3: Public Reaction to the Interim Plan*, p. 28.

33 *Wolverton and North Bucks Express*, 11 October 1968.

34 Kitchen, 'Silent majority', p. 754.

35 Kitchen, 'Silent majority', p. 754.

36 Howard Newby, *Green and Pleasant Land? Social Change in Rural England* (London: Hutchinson, 1985), pp. 229, 232, 236; Schaffer, *The New Town Story*, pp. 81–2.

37 Anon., '"Sit tight" advice to new city farmers', *North Bucks Times*, 10 July 1968.

38 Anon., 'Farmers protest at new city plans', *Slough Express*, 4 December 1964.

39 Anon., 'Farmers protest at new city plans', *Slough Express*, 4 December 1964.

40 Anon., 'Bitter blow to many farmers', *North Bucks Times*, 18 January 1967; Anon., 'We deplore land loss but will pull together', *North Bucks Times*, 18 January 1967.

41 Anon., 'Farmers to fight new town plan', *The Times*, 15 April 1966.

42 Anon., 'Farmers ready to go to jail', *Bletchley Gazette*, 26 January 1967.

43 Anon., 'Farmers to fight new town plan', *The Times*, 15 April 1966; Anon., 'Farmer will emigrate', *The Times*, 13 January 1967.

44 Ray Thomas and Peter Cresswell, *The New Town Idea* (Milton Keynes: Open University Press: DT201, Urban development unit 26, 1973), pp. 44–5.

45 University of Reading, Department of Agricultural Economics and Management, *Milton Keynes 1967: An Agricultural Inventory*, p. 30.

46 University of Reading, Department of Agricultural Economics and Management, *Milton Keynes 1967: An Agricultural Inventory*, p. 30.

47 Llewelyn-Davies *et al.*, *Interim Report*, p. 34.

48 Llewelyn-Davies *et al.*, *Interim Report*, p. 34; University of Reading, Department of Agricultural Economics and Management, *Milton Keynes 1967: An Agricultural Inventory*, p. 31.

49 National Farmers Union, *Annual Report, 1968* (London: NFU, 1968), p. 22.

50 Anon., '"Sit tight" advice to city farmers', *North Bucks Times*, 10 July 1968.

51 Anon., 'Tenant farmers: at least five years compensation', *Bletchley Gazette*, 24 February 1967; Anon., 'Fight is still on, says NFU', *North Bucks Times*, 1 February 1967.

52 University of Reading, Department of Agricultural Economics and Management, *Milton Keynes 1967: An Agricultural Inventory*, p. 31.

53 University of Reading, Department of Agricultural Economics and Management, *Milton Keynes Revisited: 1971*, p. 12.

54 University of Reading, Department of Agricultural Economics and Management, *Milton Keynes 1973: Case Studies in a Dwindling Agriculture* (Reading: University of Reading, miscellaneous study no. 57, 1974), p. 8.

55 A. K. Giles, 'The impact of urban development on agriculture: a case study of Milton Keynes', in Ray Thomas (ed.), *Perspectives on New Towns Development: Proceedings of a*

Conference Organised by the New Towns Study Unit, and the Regional Studies Association at Walton Hall, 15 November 1975 (Milton Keynes: New Towns Study Unit, Open University, 1976) p. 59.

56 Giles, 'Impact', p. 61.

57 University of Reading, Department of Agricultural Economics and Management, *Milton Keynes 1973: Case Studies in a Dwindling Agriculture*, p. 1.

58 University of Reading, Department of Agricultural Economics and Management, *Milton Keynes Revisited: 1971*, p. 8.

59 National Farmers Union, *Annual Report, 1968*, p. 22.

60 University of Reading, Department of Agricultural Economics and Management, *Milton Keynes 1973: Case Studies in a Dwindling Agriculture*, p. 5.

61 University of Reading, Department of Agricultural Economics and Management, *Milton Keynes 1973: Case Studies in a Dwindling Agriculture*, p. 7.

62 Chris Binding, 'Angry farmers warn: we shoot to kill', *Milton Keynes Gazette*, 14 February, 1975; Eugene Fisk, *People in their Place* (Milton Keynes: People's Press, 1985), 'The farmer'.

63 University of Reading, Department of Agricultural Economics and Management, *Milton Keynes 1973: Case Studies in a Dwindling Agriculture*, p. 7.

64 A. K. Giles and D. J. Ansell for University of Reading, Department of Agricultural Economics and Management, *Milton Keynes 1967–1985: The Farming Story* (Reading: University of Reading, miscellaneous study no. 73, 1985), p. 14.

65 MKDC, *Milton Keynes Employment Survey, 1990* (Milton Keynes: MKDC, 1990), pp. 12–13.

66 David C. Thorns, *Fragmenting Societies: A Comparative Analysis of Regional and Urban Development* (London: Routledge, 1992), Table 3.1, p. 72.

67 MKDC, *Milton Keynes Employment Survey, 1990*, p. 17.

68 MKDC, *Plan for Milton Keynes*, vol. 2, p. 98.

69 MKDC, *Plan for Milton Keynes: Technical Supplement No. 3: Public Reaction to the Interim Plan*, pp. 34–5.

70 MKDC, *Plan for Milton Keynes: Technical Supplement No. 3: Public Reaction to the Interim Plan*, pp. 30–1.

71 MKDC, *Plan for Milton Keynes: Technical Supplement No. 3: Public Reaction to the Interim Plan*, pp. 36–7.

72 MKDC, *Plan for Milton Keynes*, vol. 1, pp. 57–60.

73 Kitchen, 'Silent majority', p. 754.

74 MKDC, *Plan for Milton Keynes: Technical Supplement No. 3: Public Reaction to the Interim Plan*, pp. 35–6.

75 MKDC, *Plan for Milton Keynes: Technical Supplement No. 3: Public Reaction to the Interim Plan*, pp. 37–9.

— 5 —

Who Moved to Milton Keynes?

If you dislike suburbia, then you will never like Milton Keynes, which is a suburban city. It lacks the patina of human experience, the serendipity, the neurotic edge of a traditional city. But if you're fed up with the squalor, the depletions, the sheer inefficiency of metropolitan life, it can look awfully enticing.
Laurence Marks, 'City of sky and myth', *Observer Review*, 19 January 1992

This chapter looks at the many different groups of people who have moved to Milton Keynes since its earliest days as a new city. It also argues that, because the development corporation attempted, between 1970 and 1992, to encourage the formation of a social mix which reflected the wider national class profile and also the growing diversity of ethnic groups, the experiences of moving to Milton Keynes may be viewed as representative of a great many people who have moved home in England since 1970. As a recent article on Milton Keynes has noted, however, the new city has grown a predominantly younger population than is found in most English towns and cities.[1]

MIGRATION TO MILTON KEYNES

One of the first questions to ask about migration to Milton Keynes is where did the migrants come from? The answer can be seen in Table 2,[2] which clearly illustrates the predominance of London and the South East, especially in the early years. From the later 1970s, a widening of the geographical origins of migrants becomes more apparent, a trend continued since.

TABLE 2: PREVIOUS RESIDENCE OF HOUSEHOLDS MOVING TO MILTON
KEYNES, 1968 TO 1983 (PERCENTAGES)

Years	1968–73	1974–77	1978–80	1981–83
London	48.5	46.5	35	30.6
South East	30.3	35.1	37	41.1
Other UK	16.8	15.7	24	25.2
Overseas	3.6	2.3	4	3.0

TABLE 3: PREVIOUS RESIDENCE OF HOUSEHOLDS FROM SUB-REGION
AND SURROUNDING COUNTIES (PERCENTAGES)

Years	1968–73	1974–77	1978–80	1981–83
Sub-region	5.7	5.8	4.0	8.3
Bucks	2.1	3.1	2.9	4.9
Beds/Northants	4.2	7.7	7.4	10.1
Total local	12	16.6	14.3	23.3

We know from MKDC's glossy abstracts of their own household surveys, the *Milton Keynes Insights*, that by the late 1980s the rate of migration from London had settled at 'only about one third of newcomers' with the majority 'moving from other parts of the South East'.[3] That figure was broadly the same in 1990, when Londoners still accounted for about a third of migrants to Milton Keynes. Those from the South East of England, which included the 'sub-region' of Milton Keynes, accounted for 41 per cent of migrants. The rest of England and the UK provided 20 per cent of migrants by 1990, whilst incomers from overseas had increased to 4 per cent of the total.

What was the 'sub-region' of Milton Keynes, a term that suggests a region subordinate to the new city? MKDC defined it, geographically, as the five-mile radius from the borders of the designated area of the new city. The sub-region was thus based within the counties of Bedfordshire, Buckinghamshire and Northamptonshire. Between the years 1968 and 1980, the percentage of all migrants moving to Milton Keynes from the sub-region never exceeded 6 per cent, but this began to grow during the 1980s. By 1983, for example, the sub-region accounted for 8.3 per cent of migrants to Milton Keynes. This figure, in turn, reflected increased levels of local migration to Milton Keynes, from the rest of the counties of Bedfordshire, Buckinghamshire and Northamptonshire *beyond* the sub-region. Table 3 (see above)[4] illustrates the growing level of migration from Beds, Bucks and Northants, both within the sub-region and beyond it.

Some important explanations deserve to be made about these figures. The predominance of Londoners during the first 10 years of migration to the new city reflected in part the dispersal policies of the Greater London Council (GLC). For most of the postwar period, the government of London had been engaged in a 'spread the people' attempt to thin out London's population, notably in those boroughs with pressing accommodation shortages, and the new towns had been the major receptors of the dispersed population.[5]

The mechanisms through which this relocation took place were the New and Expanded Towns Scheme (NETS) and which was later termed the Direct Nominations Scheme. The predecessor of the Greater London Council, namely the London County Council, which was abolished in 1965, had laid the basis for such planned dispersal of population with its Industrial Selection Scheme (ISS). The ISS was central to the workings of the Town Development Act of 1952, an Act that allowed for the expansion of a number of existing new towns such as Bletchley, Swindon and Northampton. From the early 1950s, the ISS offered workers in London the opportunity to gain a better home, and also employment, in one of the eight postwar new towns built to relieve London of its pressure-point population. MKDC's Household Survey for 1976 made it clear that the only difference between the ISS and NETS 'was the change of name'.[6]

The North Bucks area had long been a recipient of urbanisation, including planned population dispersal.[7] Bletchley played host to newcomers, from a number of northern and central London boroughs, following the Second World War. Councillors in Bletchley, keen to see their town grow and prosper, had utilised the wartime town and country planning legislation, and also the Town Development Act of 1952, to get subsidised land for building homes, attracting employment and inducing Londoners to move there.[8] The Lakes Estate, moreover, built during the 1960s, and discussed in an earlier chapter, was an overspill estate of Londoners. In a number of ways, Bletchley provided a dress rehearsal for the later experience of Milton Keynes, a town that would include Bletchley.

By the end of the 1960s, however, the ISS and its role in creating new and expanded towns full of Londoners was adjudged a failure, for two reasons. It had not moved as many people as had been anticipated by government. Moreover, the ISS had proved to be quite inadequate to the much-valued planning goal of creating 'an industrially and socially balanced community' in the new towns.[9] For the most part, they had attracted a disproportionate working-class population and not enough professional middle-class households.[10] It was just this sort of residential and socio-occupational imbalance that Milton Keynes Development Corporation wished to avoid.

Better housing and more secure employment were the two major reasons why people moved to Milton Keynes through the planned dispersal schemes. Many in housing need in London had good reason to pack their bags and journey up the M1, the A5 or the mainline railway to Milton Keynes. In this sense, using NETS was a mode of self-help, a way of bettering the circumstances and opportunities of one's household.

Basically, NETS worked liked this: any Londoner could register with the scheme, either directly through the GLC housing department or with their London borough housing department. Applicants had to give details of their present housing conditions, a personal employment record and work skills. They were then placed on a register for employers to consult, especially when labour shortages occurred. Skilled workers were not as heavily encouraged to sign on as unskilled workers, whom the scheme was primarily intended to benefit. Skilled workers were supposed to utilise job centres. MKDC had arrangements with various London boroughs to facilitate the movement of likely employees to the new city. But by 1973 it became clear to MKDC that NETS was failing in its intention to facilitate unskilled workers to move to Milton Keynes. One reason for this was that existing local workers were filling up job vacancies quite quickly by themselves.[11]

There were other problems with NETS. It was becoming increasingly unpopular with many planners and politicians and writers on urban affairs who argued that such policies speeded up decentralisation and drained London of social capital.[12] More directly for MKDC and its needs, however, the administration of NETS had produced a complex bureaucratic procedure which did not endear itself to employers. They could and did bypass the system and take more direct and traditional means of recruitment. The official consequence of this was a policy change by MKDC, and the addition of another scheme of assisted migration, namely the Direct Nominations Scheme (DNS) in 1975. The DNS was established in conjunction with the Greater London Council and the London boroughs of Brent, Camden, Hackney, Hammersmith,

Islington and Lambeth. Each borough, with the exception of Lambeth, where housing need was particularly acute, was north of the River Thames. Most Londoners migrating to Milton Keynes were from the northern half of the capital and, of those, the majority came from the outer London boroughs rather than the inner ones.[13]

As Milton Keynes became more established, however, the process of in-migration became a more self-sustaining one, and the role of these official dispersal schemes diminished. London began to supply less people anyway, as was evident in a previous table. After 1980, more and more people moved to live in Milton Keynes from the sub-region, that area of a five-mile radius from the borders of the new city. And more and more people migrated from elsewhere in the UK, and from overseas.

The usage of the ISS, NETS and the DNS had been one important component of a wider strategy by the development corporation to recruit a mixed labour force that would provide the basis for a mixed and dynamic social structure. This entailed an emphasis upon diversification in the local economy in order that it would open employment opportunities to as wide a range of people as possible. As the *Plan for Milton Keynes* argued, 'the city should be offering the widest possible range of choices of jobs, and doing this in a way which gives all the residents the opportunity to make the most of their capabilities'.[14] There was a chicken-and-egg intention here: a varied range of jobs would attract workers of differing skills, abilities and interests, and, when those people came, thus the social structure would become more diverse, and that in turn would provide a flexible labour force, essential in the attraction of subsequent companies. It was a key component within a wider strategy to provide the 'space, labour availability, services, access, and environment' that would tempt firms in, and enable them to flourish. These economic considerations were inextricably bound up with the issue of social mix or social balance. Getting a mix of occupational classes, it was hoped by MKDC, would create a balanced population.

Other strategies were adopted so that Milton Keynes would become a city that was socially balanced. Among the most important indicators of this balance were occupational class, age and ethnic grouping. We will look at each one in turn.

TABLE 4: SOCIO-ECONOMIC PROFILE OF MILTON KEYNES
HOUSEHOLDS, 1968 TO 1988 (PERCENTAGES)

Years	1968	1973	1976	1983	1988
Professional–managerial	10	13	18	17	20
Intermediate	20	19	20	39	37
Skilled manual	35	49	44	24	22
Semi- and unskilled manual	35	19	18	20	21

SOCIAL BALANCE

Milton Keynes Development Corporation's *Household Surveys*, and those of the Borough Council from 1992, provide the details necessary to produce a picture of the changing occupational class structure of Milton Keynes. This is what sociologists and social historians term 'objective class', the judgement of wealth and social status by employment. ('Subjective' class refers to class consciousness and perceptions of class, perceptions which are often very different to those based upon occupation.) The household surveys utilised four major categories of Socio-Economic Group (SEG), namely 'professional–managerial'; 'intermediate'; 'skilled manual', and 'semi- and unskilled manual'.

Between 1968 and 1988 the shifting percentages of these broad categories revealed the broad changes taking place within the occupational structure of the migrants to Milton Keynes, and hence the changes occurring in the class composition in the aggregate number of households. Put simply, Milton Keynes became an increasingly middle-class city following the peak of skilled and semi- and unskilled households during the middle of the 1970s. Table 4 (see above)[15] illustrates these trends, trends replicated more generally across England.

Milton Keynes thus directly shared in the much-documented rise of the service sector in the concluding third of the twentieth century, a trend that was already in existence, but which accelerated and expanded with the worsening of Britain's manufacturing problems during the 1970s. The new city was conceived and then born into decades of de-industrialisation and service sector growth. The growth of the 'financial district' between Central Milton Keynes and the rail station was one obvious consequence of this, but so too was the rise and rise of the Open University and the expansion of secondary educational provision as the population grew. The opening of the hospital in 1981 also increased the size of the public sector bureaucracy in the new city, as well as of course the number of doctors, nurses, skilled technicians and so on. All of these places of work required ancillary manual workers, but they were not the largest proportion of the in-house work-forces.

Yet there was also a local factor influencing these figures. The sharp rise and fall in the number of skilled manual workers as a percentage of the working population also reflected the demise of those planned dispersal schemes from London, outlined above, and also the fact that the early phase in the Milton Keynes' infra-structure, notably the laying of main grid roads, drains, sewers and cables, was largely completed by the end of the 1980s. Subsequently, less labour was needed to finish off the extensions of Milton Keynes. It is clear from MKDC's *Milton Keynes Planning Manual*, in 1992, that, whilst large parts of the city remained to be built in 1992, most of the groundwork had been extensively laid down over the 9,000 hectares of the new city.[16]

Given the winding-up of MKDC in 1992, the borough council and the Commission for New Towns compiled statistics on the changing occupational structure of Milton Keynes during the 1990s. Although the categories used were not quite the same as those of MKDC, with, for example, the catch-all term 'manual' replacing the more specific skilled/semi-skilled/unskilled cat-egories, nonetheless the figures illustrate that the decade contin-ued the trends of previous years. A 1993 report by Milton Keynes Borough Council, based on the 1991 Census, illustrated that pro-fessional and managerial groups accounted for over 21 per cent of employed people in the new city. Those in 'intermediate' work, that is, clerical and administrative, comprised 36 per cent of the working population, with manual workers numbering 41 per cent.

'Compared to Britain as a whole', argued the report, 'the new city has slightly more households in the skilled non-manual classes, with fewer in the professional/managerial and technical classes'.[17] Milton Keynes was thus home to a growing profes-sional and managerial class, and to the continuing rise of the number of occupations falling within the rather diverse range of 'intermediate and clerical–administrative' categories. This has led to an imbalance of the population in favour of more affluent groups.[18]

Social balance was not only about occupational class. As noted above, age was a significant factor in new towns. The earlier new towns, along with many interwar and postwar suburban new estates, were the places where decent housing was more likely to be achievable for those seeking to raise a young family, and for those with or without children who were looking for a bright new home that reflected their sense of higher expectations than those of their parents.[19]

In line with the official expectations outlined in the *Plan for Milton Keynes*, the residents of Milton Keynes have tended to be, on average, younger than those of established older towns. In 1976, the Household Survey found that 56 per cent of workers in Milton Keynes were aged between 20 and 39 years old, as against 41 per cent nationally. But as these families grew older, the numbers of people in the more advanced age brackets began, naturally, to increase.[20] This was further augmented by the follow-on migration of many older members of the family, the parents of migrating offspring, who moved to Milton Keynes to be near their children and often their grandchildren. Thus as a result of internal ageing, as it were, and also incoming elderly migrants, MKDC reported in 1991 on the 'substantial increase' in elderly people within the new city during the previous 10 years.[21]

Nonetheless, by 1991 Milton Keynes was still a younger place, in terms of both people and age of environment, than most other towns and cities in England. The *Milton Keynes Population Bulletin* noted that, in contrast to national trends, the number of young adults (aged 16 to 24 years) in Milton Keynes had increased rapidly since 1981, an increase of some 54 per cent from 13,800 to 21,300. That compared with a static level in England and Wales.[22] By the year 2000, Milton Keynes had higher percentages of people aged 50 and below than the average of the total population, and lower proportions for those above 50 than the average percentage of the national population.[23]

Ethnic mix was also an important indicator of social balance. The *Plan for Milton Keynes* had noted the emerging problems of racism and racial conflict in urban areas.[24] The very fact that this observation was made stemmed from the appalling problems of some of America's city centres, that were apparent in the later 1960s, when Milton Keynes was being planned. Racial tensions, moreover, had intermittently blown up in English cities since the Notting Hill and Nottingham riots of 1958. There were further indications during the formulation of the *Plan for Milton Keynes* that race and immigration were potentially fraught issues for the new city. In its survey of what people felt about the proposed

TABLE 5: ETHNIC CHARACTERISTICS OF MILTON KEYNES
NEW CITY, 1991

White	*133,596*	*93.3%*
Other	*9,542*	*6.7%*
Black Caribbean	1,551	16.3
Black African	478	5.0
Black Other	636	6.7
Indian	2,659	27.9
Pakistani	800	8.4
Bangladeshi	660	6.9
Chinese	634	6.6
Other Asian	891	9.3
Other	1,233	12.9
Total	*143,138*	

plan, MKDC found that 'Some people wanted to know what kind of people would come to the city', with a number of the questioners asking 'whether coloured people would be expected and if they were, whether they would tend to settle in poorer housing areas in the city'.[25] Ultimately, in its 1970 Plan, MKDC dealt in vague terms with the notion that 'the physical and institutional structure of cities will influence the ease and speed with which minority groups can fully share the opportunities open to the majority'.[26]

The *Plan for Milton Keynes* did not give any detailed or strategic undertaking to specifically recruit a black population that accurately or even approximately would represent the numbers of blacks of the wider national population. Nonetheless, it appears from the available statistics on ethnicity in Milton Keynes that the new city was not unsuccessful in attracting minority groups of colour. Some significant patterns and pictures can be identified in the ethnic evolution of Milton Keynes.

By 1981, of those ethnic groups born outside the UK, people of African origin, both from the Caribbean islands and from East Africa, numbered a little over 1,130; Indians numbered 614, Bangladeshis 248, 'New Commonwealth' 642 and Pakistanis 150. In addition, 859 people of African origin, 433 Indians, 42 Bangladeshis, 485 'New Commonwealth' and 106 Pakistanis were born in the UK. In total, this amounted to 4,725 people, less than 4 per cent of the local population.[27]

The 1991 Census gave a clearer picture of how the groups were evolving in Milton Keynes. Table 5 (see above)[28] is drawn from the borough council's analysis of the 1991 Census for the new city, and of subsequent trends during the 1990s. They illustrate both the major groups that had settled in Milton Keynes by 1991, and those that were moving to the new city, whether from within Britain or from abroad, during the decade.

The introduction of the Chinese category was interesting not only in itself but because subsequently, during the 1990s, the Chinese population began to grow more quickly than before. During the latter half of the decade, the Commission for New Towns, the chief development agency that took over from MKDC, made overtures to the Hong Kong Chinese who were fearful of remaining in the city once the Chinese communist regime took over from 1997. Both before and since British hegemony ended in the ex-colony, the Hong Kong Chinese were migrating in their thousands to Britain and elsewhere, including Milton Keynes, adding to the small number of mainland Chinese people that already lived in the new city.

By 2000, the settlement of Asians and blacks within the new city revealed quite gentle levels of clustering within a general pattern of dispersal. This was evident from the council's ward profiles. Bangladeshis, for example, were most concentrated in Bletchley and Fenny Stratford, yet even here they were less than 5 per cent of the local populations. Most of this in-migration had occurred before 1970, however, and it was heavily loaded into those older parts of the city made up largely of terraced housing that existed before the designation of Milton Keynes. Bangladeshis were also to be found in some of the poorer gridsquares, but in most of the residential estates they usually made up less than 1 per cent of the population, and less than 0.5 per cent in some. None were recorded in the wealthy gridsquares of Emerson Valley, Westcroft and Shenley Brook End that made up the Emerson Valley ward.[29]

Pakistanis were also to some extent more numerous in older and poorer parts of the city, such as Wolverton, where they numbered just over 2 per cent of the population, and they were dispersed in low numbers around some of the gridsquares. As with Bangladeshis, however, none were recorded in Emerson Valley ward. Indians, by contrast, the largest ethnic group of colour in Milton Keynes, made up more than 1 per cent of the population in Emerson Valley and some of the relatively wealthier gridsquares, suggesting less socio-economic segregation from the middle classes than Bangladeshis and Pakistanis. They were, however, represented in almost all gridsquares and in the older settlements such as Bradwell and Wolverton.[30]

Furthermore, both Chinese and Japanese groups were also dotted across many different gridsquares in Milton Keynes by the year 2000, usually in quite tiny fractions of a percentage. There appeared to be no clustering on any significant scale, although a small Hong Kong Chinese community established itself on Kents Hill from the mid-1990s, and the Japanese had built their own-language school.[31] This is discussed further in the next chapter.

Black African Caribbeans and black Africans were also spread around most areas of Milton Keynes, and they were no more or less numerous in the older towns and villages such as Bletchley, Fenny Stratford, Bradwell and Wolverton.[32] Theirs was perhaps the widest and thinnest spreading of all groups across the new city.

CONCLUSION

In 2000, the ethnic composition of Milton Keynes was about 94 per cent white. However, it was not the bastion of the white British-born working classes that most of the earlier postwar new towns in the South East of England had become at the same stage of their development. Milton Keynes was also a city whose occupational profile mirrored the changes occurring in the English economy and that meant a diminishing number of manual workers and a growing proportion of white-collar and non-manual households. It was, furthermore, a relatively younger city in terms of both demographics and its built environment than most other towns and cities in England. In this, Milton Keynes was closely representative of the first generation of most of the new communities that were built during the twentieth century.

With all due deference to the younger age profile of Milton Keynes noted above, we need to acknowledge that a demographic transition is now under way in the early twenty-first century: the population of the new city is ageing. The 2001 Census revealed that the number of people aged 60 years and over had been growing quite markedly in the 1990s.[33] There is no cause for surprise there, for many people who had moved to the new city during the 1970s who had been in their 40s, or those who were by no means young when they moved to Milton Keynes in the 1980s and 1990, had reached 'old age'. This ageing process had been augmented with chain migration, as parents or grandparents moved to be with their offspring or grandchildren.

Milton Keynes is still, at the time of writing, one of the youngest cities in the UK. To what extent this will continue depends on the future migration cohorts, and the plans and provision for the new city's population.

NOTES

1 Robert Shipley and Steven Gammon, 'The six planning goals of Milton Keynes: a third decade report card', *Planning History*, 24, 1 (2002), p. 40.
2 This table is adapted from MKDC, *Milton Keynes Household Survey, 1983: Demographic Report* (Milton Keynes: MKDC, 1984), Table XVIII, p. 32.
3 MKDC, *Milton Keynes Insight* (Milton Keynes: MKDC, March 1989), p. 2.
4 MKDC, *Milton Keynes Household Survey, 1983; Demographic Report* (Milton Keynes: MKDC, 1984) Table XVIII, p. 32.
5 Andrew Saint, '"Spread the people": the LCC's dispersal policy', in Andrew Saint (ed.), *Politics and the People of London: The London County Council, 1889–1965* (London: Hambledon, 1989), pp. 215–36.
6 MKDC, *Household Survey, 1976: Seven Years On, Technical Report 2* (Milton Keynes: MKDC, 1977), p. 3b.
7 Pat Mortimer, 'Urbanisation in North Buckinghamshire, 1930–1970' (Milton Keynes: unpublished M.Phil., Open University, 1986).
8 Marion Hill (ed.), *Bigger, Brighter, Better: The Story of Bletchley 1944–1966, As Told by its Residents* (Milton Keynes: Living Archive Project, 1996), *passim*.
9 B. J. Heraud, 'The new towns and London's housing problem', *Urban Studies*, 3, 1 (1966), pp. 8–21.
10 B. J. Heraud, 'Social class and the new towns', *Urban Studies*, 5, 1 (1968), pp. 33–41.
11 MKDC, *Milton Keynes: Seven Years On: The Summary Report of the 1976 Household and Employer's Surveys* (Milton Keynes: MKDC, 1977), pp. 18–23.
12 Heraud, 'The new towns and London's housing problem', pp. 10–15; Paul Lawless, *Britain's Inner Cities: Problems and Policies* (London: Harper and Row, 1981) p. 223.
13 MKDC, *Household Survey 1976: Seven Years On, Technical Report 2*, p. 8.
14 MKDC, *Plan for Milton Keynes*, vol. 2, p. 117.
15 This table is adapted from the following: MKDC, *Four Years On: The Milton Keynes Household Survey, 1973, Summary Report* (Milton Keynes: MKDC, 1974) Fig. 2 between pp. 8 and 9; MKDC, *Seven Years On: The Summary Report of the 1976 Household and Employer's Surveys*, Fig. 1.9, p. 11; MKDC, *Milton Keynes Household Survey, 1988: Employment Technical Report* (Milton Keynes: MKDC, 1989), Table 1, p. 4.
16 MKDC, *Milton Keynes Planning Manual* (Milton Keynes: MKDC, 1992)
17 Milton Keynes Borough Council, *People and Work in Milton Keynes: A Profile of Settlements from the 1991 Census* (Milton Keynes: Milton Keynes Borough Council and the Commission for New Towns, 1993), Appendix B.
18 Shipley and Gammon, 'Six planning goals', pp. 36–45.
19 Mark Clapson, *Invincible Green Suburbs, Brave New Towns: Social Change and Urban Dispersal in Postwar England* (Manchester: Manchester University Press, 1998), pp. 62–95.
20 MKDC, *Household Survey, 1976: Seven Years On: Technical Report 3: Employment* (Milton Keynes: MKDC, 1977), p. 6.
21 MKDC, *Milton Keynes Population Bulletin, 1991* (Milton Keynes: MKDC and Chesterton Consulting, 1991), p. 25.
22 MKDC, *Milton Keynes Population Bulletin, 1991*, p. 23.
23 Milton Keynes Council, *Facts and Figures, 1999–2000* (Milton Keynes: Milton Keynes Council, 1999), p. 45.
24 MKDC, *Plan for Milton Keynes*, vol. 1, p. 10.
25 MKDC, *The Plan for Milton Keynes: Technical Supplement No. 3: Public Reaction to the Interim Plan* (Milton Keynes: MKDC, 1970), p. 14.
26 MKDC, *Plan for Milton Keynes*, vol. 1, p. 10.

27 Statistics based upon Dave Middleton and Stewart Palmer, *Blacks Need Not Apply: A Report into the Problems of Unemployment among Ethnic Minorities* (Milton Keynes: Campaign Against Poverty, 1985), p. 4.
28 Milton Keynes Borough Council, *People and Housing in Milton Keynes: A Profile of Settlements from the 1991 Census* (Milton Keynes: MKBC, 1993), Appendix B.
29 Milton Keynes Council, *Facts and Figures, 1999–2000*, p. 76 for Emerson Valley.
30 Milton Keynes Council, *Facts and Figures, 1999–2000*, p. 148 for Wolverton; Ward Profiles, *passim*.
31 Milton Keynes Council, *Facts and Figures, 1999–2000*, pp. 50, 72, 148, and Ward Profiles, *passim*; William Underhill, 'No place like it for Eastern promise', *Daily Telegraph*, 23 January 1992.
32 Milton Keynes Council, *Facts and Figures, 1999–2000*, Ward Profiles, *passim*.
33 Anon., 'Council's growing problem', *Milton Keynes Citizen*, 2 November 2002.

6

Settling In

The trouble is, say 'new town' to most British people who
have seen only one or two and the immediate picture is an
overgrown estate of municipal housing and a draughty
shopping precinct. That is why Milton Keynesians insist that
people must visit their city to understand what it's all about.
Doreen King, 'Twenty years on, and still going strong',
The Times, 16 November 1987

The experience of moving to a new city with a far from positive
reputation might be considered depressing, and perhaps one
based more on necessity than on choice. Why would one want to
leave apparently cosy old towns and cities, or even the countryside, to live in the cold suburban city that Milton Keynes was
widely touted as? And would it not have been a grim experience,
settling into this bleak new city?

This chapter assesses the reasons why people moved to the new
city, and it looks at their experiences of settling down to a fresh
new life there. It will be seen that, whilst there were fundamentally
similar encounters shared by those who moved to Milton Keynes,
there were also many different ones, and this depended on the
class and income, ethnicity and age of individuals and households.
Many different voices are quoted in the chapter to illustrate both
the commonality and the diversity of experiences that went into
the social making of the new city.

WHY DID PEOPLE MOVE TO MILTON KEYNES?

The major reasons why people moved to Milton Keynes are
broadly very similar to the main reasons why most people move

TABLE 6: REASONS FOR MOVING TO MILTON KEYNES (PERCENTAGES)

Years	1968–73	1974–78	1979–83	1984–88
Employment	30.9	28.1	31.1	38.9
Housing	33.1	34.2	32.3	33.3
Kin	27.2	26.3	24.2	17.5
Environment	6.3	9.5	8.6	7.8
Other	1.9	1.9	3.4	2.2
Not stated	0.6	0	0.4	0.3

home at least once in their life: they want better housing, or higher-paid or more secure employment. Sometimes the two went together. They also moved to be nearer to family, or to move to an environment which they felt, generally, to be an improvement on the place in which they were currently living.

Table 6 (see above)[1] is based upon MKDC household surveys. Interesting in itself, the table is also a testament to the information-gathering exercise of the development corporation, an exercise which provided data that are useful for understanding the qualitative or subjective reasons behind internal migration and immigration to Milton Keynes, and also the rest of England, in the years since the late 1960s.

Housing and employment were continually the most important reasons for moving to the new city, despite fluctuations. However, some qualification of these ostensible findings is required in relation to kinship as a reason for moving. In fact, despite the dip in kin as a reason for moving to Milton Keynes, this factor probably remained quite constant, for a number of reasons. First, MKDC's resettlement policy until 1992 encouraged middle-aged and more elderly people to move to the new city, and this often meant the parents of younger couples.[2] A study of the Beanhill gridsquare, conducted in the spring of 1987, found that 'the most popular reason for moving to Milton Keynes was to be nearer grown-up children', a development which also brought about 'the gradual stabilisation of the population' through the movement of subsequent members of the family to the city in the wake of the original migrants.[3] There was a further reason for the apparent dip during the 1980s: more and more migrants to Milton Keynes emanated from the sub-region and nearby counties, and thus family, and also friends, were probably still within driving distance. Hence, family and friends as a reason for moving to Milton Keynes was relatively unimportant for these newcomers.

Yet, as noted above, better housing and employment remained the most important reasons for moving, and each will now be dealt with in turn. MKDC noted in 1976 that, in terms of the stimuli for all groups who moved to Milton Keynes, it was 'much more important to move for a better house than for a better job'.[4] Given the newness of most housing in Milton Keynes, this was hardly surprising, and Table 6 shows that the pursuit of improved housing remained a major motive for moving to the new city.

IN PURSUIT OF BETTER HOUSING

Many people who settled the earliest estates referred to themselves as the 'pioneers'. It was as if, in common with the migrants who moved westwards across nineteenth-century America into unsettled territory, they felt they were moving from an older civilisation to a newer life, and blazing a trail for those who would come later. Yet they also had much in common with many residents of earlier new towns, who also dubbed themselves as 'pioneers'. Making the break with older urban living areas for a new housing estate was and remains a mass movement, yet it is a mass movement which is generally understudied in English contemporary social history.[5]

During the later 1960s and for most of the 1970s, the city was much rawer, and less well endowed with shops and cultural facilities, than it would later become. In 1973, MKDC undertook to investigate those people who had moved to the city since its beginnings. The results of the survey were published as *Four Years On: The Milton Keynes Household Survey*.[6] Some of the findings were made available to a wider audience in the popular sociological periodical *New Society* in August 1974, in the form of an article by a local community worker for MKDC, who was concerned with arrivals work. These arrivals workers personified the concern of the development corporation to monitor the earliest experiences of settlers, and to ensure things went as smoothly as possible, not just for the people, but also for MKDC.

Particular interest was shown towards poorer households, or those who had been in housing need. Many poorer early migrants from London, for example, were in housing need. They moved to live in housing built by and rented by the development corporation. MKDC's definition of housing need was any household 'that used to live in overcrowded conditions, or shared a dwelling with another household or lacked an indoor toilet, kitchen or bath'.

Furthermore, if any respondents interviewed by MKDC felt their previous dwelling was overcrowded, in poor physical condition and therefore in need of repair, the development corporation 'defined that household as in housing need'.[7]

People in such conditions naturally wanted to escape from them. The following examples clearly illustrate the attraction of new and better housing when considering a move from an older-established area to a new town:

> It was a terrible house. For a start off, it was running with mice. The mice were in the beds, in the furniture, and it was making my children's lives a misery, and mine as well, 'cos I suffer badly from me nerves. It was half a house – very small, and we were paying almost £6 a week for it. It had two rooms and a kitchen . . .[8]

Moving could certainly be a wrench, but the new house was usually the crucial factor in the decision to go. One man, working for the Post Office in London, badly wanted his new house but felt misgivings and a sense of loss at leaving behind his family and his 'community' in Hackney, east London, for north-west Milton Keynes. 'My mum stood on the doorstep', he since recalled, 'shedding a little tear cos I think she thought we were going to the other side of the world.'[9] Another man from London, a factory manager for a sugar milling company that was relocating to Milton Keynes, was put in charge of coordinating the move. He 'sounded out the men; eight of the twelve saw it as an opportunity to get their own place'. He and his wife, for example, lived above his parents, so they were 'looking forward to having [their] own place with a garden'. Soon afterwards, his parents and other relations moved to Milton Keynes 'and didn't want to move back'. His wife spoke of 'the thrill of her own front door'. She was not homesick for London, and regularly visited friends and family there.[10] Another woman and her husband, from Watford in Hertfordshire, were among the first couples to move to the estate of Greenleys. Again, the house was the main attraction. Soon after she moved in, her sister and brother moved up to Milton Keynes, reconstituting one generation of the family in the city.[11]

It is apparent from some people's comments, however, that people felt compelled to leave London to gain the sort of accommodation they really wanted. The concept of 'choice' was much more restricted for those who could not get what they wanted where they were originally living. This was exposed in such comments as 'It wasn't Milton Keynes, it was just what the Labour

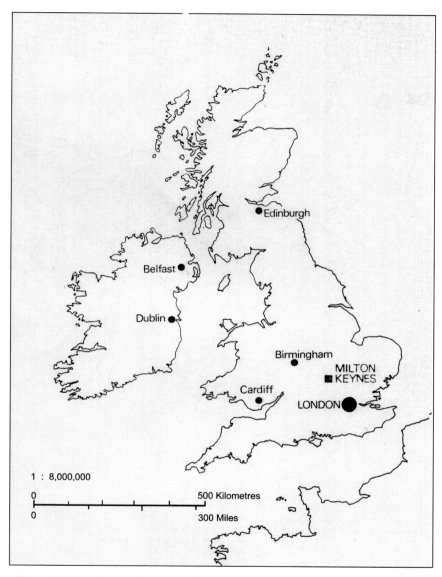

Figure 1 Map showing location of Milton Keynes in United Kingdom (Milton Keynes Development Corporation, *The Plan for Milton Keynes*; Volume 1, 1970)

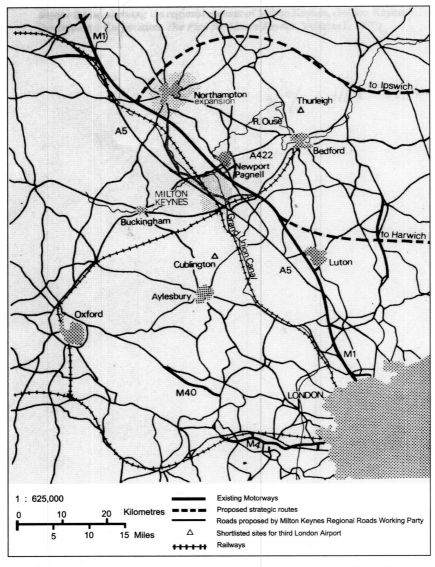

Figure 2 Map showing the regional context of Milton Keynes (Milton Keynes Development Corporation, *The Plan for Milton Keynes*, Volume 1, 1970)

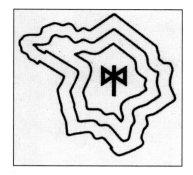

Figure 3 Icon of the Minoan double-headed axe within the shape of Milton Keynes (Milton Keynes Development Corporation)

RENTAL ESTATES	VERY OR QUITE PLEASED	DISAPPOINTED	WANT TO GO BACK
Windmill Hill Warren Bank			
Woodside			
Fullers Slade Galley Hill Hilltop Bradville 2			
SALE ESTATES			
Tinkers Bridge 5 Simpson 3 Fairfield			
Galley Hill Tinkers Bridge 4 Eaton Mill			
Hill Top Tinkers Bridge 1			

FIRST REACTION TO LIVING IN MILTON KEYNES

on Corporation estates

☺ represents 5% of particular group of residents

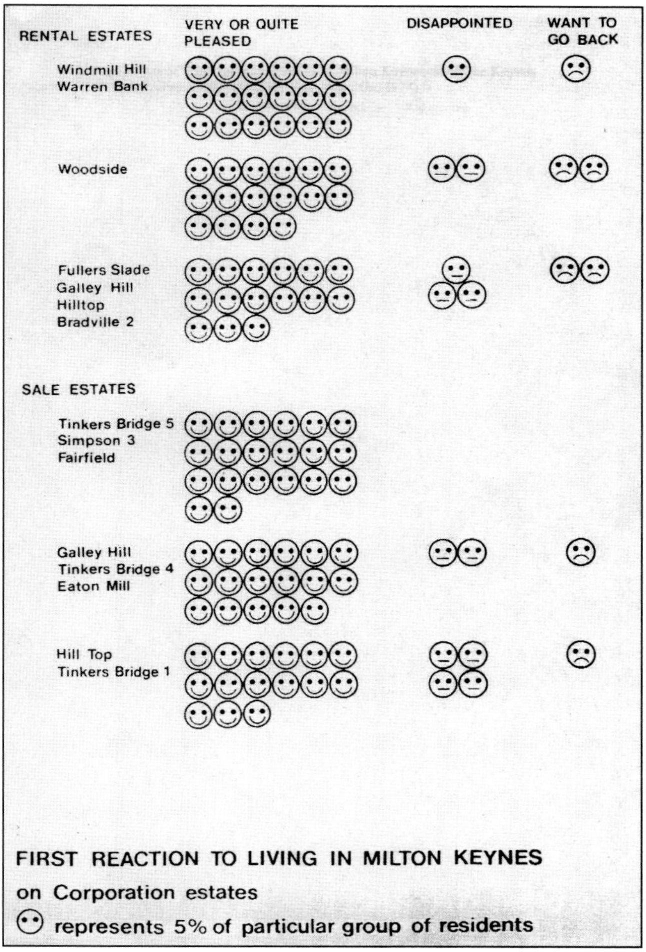

Figure 4 Smiley chart of 'First reaction to living in Milton Keynes on Milton Keynes Development Corporation estates' (MKDC, *Four Years On*, 1974)

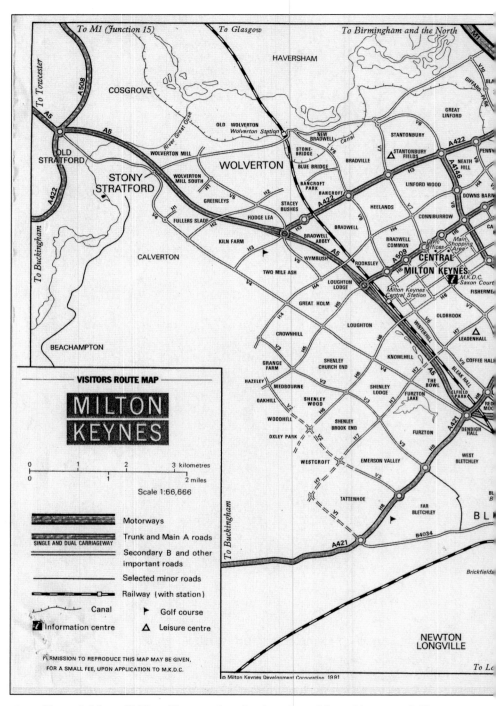

Figure 5 Map of Milton Keynes, showing location of the gridsquares (Milton Keynes Development Corporation)

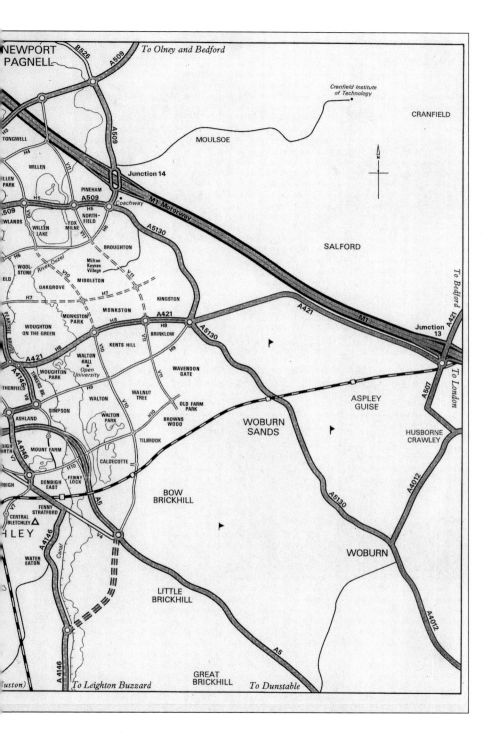

Figure 6 Netherfield housing by the year 2002. Poor weathering is clearly apparent on the fins that separate the houses (photograph by author, 2002)

Figure 7 A road sign; another signifier of the country-in-the-city (photograph by author, 2002)

Figure 8 Canal fishing, Campbell Park (photograph by author, 2002.

Figure 9 Graffiti spoils the appearance of this Meeting Place (photograph by author, 2002)

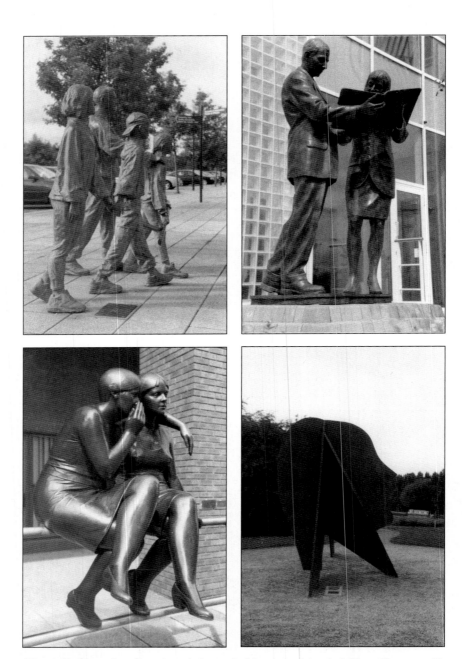

Figure 10 Changing directions in household composition in Milton Keynes will require considerable thought on the nature of current and future housing provision (photographs by author, 2002; each sculpture is in Milton Keynes)

Figure 11 New City Magazine, 1975, cover (published by Milton Keynes Development Corporation)

Beanhill
Milton Keynes
MK6

TO RENT

Beanhill is a development of 569 homes near the A5 just north of Bletchley.

The majority of the houses are single-storey and have integral carports. The number of bedrooms ranges from one to three.

There are also two-storey houses with three bedrooms. The buildings are timber frame and clad in aluminium.

The kitchen, dining room and living room have been designed to overlook the garden, so it is easy to keep an eye on the children during the day. Bedrooms are on the approach side of the house.

To cut down on carpeting costs, vinyl tiled floors have been laid in all single-storey homes and on the ground floors of the two storey homes. Each house has a telephone point, television socket and part central heating by a gas-fired warm air system. The single storey design of the houses has resulted in a wide frontage which in turn provides a large rear garden with added privacy.

The estate is divided into neighbourhood units each of which is grouped around cul-de-sac roads. This means that only the people who live in the roads will use them, so there is extra privacy and more safety for children. In each of these units there are a number of single-storey dwellings for older tenants.

The Beanhill estate will have as many as twenty separate play areas for toddlers and a meeting hall, as well as a small shopping complex.

There is good access to the M1 motorway and the A5. The main rail station at Bletchley is on the Inter-City route which provides a fast and frequent service between London (Euston), Birmingham and the North West.

Bletchley has good shopping facilities, a Sainsburys store and a Leisure Centre with attractions for all the family.

A combined First and Middle School is within walking distance of the estate.

Figure 12 Beanhill housing for rent, mid-1970s (Milton Keynes Development Corporation)

Milton Keynes Village
Milton Keynes
MK10

FOR SALE

Within the picturesque village of Milton Keynes near the site of Willen lake, is a small select development of 14 luxury bungalows built by Bryant Homes.

There are two types of bungalows — 10 have four bedrooms and four have three bedrooms, each is 'L' shaped with a monopitch rolled tile roof and encloses its own private garden which is overlooked by all the main rooms. The hall leads off to the kitchen, a large living room and the guest cloakroom. Its superbly equipped kitchen has a hatch to the dining room. The main bedroom and shower room are grouped en suite in one wing of the house and in the other wing are the two or three other bedrooms with a second bathroom. The homes have electric underfloor heating throughout and all the bedrooms have fitted cupboards. An attractive feature of the exterior elevations are the long brick 'flower boxes' that run the length of two walls. They are an integral part of the house, built in brick up to the level of the windows which overlook the secluded garden.

The paved patio in the garden can be approached from the hall, or from large glazed doors in the dining and living rooms.

Bletchley, six miles away, is the largest existing town in the Designated Area of the City. There are schools, a clinic and health centre, shops, banks, offices, restaurants, pubs, and the new Leisure Centre for all kinds of activities and entertainment. From Bletchley Station, fast direct trains will take you all over the country.

Milton Keynes village is very close to the city's main link with the M1.

Figure 13 Milton Keynes Village housing for sale, mid-1970s (Milton Keynes Development Corporation)

パーフェクト・シティー
ミルトン・キーンズ

ミルトン・キーンズは、ノース・バッキンガムシャーの田園地帯に広がる3つの町と13の村を統合・開発した都市で、ロンドンとバーミンガム、オックスフォードとケンブリッジのそれぞれの中間という理想的な位置を占めています。

ロンドン（ユーストン）と主要地方工業都市であるバーミンガム、マンチェスター、リバプール、グラスゴーを結ぶ電化幹線網（ミルトン・キーンズを経由している）が約40分で結んでいます。

現在、ミルトン・キーンズには、1982年5月にオープンしたショッピングで有名なミルトン・キーンズ・セントラルをはじめとして、ここにはキャナル・トラム、南のアレッチャリー、北のストーニー・ストラットフォード、西のウォルバートンの3つの駅があります。

1983年初頭に10万人を超えたミルトン・キーンズの人口は、現在、103,000人を超えるものへと成長しました。ミルトン・キーンズは、20万都市を目指した都市計画を進めています。

Loughtonの住宅

市内には、新高速道路が接続するように走り、安全面も全住宅の周辺から、歩道と自動車専用道路が整備されています。平均通勤時間はわずか15分足らずで交通渋滞とも無縁です。

住宅開発や雇用創出の達しのにつれて、学校やヘルスセンター、各種コミュニティ施設の整備も進められてきました。

3つのレジャー・センターでは各種室内スポーツが楽しめるほか、それぞれにプール、劇場が併設されています。また、スポーツ・フィールドも数多く、公認ゴルフ場も2コースあります。

また最近、ニューシティーとの457,290平方メートルの緑地に、ミルトン・キーンズ第2の見どころの大温室をつくり上げ仕事に着手しました。

さらに、ミルトン・キーンズ近郊にはさまざまな種類の大型ショッピング・センターがあってヨーロッパの大型ショッピング・センター（床場面積：約93,000平方メートル）があり、デパートや個人商店など140を超える店舗が軒を並べています。このほか、大規模な屋内装飾展示場を2回開かれる育児市場もあります。

その他、市内にある大きなレジャー・オブ・ファーマーエステートショップをはじめ、エンジョイ・ファーマーズ・マーケットは、街の様々な施設・技能地の様々な種類のローカル・センター、旧市街の各種と、本センターなどで行なわれています。

セントラル・ミルトン・キーンズのショッピング・エリア

湖畔のパブ

芝生でのクリケット

ミルトン・キーンズ近郊には、商工業への応用研究に重点をおいた工業技術や経営専門の分野で、国際的にも高度な研究の実績をあげています。フィールド工科大学があり、毎年、5,000人ほどの学生が大学院や短期コースに学んでいます。さらに、ミルトン・キーンズの学生数は経営約50を国内には、商工業の各種実務のコースにも応える訓練・教育機関が多数あります。また、オックスフォード大学やケンブリッジ大学も近く、車で90分足らずです。

ミルトン・キーンズは、さまざまな技能をもつ豊かな労働力に恵まれています。なかでも、ここには若年労働者の割合が高く、20〜40才の労働者が全労働者に占める割合は、60%にのぼり、全国平均の40%を大きく上回っています。労働調査結果ても、シフト制も順調に機能しています。また、無断欠勤率や転職率、病気などによる欠勤率も低く、失業率も全国平均的なを下回っています。

雇用めぐるまったく新しい解雇産業に対する適応性も不可欠です。ミルトン・キーンズには、こうした要求に対し、トレーニング施設や訓練機関を数多くあるようなハイテクシェーラーの失業者に最新的テクノロジーの基礎技能を習得させ、実務に即戦力をもたせることを目的に、政府機関が設立したミルトン・キーンズ・インフォメーション・テクノロジー・トレーニング・センターもそのひとつ。これにより、先端技術産業の分野における熟練労働市場も、一層、強化・増大されます。

Exchange offered us was Milton Keynes.'[12] Yet lack of choice was not just experienced by those within public sector housing but also by those on the lower rungs of the private housing ladder. In the case of one teacher and his family, living in London, this was exacerbated by the age of the children, and hence the costly stage of the family life cycle: 'On the face of it', he said, 'it was a good time [to move], the kids were young and the prospect of getting decent housing in London was virtually non-existent.'[13] Yet this was not a situation of powerlessness. A 1970s study of planned migration from London to the new towns noted that, even where people were moving with their employment or taking public housing, 'choices are still being made', and those choices were of 'particular importance just because opportunities were so limited'.[14]

Milton Keynes Development Corporation was adept at presenting the new city to potential migrants as a place where good housing, especially for those with limited opportunities to improve their accommodation, was available. In publicity materials, for example the glossy *New City* magazines of the mid-1970s, attractive photo-articles played to the positive experience of moving from old and overcrowded housing to the spacious modern housing in the green fields of Milton Keynes. MKDC also produced brochures and folders with illustrations and descriptions of the housing on offer. It is interesting to note, moreover, that the 'traditional' terraced housing areas of working-class housing, such as East London, and the inner London boroughs of South London, were chosen for comparative purposes, rather than outer London boroughs, where housing was, for the most part, newer. One such example was of a couple from Brixton, with young children, living in a terraced house with the husband's parents. Milton Keynes opened up a new and pleasing prospect for this couple. As its policy dictated, housing officers from MKDC showed them around different show houses, and the couple made their choice. It was now up to the head of the household to get a job in the area before they were allowed to move in. Once he had achieved this, the house move was completed, the keys were handed over and the family moved in. 'You'll have to ask me down so I can have a proper bath,' said the husband's mother, back in Brixton.[15]

Not everyone was from London, however. One man who moved to Milton Keynes from Luton, in 1972, had learned about the new city from a brochure in Luton Town Hall. He was single, which he complained kept him towards the bottom of the Luton council house waiting list, although he had a pregnant girlfriend. He was, however, grateful for the ostensibly more liberal regime in Milton Keynes where 'it seemed you didn't have to be married to get a house quickly'. He and his partner were given a house in Netherfield, but they 'didn't want to go there'. They did not like the metallic modern appearance of those houses. They wanted 'a brick house, and didn't want a three storey town house', which they felt was 'ridiculous' for a couple with a baby on the way. But that was what they got and, whilst it was a welcome break with the Luton waiting list, they felt they had little choice in the matter. The man also had to take employment in Milton Keynes before the move could be completed.[16]

There were other, connected, reasons to move to Milton Keynes. Many felt that the area that they were living in prior to the move was deteriorating, 'going down', and not simply in a physical sense, but in terms of social change. This was felt to be potentially undermining to those with aspirations for their family. A new house also often meant a better environment. Hence a West Indian couple, interviewed by workers of the development corporation, told of how they had moved to Milton Keynes from South London as a result of the obscene language and threatening behaviour of their neighbours. They did not wish for their young children to be raised in the area, and welcomed 'the peace and clean of the open streets' of Milton Keynes. As the woman stated, 'I like to keep an eye on the children all the time, and there was a garden here, so I could see them.'[17]

A Pakistani couple moved to Milton Keynes from London in 1980 for both improved housing and nicer surroundings. Their experience rang true not only for Pakistani movers to Milton Keynes, but for Londoners more generally. 'In 1980', they stated, 'we were living in London, in Islington':

> The housing wasn't very good. I would say Milton Keynes was much better than expected. We moved into Conniburrow and couldn't believe it was a council house because it was such good quality. We were used to seeing council houses in London that are all dilapidated and run-down. We were quite excited by it all.[18]

New housing with a garden in the garden city appealed to migrants from cities other than London, cities that are often held up by fashionable international architects as successful examples of high-density and high-rise urbanity. During the 1990s, Milton Keynes Development Corporation targeted business people living in Hong Kong who were fearful at the consequences of communist Chinese rule in that city-state once British rule ended in 1997. They showed them promotional videos of the new city. It is not extravagant to argue that the subsequent migration of Hong Kong Chinese people to Milton Keynes is almost a global expression of the suburban aspiration. This may be described as a desire to move from the overcrowded and dense city centres to lower densities and the more spacious greenery of new estates made up mostly of houses with gardens. An article in the *Independent* in the summer of 1998, entitled 'How Milton Keynes has become "little Hong Kong"', found that the newness and the space of Milton Keynes were very appealing to aspiring Chinese families. 'Charles and May Tien and their eight year old daughter Sarah', the report found, 'recently exchanged their matchbox on the 16th floor of a high-rise in Hong Kong for a spacious home on Kents Hill, a housing development on the east of Milton Keynes':

> And they are still marvelling at the difference. 'Our apartment was very small and obviously we had no garden or outdoor space at all', said Mr. Tien. 'We looked straight in the window of the apartment in the block opposite to ours, less than 50 metres away. Now we are living in a clean, healthy place with green fields to look at. It is like living in the countryside and the town at the same time'.[19]

From another country of the Pacific Ocean rim, the Japanese have settled in Milton Keynes in some numbers since the new city began, and especially since the boom years of the later 1980s. Most Japanese households came with their company: there were 47 Japanese firms in Milton Keynes by 1994, making the Japanese the second largest group in terms of foreign direct investment in the new city, after the Americans.[20] Here was a further example, perhaps, of workers who came because their work necessitated the move, yet who were able to improve their housing and environment as a consequence. A not uncommon word used by the Japanese to describe Milton Keynes was 'utopia'. Milton Keynes was not only convenient to business location. It served the suburban aspirations and needs of the incoming Japanese population very well.[21]

In sum, then, good-sized housing with a garden was actively chosen by many people from a variety of countries. The planned 'Anglo-American suburb', of which Milton Keynes was, and still is, a particularly large-scale expression, appealed well beyond

England and America. During the last two decades of the twentieth century, it was one of many fast-growing examples of what the
cultural historian Anthony D. King termed 'globurbia'.[22]

Before Milton Keynes was born, the earliest migrants to the new
town of the 1940s and 1950s had also viewed themselves as pioneers, for the obvious reason that they were the first people to
embrace the promise of a new community in a new territory.
Milton Keynes continued this planned postwar migration from
traditional areas of terraced housing or flats in the hearts of older
towns and cities, and into raw new estates of housing, where
established networks of family and friends were absent or barely
in existence. Here, people made new lives for themselves, sometimes looking back over their shoulder at what they had lost, but
determined to build a brighter and more prosperous future than
had been available to them before the move. Many different narra-
tives encompassing these experiences may be found in the
archives of the new city, and in a number of publications that give
expression to people who settled in Milton Keynes during its first
decade.[23] The collection of testimonies by Jane Turner and Bob
Jardine, *Pioneer Tales* (1985) was one such publication that detailed
early accounts of settling in to the new city, but there were others.
Some of these were gathered by the Milton Keynes Development
Corporation, but any suspicion that these were cunning corporate
attempts to validate the Milton Keynes project by digging up
favourable comments from grateful newcomers may be quickly
dispelled by an examination of the complexity of MKDC's findings. However, before we undertake this examination, as it were,
we need to know why MKDC undertook to get this information in
the first place.

The *Plan for Milton Keynes* had promised to 'provide for a wide
range of living conditions, to attract a full range of social and economic groups'. It aimed to create 'a safe, convenient and agreeable
environment at a reasonable cost'.[24] Reasonable cost was thus an
important consideration: excessive spending would be criticised
and perhaps curtailed by the Ministry of Housing. Yet MKDC also
had to meet the standards of house building laid down by the
Parker Morris report, *Homes for Today and Tomorrow*, published in
1961. The report had recommended bigger rooms and minimum

room sizes than had been the case for hundreds of thousands of speculative semi-detached houses built during the Conservative government's housing boom of the 1950s. The Parker Morris report also called for better fittings in kitchens and bathrooms, adequate storage space and newer and more flexible layouts of internal space to accommodate the needs and aspirations of British households as people became wealthier.[25] Its guidelines were mandatory for public housing. This meant that the development corporation had to meet quite high standards with a lower budget than it would have liked, and hence it argued that 'rationalised building methods will be necessary for a considerable proportion of the dwellings to be built'.[26]

As a result, most of the early pioneers to Milton Keynes moved into 'rational housing schemes', schemes that were often very unlike the appearance of traditional housing, a point made in previous chapters. Some of the residential housing on the gridsquares was designed by a number of eminent architects and architectural practices during the 1970s. Beanhill, for example, was designed by Norman Foster Associates, whilst the architects of Netherfield included the up-and-coming modernist Jeremy Dixon. Other estates, such as Bradville, Coffee Hall, Fullers Slade, Galley Hill, Greenleys, Stantonbury and Tinker's Bridge, were built according to industrialised building methods which employed non-traditional materials. Resident's reservations about such housing appear to have surfaced quite quickly. MKDC felt that their public housing gridsquares exhibited a 'tremendous variety of solutions and creative opportunities to design', yet that was no justification for top-down complacency. They also undertook 'feedback' sessions with local residents, 'in a positive exercise in participation with the Corporation', in order to enhance and render more democratic the relationship between housing designers and consumers.[27]

What did the corporation discover about pioneers' attitudes to new housing, to new estates and their amenities and to the experience of settling in to a barely developed new urban experiment? They discovered, in fact, a diverse range of views about the new city, many of which were warm and appreciative, some of which were balanced and evaluative and many that were downright critical. There was, for example, much criticism of experienced shortcomings in many aspects of design: houses with downstairs washrooms or WCs as well as upstairs were preferred to those with a single bathroom. The absence of windows in bathrooms was disliked. Yet the fact of an internal bathroom was a welcome novelty for some. Larger bedrooms were preferred to smaller ones, and houses with separate dining rooms were favoured over those without. There was a good deal of criticism of heating systems, as many dwellings 'are not found to be well designed for warmth'. Places with full central heating were most popular. Whilst all lounges and living rooms in MKDC houses or flats met Parker Morris requirements that the space should accommodate three easy chairs, a settee, a television set and some space for a few other items of furniture, nonetheless there was a clear preference for the largest living rooms, those over 15 square metres. Another common complaint was that noise insulation between terraced and semi-detached houses was often poor, and most families did not feel that their houses were particularly well designed to ensure peace and quiet. Lesser levels of storage provision were also criticised.[28]

External features of housing produced some strong reactions. People were generally conservative in their tastes, expressing a clear preference for brick finishes or white rendering, and a 'marked dislike' of such materials as cedar boarding or aluminium. One resident stated that 'white paint instead of the hideous colours applied at the moment could make a world of difference'.[29] An early resident of Galley Hill complained that the pink-and-white two-tiered exteriors of the housing resembled 'rows of false teeth'.[30]

Despite such criticisms, housing provision for rent met with broad approval. For the development corporation, Rowan Mactaggart, who worked on housing policy in the Corporate Planning Group, argued that 'the variety of housing in Milton Keynes seems fully justified':

> and more families enjoy life in the new city. On the five [estates] surveyed, between 83 and 95 per cent of residents were pleased with life in Milton Keynes, and only four families out of the 290 covered wanted to return to wherever they had come from.[31]

Such statements invite suspicion that MKDC petitioned their residents in order to validate their early public housing designs. After all, residents had no chance for an a priori contribution to the design of their housing. The writer Beatrix Campbell has pointed out that often in the postwar years local tenants had certainly been consulted on housing issues and plans, but usually only to ratify completed schemes or to provide token input.[32] Thus, it follows that their wishes were not really fully acted upon. MKDC was, to some extent, guilty of this. Looking back on the early 1970s, even ex-members of the development corporation, or consultants working for it, have been critical of the view of the Chief Architect that he himself and his advisors knew best and that 'there was no client' when it came to housing design.[33] Nonetheless, MKDC does appear to have learned quickly from some of its earliest mistakes: residents' continuing dissatisfaction with some of those rational housing schemes provided a stimulus for MKDC to commission the study by Jeff Bishop, of Bristol University's School of Advanced Urban Studies, whose aim was to study people's perceptions of their city and their housing. This provides us with some valuable information on the values and experiences of 1970s settlers into Milton Keynes.

Bishop's research was undertaken from 1979 to 1981, and published in 1986. One writer in the *Architects' Journal*'s 25th anniversary issue on Milton Keynes saw Bishop's study as 'a watershed in the development of the town because it offered clear guidance on the way the residents saw the place and wanted it to develop'.[34] Following Bishop, and also as a consequence of residents' campaigns (see Chapter 8), the flat roofs of rational housing developments were replaced with pitched ones, and exteriors and interiors were modified to become more user-friendly. This led one writer, also contributing to the same edition of *Architects' Journal*, to lament 'the indignity of pitched roofs' in lieu of what was originally there.[35] Yet clearly that writer did not understand the importance of residents' perceptions of their houses, and of their need to feel comfortable with their housing. This was at the heart of settling in to a new town, and to settling down more generally. Hence the modifications to Beanhill and the other estates were to become popular with the residents. The alterations helped to change the perceived character of the estate. One researcher from the Open University, concerned with the 'felt needs' of the city's poorer citizens, found that 'Beanhill has become one of the more popular estates – there is even a waiting list of people wanting to move onto the estate'.[36] In a very real sense, through their active criticism of early rational housing, the pioneers of the 1970s had blazed a trail of housing improvements that subsequent newcomers would enjoy.

In terms of the material environment, it was not only housing that helped people to settle down. The garden also had a role to play, and, for the majority of those who moved to Milton Keynes, it was a considerable asset. All families with children wanted a garden. The *Residential Design Feedback* found, unsurprisingly, that for the most part larger back gardens were preferred to small ones, although elderly people were less inclined to want a large garden. A garden with privacy was favourable to one that was overlooked. Enclosed front gardens were preferred to open frontages, although car users were less fussy on that score.[37] For some, moreover, a garden, no matter what size, was a luxury they had never had before. The Open University historian Arthur Marwick, a social historian of postwar Britain, understood the significance of the following anecdote:

> When [the] community television station, as an April Fool's joke for 1979, broadcast a message saying that the entire city (100,000 inhabitants, half the planned total at the end of the decade) was to be ploughed back into the ground, a viewer declared that he was not going to go back to London: 'Milton Keynes had given him a garden, something he'd never had before, and he was damned if he was going to give it up now'.[38]

And for those with only small gardens or for that matter with no garden at all, for example those living in flats, a generous provision of attractive landscaping and public parks was appreciated. Yet it is clear that even here people valued *private* outdoor space just a little bit more than shared open spaces The *Residential Design Feedback* found that 'Major public space is enjoyed, but it should not be provided at the expense of more important features':

> On some schemes 50 per cent of families said it was like living in parkland, and nearly all families valued the sense of spaciousness given by the public open space. However, in cases where families felt that there was insufficient land available in gardens, playspaces or allotments, they were quick to suggest that some public open space could be reallocated to these uses.[39]

Yet an insistence upon privatism should never be allowed to obscure the active neighbourliness and sociability during the earliest days of the 1970s estates. And it was simply because the estates were so new, and so environmentally raw, that MKDC set out to assist in the making of a community consciousness and a sense of local belonging. Those briefings from Melvin Webber about 'community without propinquity' were in no way intended to deny community *with* propinquity. Hence Colin Ward has described the efforts of arrivals workers, the ground workers of MKDC's social development programme, as 'smoothing the path for its incoming citizens'.[40]

Arrivals workers had a varied task, one that was more facilitating and responsive in intent rather than proactive and nanny-state-like. New arrivals were given help in establishing local associations, clubs, community newspapers and all manner of arts, crafts, sports and leisure groups. One man, for example, established a football team at Greenleys which, he felt, was 'almost like a family'. And most gridsquares had a community newspaper within a few years, some of whose names reflected a new-found sense of place: *The Noose, Simpker, Brad, Beanstalk, Netherfield News* and *The Windmill Whistle* were just some of these informal and bespoke publications. Roger Kitchen, who worked for MKDC, which helped to subsidise these papers, wrote in 1975 that 'In a new estate where people are strangers to one another':

> the printed word is the cheapest, quickest, and easiest way to achieve a basic level of communication between neighbours. Less than a year after the first resident had moved in, *The ?* advertised weekly meetings of more than ten clubs, catering for all ages and for a variety of activities.[41]

Being involved in a community newspaper was of course a great way to meet people. For Sandy Cunningham, an editor during the early 1970s, putting together an issue of the paper was a way to escape the 'housewives' set. With her tongue firmly in her cheek she wrote that 'to belong to this set':

> you need to be tied to a home with several young children, to be able to discuss in great depth the soap powder which will wash nappies whitest, and generally to have the knack of being able to talk for hours without actually saying anything. In a few weeks of moving to Milton Keynes I was given the opportunity of relinquishing my subscription to this club, and it all came about because of our local community newspaper.[42]

And, beyond those activities that were assisted by MKDC, good old-fashioned and spontaneous neighbouring was also much in evidence, as oral testimonies of early Milton Keynes illustrate. One retired woman, who had moved to the new city from London in 1972, remembered the muddy bleakness of her estate, but this was compensated for by its friendliness:

The young people have adopted us and we're 'grandparents' to most of the children. We've got marvellous neighbours but we didn't realise how wonderful they were until I was taken ill and had to have a pacemaker. They then came up trumps. Also, when Bill was in hospital they gave me a lift to Northampton every day so he never went without a visitor. They did it out of kindness.[43]

A little girl who moved to the Stantonbury estate in the 1970s remembered that 'When we moved in':

the next door neighbour came out and said are you moving in and my mum said yes and he said well if theres anything you need me and my missus are only next door and my names George.[44]

And let us not forget Jack Trevor Story, a 1970s migrant from London to Milton Keynes, who was mentioned in Chapter 1. He also knew that if he was going to make anything of his life in Milton Keynes, he would have to be actively involved. For example, he mixed with what he called the 'Milton Keynes art belt', notably the sculptress Liz Leyh, who made the concrete cows, and the painters Fionulla Boyd and Les Evans, whose mural of the new city now adorns the Milton Keynes Library in the city centre. Boyd and Evans were 'artists in residence' in Milton Keynes during the early 1980s, and are now regarded as significant and powerful landscape painters.[45] Story met and drank with many other people who were active in the promotion of art and culture in the raw new city. He was, for example, involved with Inter-Action, a youth project based in a large Victorian house by the Grand Union Canal. And most significantly he took classes to encourage working-class writing in Milton Keynes. Story has also been credited with discovering one of the city's local artists, Bill Billings.[46] Billings was still working at the time this book was written.[47]

In common with Story, even if they did not share his complicated personal life, most newcomers were well aware that stopping in at home for too long was anti-social and soul destroying and that making new friends and neighbours was an essential activity when settling in. These testimonies were also representative of all those pioneers who moved to Milton Keynes during the 1970s, and who were neither credulous nor passive in their attitude to their new home in their new city. Nor were they privatised and individualistic to the exclusion of social activities. This continued to be true, but, as noted, the origins of migrants to the new city became more diverse after 1980, and the city was more 'established' by then in terms of amenities.

SETTLING IN: THE YEARS SINCE 1980

Those who moved in since 1980, when the town was more established and when there were more things to do in Milton Keynes, cannot really be viewed as the original settlers or pioneers. Nonetheless their experiences of moving to a new housing estate and to a new town may be viewed as broadly representative of that continuing phenomenon in late postwar England. People still wanted and needed to make friends and neighbours, and to enjoy a comfortable new home. This was true of both those estates built during the 1970s, and also the new ones begun after 1980. As a study of Beanhill summarised in 1988, most of the original residents had been long settled, and new ones were coming to live on or near the estate, including relatives. The study recorded frequent and regular contacts between members of most families. Here, then, was an example of that 'chain migration', the follow-up migration of relatives and sometimes friends, which contributed to the maturation of the new city.[48]

The gridsquare of Walnut Tree, whose construction was begun during the 1980s, was studied by Milton Keynes Development Corporation. MKDC wished to find out how in-migration and settling in was continuing to happen in its newest housing developments. Walnut Tree was a mixed-tenure estate, composed of both owner-occupied homes and housing association homes for rent or shared ownership. Housing values were mixed, but tended towards the lower end of the owner-occupied scale. However, the northern section of the estate near Walton Road was made up of many larger detached homes, as well as semi-detached homes, for owner occupation.[49]

The Walnut Tree study dealt with the question of how far the residents on the estate, and a number of others in official positions, felt that it was becoming a 'community' with its own sense of identity. In all, 34 people were interviewed, most of whom lived on Walnut Tree. The majority were community leaders, organisers of local voluntary groups. Others interviewed included a number of church leaders from the ecumenical church on the estate, representatives from charitable organisations, social workers, the police, a health visitor, a general practitioner and a money advice worker from the council.

Unlike earlier MKDC surveys, the report was not primarily a sounding board for residents to air criticisms of their housing or of the design and facilities of the estate. Nonetheless, a number of complaints had surfaced regularly enough to be noticed by those involved in the study. These complaints were based upon those problems which so often faced settlers in the new communities of twentieth-century England: the lack of shops in the early days; the absence of a frequent and regular bus service, which was made worse by the rather isolated position of Walnut Tree on the city's eastern side; the messy problems of mud and traffic and building-site construction traffic; and the lack of a proper meeting place.[50] A meeting place was opened, however, towards the end of the 1980s.

The report contained mixed information about the nature and extent of community formation on the estate. The local organiser for the National Childbirth Trust, who lived on Walnut Tree, felt that at first there was 'not a strong community feeling' due to so many people commuting to work or going back to their original towns for weekends, but this was 'getting better now that the Meeting Place was open and the population was larger'. A worker for the Children's Society also thought that the lack of an early shop inhibited the 'gelling' of the community. Moreover, she observed another key pattern in the settlement of estates: there was a growing sense of class and status differences based upon property prices and the residential tones of varying streets. A head of a local school concurred that there was a divide through the estate between the wealthier top half and the southern half. A health visitor detected 'some community feeling in the areas' but she also observed 'a tendency for groups to become cliques'.[51]

The Milton Keynes Housing Association, which had its largest client group of renters on the estate, felt that 'feedback from tenants is mixed, with people either liking or not liking the quietness'. Yet no tenants as of December 1990 had expressed a wish to move away 'which is a good indicator of satisfaction'.[52]

MKDC finished off their Walnut Tree study with a number of observations confirming that community formation was taking place and would continue to do so. They pointed out that 'neighbourhood networks have been formed and can be identified' and that residents 'are beginning to identify Walnut Tree as "home"'. Community facilities at the local school, at the shops, and in the meeting place were completed or nearing completion, and most local community organisations, following practical help from MKDC's neighbourhood workers, were now able to sustain themselves on their own.[53]

In fact, what had occurred on Walnut Tree, as on the other estates, was that most people, following some early difficulties, settled into their new home and sought out alliances and friendships with those whom they felt were most like themselves. The description of such groups as 'cliques' illustrates both a sense of common internal feeling within that 'clique' and also a sense of difference or even exclusion from others. This was nothing new. A great deal of research both into interwar suburban housing estates and also into earlier postwar housing developments found a similar pattern of early mixing and mutual helpfulness, quickly followed by a more selective pattern of sociability. This was true of new peripheral estates in interwar London, in Oxford, Swindon and Worsley near Salford during the 1950s, and in a variety of new towns during the 1950s and 1960s.[54] Milton Keynes was the latest and the largest of many postwar new residential areas whose patterns of community and association were very soon established, and grew and developed over time.

Finally, most of those earlier interwar and postwar surveys also discovered that, once people had settled down into their new home in their new estate, a sense of local patriotism usually emerged. Local pride in one's city was, and remains, an unambiguous signifier of local identity and of having settled down. In 1992, as Milton Keynes celebrated its 25th birthday, a *Daily Telegraph* reporter, interviewing locals in the shopping building, found that many who had moved to Milton Keynes had few or no regrets. Here are just two comments:

> 'I never wanted to come to Milton Keynes when we moved here nine years ago', said Mrs. Verna Nicholson, walking past the [concrete] cows with her dog Dixie. 'But now we love it. You have open views, parks, no traffic jams.'

> 'I'm very proud of Milton Keynes. When I go to London people make fun of it, but I love living here.'[55]

And in her book on Milton Keynes, *Tales of the City*, published in 1999, the Open University's Ruth Finnegan found many similar comments that emphasised 'the place of "place"', as Finnegan termed it. 'I love Milton Keynes, I love the area, and I love the fact that you can be in the countryside within five minutes walk' was one such comment.[56] Many similar comments were made, at different times, during the 1990s. They emphasised 'the linear parks', 'the canal', 'the quality of the landscaping', 'open spaces and trees' and the fact of being 'close to footpaths and countryside'.[57]

CONCLUSION

A recent study of suburbanisation paints a general picture of an urban population, once huddled into small housing in terraced streets, that increasingly enjoyed the move outwards to more spacious suburbs and better housing. In general, the urban population of the 'English speaking world' voluntarily undertook a collective move away from '"streetscapes" dominated by fairly continuous building facades':

> To more open 'landscapes' in which dwellings, mostly detached or semi-detached, are separated from the road, and often from one another, by private gardens. The change from a closed 'streetscape' to a more open 'landscape' was initially a middle-class phenomenon . . .[58]

But this huge and ongoing change was increasingly shared by working-class households too, and also a by a multiplicity of ethnic and religious groups. And as people moved from materially worse, closer-built housing to more private and comfortable housing, they developed the neighbours, friendships, associates and acquaintances to match. And people enjoyed the social, as well as the material, opportunities that accompanied the move from one type of housing to another. The social experience is discussed more fully in Chapter 8.

It is clear that Milton Keynes played a major part in promulgating this democratic mass migration in the years between 1967 and today. The suburban-style city was actively sought after by many thousands of people who subsequently did their best to settle in as happily as possible.

NOTES

1 MKDC, *Milton Keynes Household Survey, 1988: Demography Technical Report* (Milton Keynes: MKDC, 1989), p. 30.
2 MKDC, *The Plan for Milton Keynes*, vol. 2 (Milton Keynes: MKDC, 1970), pp. 127–8.
3 Penny Liddiard, *Milton Keynes Felt Needs Project: A Preliminary Study of the Felt Needs of*

People Living in Relative Poverty on a Milton Keynes Housing Estate (Milton Keynes: Department of Health and Social Welfare, Open University, 1988), p. 31.

4   MKDC, *Milton Keynes Seven Years On: The Summary Report of the 1976 Household and Employers' Surveys* (Milton Keynes: MKDC, 1977) p. 18.
5   Two exceptions are Mark Clapson, *Invincible Green Suburbs, Brave New Towns: Social Change and Urban Dispersal in Postwar England* (Manchester: Manchester University Press, 1998); Elizabeth Roberts, *Women and Families: An Oral History, 1940–1970* (Oxford: Blackwell, 1995).
6   MKDC and Social and Community Planning Research, *Four Years On: The Milton Keynes Household Survey* (Milton Keynes: MKDC, 1974).
7   MKDC, *Four Years On;* 'Summary', p. 6
8   Quoted in Roger Kitchen, 'Moving to Milton Keynes', *New Society*, 22 August 1974, pp. 478–9.
9   Living Archive Project (LAP), NCY/0043, Tape 179, transcript.
10   LAP, NCY/T007, Tape 183; transcript.
11   MKDC, *New City: Milton Keynes* (Milton Keynes: MKDC, 1975), pp. 2–7.
12   Kitchen, 'Moving to Milton Keynes', p. 479.
13   Jane Turner and Bob Jardine, *Pioneer Tales: A New Life in Milton Keynes* (Milton Keynes: People's Press, 1985), p. 23.
14   Nicholas Deakin and Claire Ungerson, *Leaving London: Planned Mobility and the Inner City* (London: Heinemann, 1977), p. 2.
15   MKDC, *New City, Milton Keynes* (MKDC: Milton Keynes, 1974), pp. 4–12.
16   LAP, NCY/T001, Tape 186, transcript.
17   MKDC, *Milton Keynes* (Milton Keynes: MKDC, 1988), p. 36.
18   Turner and Jardine, *Pioneer Tales*, p. 69.
19   Matthew Brace, 'How Milton Keynes has become "Little Hong Kong"', *Independent,* 6 July 1998.
20   Alexander Roy, *The Impact of Japanese Investment on the New Town of Milton Keynes* (London: South Bank University Best Masters Dissertation in International Business, published by dissertation.com, 1998), p. 9.
21   William Underhill, 'No place like it for Eastern promise', *Daily Telegraph*, 23 January, 1992; William Underhill, 'A monument to approval by Japanese investors', *Daily Telegraph*, 23 January 1992.
22   Anthony D. King, 'Reworlding the city', *Planning History*, 22, 3 (2000), pp. 5–16.
23   The Living Archive Project in Wolverton has long been gathering the testimonies of migrants to the new city: Living Archive. It can be contacted at The Old Bath House, 25 Stratford Road, Wolverton, Milton Keynes, MK12 5LR, UK.
24   MKDC, *The Plan for Milton Keynes*, vol. 2 (Milton Keynes: MKDC, 1970), p. 91.
25   John Burnett, *A Social History of Housing, 1815–1985* (London: Routledge, 1991), pp. 306–10.
26   MKDC, *The Plan for Milton Keynes*, vol. 2, p. 91.
27   MKDC, *Residential Design Feedback: Report of Studies* (Milton Keynes: MKDC, 1975), pp. 1–2.
28   MKDC, *Residential Design Feedback*, pp. 125–31.
29   MKDC, *Residential Design Feedback*, pp. 109–11.
30   LAP, NCY/T007, Tape 103; transcript.
31   Rowan Mactaggart, 'Newcomers to Milton Keynes: getting their housing priorities right', *Architectural Design*, XLV (1975), p. 766.
32   Beatrix Campbell, *Wigan Pier Revisited: Poverty and Politics in the '80s* (London: Virago, 1984), p. 53.
33   See comments by Walter Bor and Peter Waterman, in Mark Clapson, Mervyn Dobbin and Peter Waterman (eds), The *Best Laid Plans: Milton Keynes since 1967* (Luton: University of Luton Press, 1998), pp. 54, 84, 86.
34   Tim Mars, 'Little Los Angeles in Bucks', *Architects' Journal*, 15 April 1992, p. 26.
35   Ruth Owens, 'The great experiment', *Architects' Journal*, 15 April 1992, p. 32.
36   Liddiard, *Milton Keynes Felt Needs Project*, p. 27.
37   MKDC, *Residential Design Feedback*, pp. 19–22; Mactaggart, 'Newcomers', p. 766.
38   Arthur Marwick, *British Society since 1945* (Harmondsworth: Penguin, 1987), p. 198.
39   Mactaggart, 'Newcomers', p. 766.
40   Colin Ward, *New Town, Home Town* (London: Caloutse Gulbenkian Foundation, 1993), p. 55.

41 Roger Kitchen, 'Community newspapers', *Architectural Design*, XLV (1975), p. 762.
42 Sandy Cunningham, 'From soap suds to soap box', *Architectural Design*, XLV (1975), p. 760.
43 Turner and Jardine, *Pioneer Tales*, p. 13.
44 The People's Press, *This Place Has its Ups and Downs, or Kids Could Have Done it Better* etc. (Milton Keynes: People's Press, 1977), Toni, age 9 (no page numbers).
45 Nikolaus Pevsner and Elizabeth Williamson, *The Buildings of England: Buckinghamshire* (Harmondsworth: Penguin, 1994), pp. 488, 492–3; F. Boyd and L. Evans, *American Paintings* (London: Nicola Barker and Angela Flowers Gallery, 2000).
46 Jack Trevor Story, *Dwarf Goes to Oxford* (Milton Keynes: Leveret Press, 1987).
47 Robert Cook and Andrew Shouler, *Milton Keynes in the News* (Stroud: Sutton Publishing, 2001), p. 45; Anon., 'Storyteller: Jack's view of city goes on TV – nationwide', *Milton Keynes Mirror*, 10 August 1977.
48 Liddiard, *Milton Keynes Felt Needs Project*, p. 31.
49 MKDC, *Walnut Tree Neighbourhood Review, July through December, 1990: A Report on the Community Development Programme Undertaken by MKDC between 1987 and 1990* (Milton Keynes: MKDC, 1990), pp. 1–2; and writer's own observations.
50 KDC, *Walnut Tree*, pp. 1–5.
51 MKDC, *Walnut Tree*, pp. 20, 28, 32.
52 MKDC, *Walnut Tree*, p. 34.
53 MKDC, *Walnut Tree*, p. 14.
54 Clapson, *Invincible Green Suburbs*, pp. 96–120.
55 Robert Hardman, 'How the "truly classless society" of Milton Keynes learned to love life in themed grid squares', *Daily Telegraph*, 20 January 1992.
56 Ruth Finnegan, *Tales of the City: A Study of Narrative and Urban Life* (Cambridge: Cambridge University Press, 1999), p. 131.
57 The Planning Exchange, *The New Towns Record*: 'Residents Questionnaires: Milton Keynes' (Glasgow: The Planning Exchange, CD Rom, 1996).
58 J. W. R. Whitehand and C. M. H. Carr, *Twentieth-Century Suburbs: A Morphological Approach* (London: Routledge, 2001), p. 1.

7

The Unsettled: Social Problems in a Suburban City

> The spirit of St. Etienne resides in several select sites and states of mind. The smell and sheen of a dismayed seaside town the day after summer . . . sorrow, often so sumptuous that it feels like pleasure . . . the lonely splendour of the first Model Home in Milton Keynes.
>
> Julie Burchill, liner notes to St Etienne, *Too Young to Die: Singles, 1990–1995* (Heavenly Records, 1985)

When people move on to a new home, they are usually also looking for a fresh beginning and a better life. But not everyone who moved to Milton Keynes was able to achieve this. Some people felt profoundly unhappy once they had moved to the new city, and were unable to settle down. Some sociologists termed this problem 'the new town blues'. Others, who stayed on in the new city, were upset and disorientated by the afflictions of poverty and unemployment. Their story is a different one from those told in the previous and next chapters.

It is important to discuss these social problems in this ostensibly bright new city. They tarnished the success of the broad mission upon which Milton Keynes was founded during the 1960s, namely new housing and full employment within a garden city designed to offer every inhabitant the benefits of a planned and convenient environment. Furthermore, our received images of poverty and social breakdown are still usually associated with run-down council estates on the edges of older towns, or with decaying Victorian-built inner cities. Yet today, if we look beyond the glitzy shops of the city centre and beyond the tree-lined roads and the leafy redways, it is possible to identify unkempt housing and shabby and vandalised parts of the poorer gridsquares. Graffiti has become an eyesore in many estates. This is mostly superficial but nonetheless compelling visual evidence that deeper social problems began anew in the new city's earliest period.

THE UNSETTLED (I): NEW TOWN BLUES

In the years prior to the designation of Milton Keynes, there had been a number of professional reports, by sociologists, housing experts and town planners, about the related conditions known as 'suburban neurosis' and 'the new town blues'.

By the time Milton Keynes was being planned, the 'new town blues' were much talked about in serious newspapers and journals and on the television. Sociologists had visited earlier new towns such as Harlow and Crawley and they had discerned a sense of disquiet amongst many women there. The alleged condition of 'Crawley neurosis', and the pram-pushing automata-mothers of Harlow and of other new towns, were convenient ways of denigrating the postwar new towns project, even if researchers found that neurosis and worry were no worse in new towns than elsewhere.[1]

Yet this was not simply an intellectual or professional concern. A popular TV drama series called 'The Newcomers', for example, which ran on the BBC from 1965 to 1969, dealt with the problems of adaptation of the Cooper family, who moved from London to the overspill new town of 'Angleton'. According to the *Radio Times* the Coopers had to 'grapple in a dazed way' with the problems of being uprooted and with the transitional difficulties they faced when settling into the new housing estate. Such problems were particularly felt by Mrs Cooper, wife and mother of two, but also a career woman in London. She appeared particularly vulnerable to the 'problems of loneliness and boredom', as the *Radio Times* put it, because she had lost her older network and apparently her sense of purpose.[2]

Both the Ministry of Housing and Local Government (MHLG) and Milton Keynes Development Corporation were aware of the attention towards the new town blues, but felt the problem was exaggerated. The MHLG argued in its *Needs of New Communities* report, published in 1967, that 'certainly problems do exist' but 'they can be dealt with before they become serious'.[3] The MKDC adopted a similar line, noting that newcomers to Milton Keynes would experience some of the social and economic difficulties that other new towns had been through.[4] These would be temporary, it argued, but nonetheless it felt that 'the fact that even though "new town blues" may not be permanent' should not mean 'the reality of their anxieties can be ignored'.[5] As the Plan noted, higher aspirations and expectations motivated people to move to new towns, and away from older areas where entertainment, shopping and public transport often existed. Milton Keynes would not possess these to the full extent in earliest days, and MKDC's social development programme would therefore attempt to identify the difficulties that would arise, and to act upon them where possible.[6]

Arrivals workers for the corporation met with newcomers to encourage a feeling of belonging and of being cared for. Moreover, MKDC's Household Survey of 1973 asked people who had recently moved onto 'new town estates' what problems they had experienced upon arrival. Only 25 per cent of households had not experienced any problems, while the following practical difficulties were most frequently mentioned:

Poor public transport to shops	24%
Local shops expensive/inadequate	18%
Poor public transport to work	17%
No hospital	17%
Mud and rubbish from construction	16%
Poor workmanship of house	12%

As noted, MKDC arrivals workers endeavoured to visit all newcomers, but about 33 per cent of people complained or lamented that they had not been visited. Yet those who had received a call had found it 'very' or 'fairly' useful.[7]

The arrivals workers, however, were unable to address deeper-seated miseries. During the early 1970s, Roger Kitchen, an MKDC employee, wrote a short paper on the phenomenon of 'doing a moonlight'. This was a secretive nocturnal flight away from the new city, often back to the original place of departure or on to somewhere else. As Kitchen noted, the romantic and exciting image that the phrase 'doing a moonlight' evoked served to obscure the often difficult circumstances that made escape such a desperate but apparently unavoidable option. Kitchen identified a number of causes, each of which had been intrinsic to earlier postwar debates about suburban neurosis and the new town blues.

These were loneliness and feelings of isolation, marital and family stresses, and economic difficulties. In many individual cases one or more of these causes was related to others.

Loneliness was felt especially by women. This feeling was sometimes compounded by the bleak appearance of the estates in the earliest days, and the attendant lack of nearby and familiar places where people could meet with others and enjoy themselves. This was not, it must be said, a problem unique to Milton Keynes. During the 1950s, for example, the sociologists Peter Willmott and Michael Young had investigated the experience of working-class households who had moved from Bethnal Green in the East End of London to suburban housing in Essex. Many women had felt lonely, stuck at home all day while their husband was out at work, and while the children, if they had any, were at school.[8] This feeling was exacerbated in new housing areas where transport services were inadequate. People settled in more easily if they were able to go back to visit relatives and friends; if this was difficult, life was harder.

Thus, as an assistant housing manager in Milton Keynes wrote in 1975, women who did not go out to paid work were often most vulnerable to loneliness: 'outside their back door is a long stretch of open space with no view, no neighbours, nothing – they're isolated'.[9] The problem did not just afflict migrants during the earliest years of the new city. During the 1980s, on the estate of Beanhill, some of the 'felt needs' were caused by such difficulties as a 'lack of friends, unfriendly neighbours, loneliness, boredom and being at home all day on your own'.[10]

A further cause of moonlight flight was related to the first: marital problems. Once couples moved away from the familiar context of friends and relatives to a new town where they knew few if any people, they were pushed more closely together in their new home. In 1975, a spokeswoman for a tenants group in Milton Keynes, speaking on an Anglia television documentary and debate about the new city, blamed marriage break-ups as a cause of homelessness, because people felt compelled to move away, but often had no accommodation as refuge.[11] Ten years later a white witch in Wolverton, Madame Morgana, observed similar problems:

> There is great unrest with the overspills from London. We have a mixed community here, there's poverty and break-ups of marriages like it's going out of fashion, so people have to learn to find themselves . . .[12]

These interconnections between feelings of loneliness and relationship difficulties caused many people to move on. But it is difficult, as noted above, to identify these as specific to any condition of the 'new town blues'. Nationally, in fact, the Divorce Act of 1969 had resulted in a considerable rise in the divorce rate, in which Milton Keynes shared. Moreover, as we saw in previous chapters, the growing population of the designated area became increasingly weighted towards younger households, the majority of whom were couples with children or couples who were just about to have them. Divorce statistics published by the Registrar-General illustrate that, although the divorce rate was increasing among all age groups, it was at its highest among younger married couples.[13]

As will be apparent from these foregoing paragraphs, a further factor which caused strains on relationships was financial hardship. The Felt Needs project in Beanhill found that lack of money was a constant worry for many people. And it is clear that the very act of moving to a new town was costly. The considerable expense of making a new start in the city often included the expense of new furnishings, as older furniture was often unsuitable for the new place, and also higher rents. One household who moved from London to Milton Keynes in the early 1970s needed to buy 'a table, four chairs – that was £48 – a stair carpet, we got that on the HP, we paid £40 deposit – that cost £178':

> As you will understand, the time we had the flat in London, we only had the one bedroom and when we were in there we had fitted wardrobes. But before we left London, we bought some wardrobes and things second hand which cost us £35. We had to buy a single bed for the little girl. We bought a gas cooker too.[14]

In some cases, the development corporation proved to be more of a costly hindrance than a help. Its stipulation that the provision of rented accommodation would only follow the taking up of employment of the head of household sometimes meant that people were forced to commute up to Milton Keynes from London to work in their new job before they were finally able to move in. This placed increased financial and travel burdens on these new movers.[15]

Not surprisingly, such outlay and the worry it caused was felt most sharply among poorer households, many of whom rented their accommodation from MKDC. The development corporation, in fact, was well aware of this through its own data, data which referred to financial difficulties under the rather euphemistic term 'temporary requirements': 26 per cent of all households who had moved to MK since 1967 had required temporary accommodation; 16 per cent had been forced to commute at least for a short while; and 4 per cent had been forced to do both.[16] These difficulties were felt most harshly by working-class households. Qualified professionals, managers and better-paid workers in private companies were more likely to receive financial assistance to help offset the costs of moving home, unlike workers earning less than £50 a week, who needed the money most of all.[17] As one man observed, 'a lot of the trouble for other people is money, and there aren't the jobs they said they would be for women'. One older worker, recently arrived, was worried about the rent rise to £10 per week, 'and I'm paying £8 a week for food, who's going to pay the electric bill?'[18]

In its Household Survey of 1973, MKDC outlined the 'problems on moving and on arrival' and it is clear that practical and financial difficulties were central to those problems. The development corporation found that, once households had moved in, three-quarters of them encountered one or more of a variety of practical difficulties, notably poor public transport to shops and to places of employment; the expensive and often inadequate local shops; the lack of a hospital and the inconvenience of travelling elsewhere for health care; the mud and rubbish left over from construction; and the shoddy building standards of the housing.

These problems were compounded by the early physical layout of the city, which was by then merely an emerging framework, with an inadequate public transport system. Poorer and less mobile people were at a distinct disadvantage if they did not have access to a car. Such difficulties contributed to a dissatisfaction rate of one in five households by 1973. These levels of dissatisfaction were 'greater on rent estates than on sale estates'. A small but significant minority, about 8 per cent, or a little under 1 in 20, wanted to go back or move on.[19] Some of them, as we have seen, were prepared to do this if they became desperate enough.

The decision to go back was not taken lightly. Oral testimony is sparse for this area of experience, but we may infer from the following, which is in fact from somebody who decided to stay, just what a struggle life could be in the new city. An unemployed husband, who in 1978 had recently applied for a job in an as-yet unopened department store in the forthcoming shopping building in Central Milton Keynes, told the magazine *Over 21* that he and his wife had been in MK for 18 months:

TABLE 7: REASONS FOR HOMELESSNESS, 1990 AND 1991

Year	1990	1991
Relationships	73 (13.8%)	79 (12%)
Friends/relatives	218 (41.3%)	268 (40%)
Mortgage arrears	88 (16.7%)	190 (28.7%)
Rent arrears	78 (14.8%)	20 (3%)
Other	71 (13.4%)	104 (15.7%)

and in spite of all the problems here it's better than what we had before we came. We feel we owe the place a chance. If the shopping centre is successful Milton Keynes will really get on its feet. If it isn't . . . well then we'll start looking around elsewhere.[20]

THE UNSETTLED (II): HOMELESSNESS IN MILTON KEYNES

By 1992, the year of Milton Keynes' 25th birthday, a number of spectres, and not very well-dressed ones, haunted the celebrations. According to the Department of the Environment's generalised 'needs index' for housing, this brave new city had moved into 'the Homelessness Top Twenty'. In fact, the new city was the 18th worst-off in terms of housing need outside of London.[21]

Not surprisingly, then, the borough council claimed in the early 1990s that 'of all the problems faced by the council, homelessness remains the most pressing'.[22] The council had undertaken an important piece of research which enabled it to support this claim, and to 'appeal to the Government to recognise the housing problems that face Milton Keynes and to enable us to provide for those in need'.[23]

The council's statistics of the personal reasons for homelessness made depressing reading, and the picture became even more depressing when the inadequacies of both local and national housing policies are considered, inadequacies that compounded the personal difficulties and miseries of the homeless.

The personal causes of the often painful or dramatic shift from a time of seeming stability to one of rootlessness and detachment are summarised in Table 7 (see above),[24] drawn from the borough council's studies made during the early 1990s.

The breakdown of marital or partner-based relationships and the difficulties involved in a wider range of relationships between families and ostensible friends often caused people to leave their accommodation or to be forced out. Such tensions and strains, however, were viciously exacerbated in many cases by the financial hardships endured by many thousands of people in the later 1980s and early 1990s. The increasing number of repossessions caused by mortgage arrears remains a terrible indictment on the building societies and banks who forced people into homelessness, cruelly disrupted family life and dealt out untold, unquantifiable, misery. Unemployment and low pay was often a cause of mortgage arrears, because many would-be home owners had taken out mortgages without insurance due to the inhibiting extra costs of insurance. When redundancy came along, there was little that many people could do to prevent the loss of their home. The local-authority-run money advice centres in Milton Keynes found that many young households, many of them 'second generation' locals, that is, the offspring of settlers during the 1970s, were coming to them.[25] They were worried and fearful about the threat of repossession, or actually experiencing the pain of it, and looking for help.

Unemployment was also a cause of rent arrears. In Britain generally, home ownership and unemployment were at high levels by 1990, and so too was the rate of repossessions. This particularly hit younger households. A national report on homelessness by the Joseph Rowntree Foundation, published in February 1989, found that 80 per cent of the homeless were unemployed. In Milton Keynes, 60 per cent of the homeless were unemployed in 1991. For many, incomes were so low that it was nigh impossible to afford even the cheapest rental accommodation, let alone the 'low-cost' starter homes intended to help first-time buyers onto the housing ladder.[26] Many people were unable to continue paying rents when they became unemployed, and, although both the council and the development corporation resisted evictions, these nonetheless occurred.

Furthermore, the Conservative government's housing legislation since 1980 had made it easier for people to buy their council houses, and that had consequently reduced the numbers of housing available to local authorities. Hence Milton Keynes, like many other towns and cities, possessed diminishing levels of public-sector rental accommodation. Fewer council houses were still being built, but greater numbers of those in existence were sold off. This situation worsened significantly in Milton Keynes during the mid-1980s, a time of continuing in-migration to the city and also a time when the offspring of migrants during the early

1970s were looking for their own homes. In 1984, there were 2,100 people on the waiting list for a development corporation or a borough council rental home, and of these 197 (almost 10 per cent) were officially homeless. Almost all applications from homeless people were accepted in that year. By 1991, the number of people on the waiting list had risen to 2,245, but the number of homeless people within that figure had leapt to 995. There were 660 acceptances, meaning that 335 applications went unmet. Over the same period, the number of properties available to the council had declined from over 7,400 to below 6,400. Most of those left behind, as it were, were staying with friends or relatives, or lodging in temporary accommodation. As for more permanent accommodation, between 30 and 40 vacancies became available every month, and that was 'about the same number of households that are accepted as priority homeless each month'.[27]

There was, then, a shortage of housing in Milton Keynes. This was exacerbated by the growing number of young people leaving home and wanting homes for themselves. These were the second generation in the new city, the daughters and sons of the original migrants. It appears that they fell foul of the official policy distinction between 'priority' and 'non-priority' homelessness. 'Priority' meant poor families with children, and those vulnerable because of age or ill health. But in Milton Keynes 'non-priority' included those who were not new migrants, for some MKDC housing was still reserved for newcomers only. Here was an unpleasant irony in the local system of housing provision. If one was not a priority case, nor a newcomer, then one was at the bottom of the list:

> The second generation have particular problems because they are not considered a priority by any of the major housing providers. Being young they are unlikely to be earning sufficient to buy their own houses. Unless they fall into one of the Borough Council's priority categories, being pregnant for example, they will have a long wait for Borough Council housing. In general, second generation people will not be eligible for Milton Keynes Development Corporation housing because that is provided for those coming into Milton Keynes from outside to take up work.[28]

There were some echoes of the Lakes Estate and Bletchley during the 1960s here, as discussed in Chapter 4. The second generation of the 1990s could either stay with their parents or other relatives, lodge with friends or with a private owner, move away or, if they were desperate to leave home, hit the streets. There can be

little doubt that the shortage of housing, outstripped by population growth in the new city, along with the iniquitous official
discrimination between second generation youngsters and newcomers, contributed not simply to the numbers of officially registered homeless, but also to those who did not appear on any list.
They appeared, instead, outside the entrances to the shopping
building, or huddled in the underpasses. Often draped in pathetic
clothes, and sometimes accompanied by a dog, they asked for
money or just sat silently, staring down. David Aaronovitch was
just one of many people, whether visitors or locals, who have been
asked for money by the new city's young homeless.[29]

And their youth was obvious. Of the 3,536 enquiries to the
homeless charity Shelter in 1991 and 1992, it was estimated that 75
per cent were from people aged between 16 and 25 years of age.
The Milton Keynes Youth Information Service (YIS) was also
aware of this problem, noting 'a substantial increase in the number
of young people coming to them for housing':

> In the past year [1992], of the 800 young people coming for advice,
> at least half needed advice on housing. [YIS] reports difficulties in
> finding lodgings-providers, and has unquantified reports of people
> sleeping rough.[30]

As Shelter argued, the statistics of officially homeless people in
Milton Keynes understated the extent of the problem. They did not
include the 'hidden homeless', namely those who had not registered as homeless, had not applied for a home and were either
staying with people they knew or sleeping rough. Most of these
were young people.[31]

By that time, the council possessed little in the way of emergency housing or resources to remedy the situation. At the end
of the 1980s it had possessed but four hostels with a total of 29
bedrooms, which, as the new decade began, could barely contain
the problem. So how would the problem be met? One possible
solution was to build new hostels or to convert a number of existing council dwellings into hostel-like accommodation on some
of the gridsquares. In the absence of enough affordable housing,
it was at least an attempt at a solution.[32] But it was not always a
popular one with those who lived near to the location of the
hostels. Thus in the winter of 1992 to 1993 the residents of
Springfield objected to the construction of a hostel on their
estate. At a hundred-strong meeting in their local community
centre, many feelings about the homeless were articulated. One

person stated that 'these people won't care about looking after the estate. It will cause nothing but problems.' Another felt that a hostel for homeless people close by two schools and a senior citizens home was asking for trouble.

Yet there was another issue within these complaints: the lack of consultation. One woman at the meeting claimed that there was 'a great deal of anger that no one knew a thing about this'.[33] Writing to the local paper soon after the meeting one man claimed that MKDC was 'irresponsible' in the way that it had 'rushed through planning permission' for the hostel. Nonetheless, he was objective enough to point out that the hostel was 'well designed for the locality' and 'people unlucky enough to have to stay there should be welcomed to the estate, not resented'.[34] It is not unreasonable to argue that the people of Springfield were worried that they were being hastened into a close encounter with people they did not really know, many of them quite poor, and, in such circumstances, they were genuinely fearful.

Hostels were of course only a temporary solution. The most effective answer to the problem of homelessness and of the waiting list more generally would have been more affordable housing for rent. One potential source of income was the monies generated from the sale of council housing via the 'right to buy' legislation. The right to buy had existed for a number of years, but it was expanded by the Thatcher governments of the 1980s. Unfortunately, this strategy for building new houses was denied to Milton Keynes council, as to other councils in Britain, by the government's freeze on capital receipts that could be used for the much-needed purposes of council house construction. The brutal problem facing local councils during the 1980s was that they moved from the status of provider to enabler. Councils were increasingly obliged to work in harness with other organisations, notably housing associations and private property owners. The council was also able to work with private housing developers to ensure 'planning gain', that is, if private developers were allowed the land to build housing for home ownership, the council could bargain to ensure that a certain number of new dwellings were built for rent, and their maintenance and tenant management was given over to housing associations. Many such projects have been built in the new city. Leasowe Place, for example, in Bradwell Common, was part of the Tay Homes development built during the years 1992 and 1994. Short rows of small terraced houses and flats, run by a housing association based in London, sit among the three- and

four-bedroomed owner-occupied Tudorbethan houses of Forra-
bury Avenue. The large-scale council estate or gridsquare is, for
the time being at least, not on the agenda of the council. Despite
that, or rather because of it, Milton Keynes Council, which became
a unitary authority in 1997, separate from Buckinghamshire
County Council, still struggles to provide affordable housing in
adequate numbers. And the beggars, pathetically asking for
money outside Marks and Spencers or Starbucks, are still there,
and some of them have a tragic tale to tell.[35]

UNEMPLOYMENT AND LOW PAY IN A BOOM TOWN

The designation and early growth of Milton Keynes came during
a relatively unstable and declining time for the national economy.
Inflationary pressures and unemployment began to creep up as
the postwar economy moved towards the end of the boom years
that had lasted since the mid-1950s. This was partly due to the
impact of the oil embargo of 1967 and the oil crisis of 1973, both of
which hiked up the prices of oil and petrol and the goods that
depended upon them. The weaknesses of British manufacturing
were exposed by industrial strife in the form of both official and
wildcat strikes, and the stark lack of competitiveness when compared with the faster-growing economies of France or Germany.

Over the course of the 30 years from 1970 to 2000, the manufacturing basis of the British economy shrank, and the so-called 'post-
industrial' economy took its place. In one sense, this was of
considerable benefit to the local economy, which threw into relief
wider changes in the national economy. As noted in a previous
chapter, between 1967 and 1990 the service sector accounted for 32
per cent of jobs in 1967 but about 70 per cent by 1990. Milton
Keynes possessed an increasingly wide variety of occupations,
some in manufacturing, but most in 'clean' indoors work in offices,
shops, places of leisure, educational establishments, hospitals and
health centres. The reasons for building such an economy may be
understood from the negative contrast to another new town,
Corby in Northamptonshire. Its economic fortunes had been
heavily dependent upon steel, until, that is, the collapse of the steel
industry.[36] When that occurred, the impact on the local economy
and its dependent workers was devastating. The sectoral and
occupational mix of Milton Keynes was intended to avoid such an
industrial meltdown, but it was no insurance against unemploy-

ment. Nor did it engender a universally high-wage economy. Each issue, unemployment and low wages, will be discussed in turn.

Unemployment became endemic in Britain during the 1970s. It had reached a postwar high of over one million by the late 1970s. Despite this, Milton Keynes, in common with other new towns in southern England, was able to resist the high levels of joblessness associated with the declining manufacturing areas in the North and elsewhere. The construction industry, and the material demands of a rapidly growing population, created work. During the 1980s, of course, Milton Keynes continued to grow. More than that, it threw into sharp relief the booming segments of the national economy: retail, finance and banking, leisure and the public services were thriving sectors in MK during the 1980s. So where was the problem?

The problem was one of mismatch between the pace of local economic growth and the in-migration of newcomers. This was further compounded by regional inequalities. In a very real sense, the new city was sharply representative of the country's economic fortunes. Thousands of people continued to move from the North of England, and from Wales and Scotland, to look for work in the booming South East. The changing profile of the origins of MK's population – discussed in Chapter 5 – proves that many headed for, and settled in, Milton Keynes within this wider pattern of economic migration. But there was not always a job for them. As a study of Britain's 'boom towns' argued in 1985, most high-growth towns in the South East shared an extremely low unemployment rate 'by comparison with the national figure of 13.2 per cent':

> The exception is Milton Keynes, where apparently the exceptionally fast growth rate in population has outrun its rate of job growth, rapid though the latter has been. The next highest levels of unemployment [found] at Basingstoke and Bracknell are also associated with rapid population growth.[37]

(Basingstoke and Bracknell were also new towns.) According to the Milton Keynes Campaign Against Poverty, joblessness and difficulties in obtaining work were particularly problematic for job-seekers among ethnic minorities. Unemployment had a disproportionate effect upon certain groups, as Table 8 indicates.[38]

The experiences of unemployment within each ethnic group were not identical. Most unemployed African Caribbeans regularly visited the jobcentre and attended for interview with employers, yet theirs was the second highest unemployment rate after that

TABLE 8: UNEMPLOYMENT AMONG ETHNIC MINORITIES IN MILTON
KEYNES, 1984

Nationality	%	Nos unemployed	Working population	Total in city
African Caribbean	27	121	442	1,164
Bangladeshi	29	32	110	290
East African Asian	16	51	320	841
Indian	12	50	398	1,047
Pakistani	17	17	98	256

of the Bangladeshis. African Caribbeans were on average younger, and spoke English as a first language, whereas Bangladeshis ascribed their unemployment to both age and language difficulties. Yet what the African Caribbean and Bangladeshi unemployed shared was a lack of qualifications and skills that rendered them more vulnerable to long-term unemployment. This was also accompanied by a lack of confidence in oral expression or the filling in of forms. Moreover, a number of West Indians, and also Kenyans, Pakistanis and Indians, felt that they were discriminated against by employers.[39]

There was perhaps a further factor: the lack of a sizeable and established community grapevine in Milton Keynes. This was, in fact, more of a difficulty influencing the employment chances of African Caribbeans than Bangladeshis. In Bletchley, a Bangladeshi community had been in existence since the 1960s.[40] There was no such community of West Indians. In London, however, many black people had heard about jobs through friends and relatives by word of mouth or personal connection. In 1977, for example, two sociologists working from the Centre for Environmental Studies in London noted that minorities were at a disadvantage in obtaining access to information about new towns.[41] The consequent failure to build up sizeable ethnic communities tended to engender feelings of isolation in those new towns. Whilst Milton Keynes had fared better than some earlier towns, it was still not good enough. As a conference held in 1988, entitled 'Economic Development: The Milton Keynes Experience', a regional director of the Department of Trade and Industry argued that more could and should have been done 'to attract those disadvantaged groups to this city where the quality of life and economic prospects are so much more favourable' than in the inner city.[42]

Unemployment, then, was caused by population growth outstripping the rate of job creation. But MKDC appeared to be indifferent to the particular needs of and disadvantages facing certain groups within the new city. Unskilled white people, it must be emphasised, were also vulnerable. In Beanhill during the later 1980s the Felt Needs study found that, among people with health problems or with feelings of stress, 'the most frequently mentioned issue was unemployment':

> Being unemployed was not only seen as intensely stressful by itself, but it made for the build-up of pressure because of lack of money. Of people who talked about money problems in this respect, the numbers of women in the younger age group were particularly high.[43]

Beyond the problems of unemployment, there were factors in MK's economy which generated low wages. For the service sectors of Milton Keynes, with all due deference to Hunter Davies's appraisal of the Fordist scale and organisation of some of the larger places of employment, were and remain heavily characterised by small, and sometimes very small, workplaces. By 1976, only 10 per cent of firms in the service sector employed more than 35 employees, and most retail outlets had fewer than eight workers on their books.[44] The considerable widening of the city's retail base following the opening of the shopping centre in 1979, and the proliferation of office space, much of it accommodating small companies, encouraged the trend to smaller workplaces. By 1990 MKDC's Employers' Survey for that year noted 'an increased proportion of establishments employing ten or less people'. By then, 64 per cent of the workforce worked in establishments of this size, despite the fact that the number of companies employing over 100 workers had increased.[45]

This is the structural context for a discussion of the 'downside' of Milton Keynes' employment record. At the wealthier end of the service sector range of jobs, the city experienced a growing proportion of professional, managerial and intermediate white-collar occupations, as noted in Chapter 5. But this growth was paralleled by an increase in low-paid part-time jobs. The MKDC Employers' Survey for 1987 found that 90 per cent of all part-time work was heavily concentrated in the following sectors of service industries: 'retail, distribution, hotels and catering, education and "other services" . . . Hotels and catering is the only sector with the majority of its workforce working part-time'.[46] Most of those workers were women. The 1987 Employers' Survey revealed that 'the vast majority of part-time jobs are held by females'.[47] Women hairdressers, waitresses, shop assistants and checkout operators, kitchen hands, bar staff, receptionists, cleaners and ancillary staff have historically remained amongst the worst-paid workers in Britain.

The problems of low pay in these jobs were, perhaps, compounded by a lack of trades union representation. Certainly, workers in non-unionised workplaces were more vulnerable to the vicissitudes of unreasonable or incompetent management than those who were members of trades unions. The reasons for this were in some ways the inverse of the city's success, notably the youthfulness and perhaps flexible inexperience of many young workers. The dominance of small workplaces was also a major handicap to trades union organisation. As MKDC could proudly state, in one of its last glossy brochures extolling the advantages of business relocation to the new city, 'The workforce is young and adaptable and the level of skill is high':

> Industrial relations are excellent – there have been no notified disputes in the past ten years. Some companies have employees represented by one union, others by more than one, while many firms run non-union plants.[48]

The trades union movement itself was well aware of the problems of organising in Milton Keynes. In particular, the large-scale industrial plants most conducive to collective organisation were largely absent or confined to the older parts of the designated area, notably at the British Rail Engineering Ltd site in Wolverton. As a member of the local trades council argued, 'Generally, unions are finding it harder to recruit in Milton Keynes than in surrounding areas.' In 1987, Middleton Hall in the shopping building held an exhibition promoted by over 20 major unions to encourage people in Milton Keynes to sign up for union membership. The exhibition was given glamorous celebrity appeal by the appearance of Norman Willis, then General Secretary of the Trades Union Congress, and the prospective Labour candidate at the forthcoming general election, Yvonne Brownfield-Pope.[49]

Six years later, the story was much the same. In September 1993 the Business section of the *Citizen* newspaper led with the headline 'Union city blues: worried trade union leaders plan major recruitment drive'. Trade union leaders were worried, and not a little angry, about the fact that Milton Keynes Marketing was selling the city both at home and abroad as the 'number one non-union city'.

Milton Keynes Marketing had become the city's promotions agency following the winding down of MKDC. And the agency itself was well aware that the main reason for this was 'the large number of new and small companies in Milton Keynes'.[50] Newness and smallness, and the problems for trades unions, were thus good for business, and this of course attracted inward investment and created jobs.

Many unemployed and low-income households were particularly heavily represented in certain gridsquares across the city. Although the *Plan for Milton Keynes* had aimed to prevent the concentration of specific groups, it nonetheless occurred in certain estates, notably those older single-tenure public-rental estates built during the 1970s. Those who owned or were buying their home were less likely to move to these estates, and their rental status made them the first port of call for poorer groups.[51]

New estates thus developed social problems within a generation. This in turn led to a consequent negative image of particular estates within the new city. In her book *Tales of the City*, Ruth Finnegan provided the following oral testimony from a woman living on a development corporation gridsquare who was worried at the increasingly visible social problems of her 'estate'; and it was an estate of which she was very fond. This testimony is worth quoting at length because it crystallises the social and economic factors that come together to demoralise people on an estate:

> I think it is a shame, I think this particular estate has deteriorated, it seems to be getting noisier and more trouble, and it doesn't seem to be as peaceful as it used to be, and when you cruise through this estate my son and I, because he is unemployed, we are both unemployed, we will often go bird watching a lot, and we go to different woodlands. But at the same time we are interested and when a new estate goes up we will cruise the estate and look at the houses, and other respects too, just to look at the houses, look at the gardens, look at how they are developing. And this estate just does not seem to be as peaceful as other estates.
>
> Just over the last five years, about five years, it has gradually started, maybe a wee bit longer than that, it started and [I] don't think it is as bad as its reputation is. It seems to have a reputation and people talk about it, and they say 'Oh it has a terrible reputation and I wouldn't live on there' but certainly if you are living on here the rubbish and the state of the streets and the rubbish . . . And you wouldn't know it isn't all the families, it is just the odd few, and

> I wish they would do something about that. I don't like to victimise
> people or anything but think something could be done.[52]

The lack of employment and subsequent problems of household
survival made life difficult for this woman and her son, but they
were also unhappy at the way the estate had developed a bad reputation. To be associated with this particular gridsquare was to be
associated with its problems. Yet this woman's words also give a
strong and sad sense of suburbanism denied. She had moved to
Milton Keynes, and undoubtedly enjoyed its qualities of peace and
quiet, the nearness of the countryside, the cleanliness of the estate,
and the improved housing and its beloved garden. She had also
been an active coordinator of a playgroup, and had many friends
both on the estate and off it. Its environmental qualities, however,
were being eroded by the increasing appearance of litter and graffiti, the growing crescendo of foul language, and the sense that the
estate was less safe than before due to social problems. And the
growth of new housing was also cutting off access to immediate
parklands. What this woman feared, then, was what some of those
metropolitan critics of Milton Keynes, discussed in the opening
chapter, deplored the absence of. She feared the onset of a more
'urban' culture and neighbourhood: the spectre of an increasingly
busy and noisy environment was disconcerting to her.

In a number of other estates, estates barely more than a generation old, similar fears could be identified in the last years of the
twentieth century. Sentiments such as 'our estate is neglected' or
'Hodge Lea doesn't have a very good reputation' were statements
that implied a sense of being on the edge of something. This was,
it can be argued, a sense of separation from the suburban mainstream, that is, from the more comfortable estates of Middle
England, with their perceived levels of comfort, security and
respectability.[53]

CONCLUSION: *PLUS ÇA CHANGE?*

Finally, however, it is important to note that none of these developments in Milton Keynes were unique to this city in time or place.
During the 1960s, for example, a review of the literature on 'new
communities' in postwar Britain pointed to the perception that in
many new towns there was 'a low tone in part of the town', and
resentment at the appearance of social problems and at the people

who appeared to bring those social problems with them.[54] And a study of 'difficult housing estates' in Bristol, published in 1963, argued that these estates were often associated with low-income, low-status households. They manifested behaviour 'which society does not like and cannot ignore'.[55] That sentiment remains as true today as it did then. Milton Keynes was the largest, and certainly one of the latest, of all of the great new communities of twentieth-century England. It is both naïve yet also disappointing to expect that it was uniquely placed to avoid or at best minimise the creation of social problems. A number of causes were to blame: unemployment, low pay, inadequate housing stock and a predominance of poorer-quality and unpopular housing on certain estates. One or more of these factors made life unnecessarily harsh for many people in the city of dreams.

Finally in this chapter, it is important to note that the thousands of people of Milton Keynes who were not directly affected by poverty, unemployment or homelessness were nonetheless perfectly well aware of the need for adequate public services to ameliorate the social problems of the city. In 1999, Milton Keynes Council, just two years after it had become a unitary authority, took an original step in English local politics by holding a referendum on the size of the next phase of council tax increases. Three options were placed in front of the public by the council. The first was an increase in council tax of just 5 per cent, thus bringing about pressure on public services in the coming year due to inadequate funding. And that inadequacy would have been made worse by the capping or reduction in central government grants to local authorities by Westminster. The other two options offered by the council were increased council tax charges of either 10 or 15 per cent. This exercise may be seen as a unique product of the consultative relationship that MKDC had established with the public, a culture of consultation that was continued by the council.

Both local and national newspapers seized upon the results of the referendum. The *Milton Keynes Citizen* noted the 66,000 who had voted, or the 'big turn-out in first ever city budget referendum'. The *Citizen* reporter emphasised that 23.6 per cent of voters had opted for the 15 per cent rise, whilst 46.3 per cent had favoured the rise of 10 per cent. In total, then, 70 per cent of those who voted opted against the lowest option, and less than a third voted for it.[56] These results attracted the attention of the national press. The *Guardian*, notably, appeared genuinely surprised and impressed by the referendum and its result. 'Middle England yesterday turned political convention on its head', wrote their regional affairs correspondent, 'by voting overwhelmingly to increase local taxes in the country's fastest growing town by four times the rate of inflation.'[57] As the *Guardian's* leader column stated, in a city with less than 2 per cent unemployed, the people had been given the facts about the impact on public services of a low increase, and they had voted to improve those services.[58]

None of this should have really come as a surprise, despite the slight tone of bemusement in the *Guardian's* report. For the new city had never been free of problems, but neither was it bereft of the means to raise those problems as local issues in order to attempt to deal with them. The next chapter delves more deeply into the ways in which the population of Milton Keynes set about to raise issues, to solve problems, and to pursue causes, through the formation of a wide variety of associations and groups. It also shows that the wider context for this was a generally prosperous city, whose people enjoyed leisure and recreation, but who were by no means rendered apathetic by increasing affluence and the enjoyment of material goods.

NOTES

1 See, for example, P. Sainsbury and Joyce Collins, 'Some factors relating to mental illness in a new town', *Journal of Psychosomatic Research*, 10, 1966, pp. 45–51; S. P. W. Chave, 'Mental health in Harlow new town', *Journal of Psychosomatic Research*, 10, 1966, pp. 38–43.
2 *Radio Times*, 30 September 1965, 7 October 1965, 14 October 1965.
3 Ministry of Housing and Local Government, *The Needs of New Communities: A Report of Social Provision in New and Expanding Towns* (London: HMSO, 1967).
4 MKDC, *The Plan for Milton Keynes*, vol. 1 (Milton Keynes: MKDC, 1970) p. 19.
5 MKDC, *Plan for Milton Keynes*, vol. 2, p. 120.
6 MKDC, *Plan for Milton Keynes*, vol. 2, pp. 120–2.
7 MKDC, *Four Years On: The Milton Keynes Household Survey, 1973, Summary Report* (Milton Keynes: MKDC, 1974), pp. 22–3.
8 Generally, see Mark Clapson, *Invincible Green Suburbs, Brave New Towns: Social Change and Urban Dispersal in Postwar England* (Manchester: Manchester University Press, 1998), Chapter 5, 'Suburban neurosis and the new towns blues', pp. 121–55.
9 Roger Kitchen, 'Doing a moonlight' (Milton Keynes: Living Archive Project, 1975, Unpublished manuscript) p. 1.
10 Penny Liddiard, *Milton Keynes Felt Needs Project* (Milton Keynes: Department of Health and Social Welfare, Open University, 1988), p. 62.
11 On the Anglia television programme, see *Milton Keynes Gazette*, 12 December 1975.
12 Jane Turner and Bob Jardine, *Pioneer Tales: A New Life in Milton Keynes* (Milton Keynes: People's Press, 1985), p. 76.
13 Ronald Fletcher, *The Family and Marriage in Modern Britain* (Harmondsworth: Penguin, 1974) pp. 146–50.
14 Roger Kitchen, 'Moving to Milton Keynes', *New Society*, 22 August 1974, p. 480.
15 Kitchen, 'Moving', p. 80.
16 MKDC, *Four Years On: Summary*, pp. 21–5.

17 MKDC, *Four Years On: Summary*, p. 22.
18 Nicholas Deakin and Claire Ungerson, *Leaving London: Planned Mobility and the Inner City* (London: Heinemann, 1977) pp. 131–2.
19 MKDC, *Four Years On: Summary*, pp. 24–5.
20 Denise Brinig, 'What it's really like to live in Milton Keynes', *Over 21*, July 1978, p. 115.
21 MKBC, Directorate of Housing Services, *Putting Progress into Practice: Housing Investment Programme 1992–94: Strategy Statement August, 1991* (Milton Keynes: MKBC, 1991), p. 9.
22 MKBC, *Partnerships with People: Housing Investment Programme Strategy Statement for 1993–94* (Milton Keynes: MKBC 1994), p. 11.
23 MKBC, Directorate of Housing Services, *Putting Progress into Practice*, pp. 8 and 1 respectively.
24 Table based upon MKBC, *Partnerships with People* and *Putting Progress into Practice*.
25 MKDC, *Walnut Tree Neighbourhood Review, July through December, 1990: A Report on the Community Development Programme Undertaken by MKDC between 1987 and 1990* (Milton Keynes: MKDC, 1990), pp. 19, 33.
26 MKBC, *Partnerships with People*, p. 11.
27 Alan Francis, *Access to Housing in Milton Keynes* (Milton Keynes: Milton Keynes Forum Paper No. 11, 1990), p. 1.
28 Francis, *Access to Housing*, p. 2.
29 David Aaronovitch, *Paddling to Jerusalem: An Aquatic Tour of Our Small Country* (London: Fourth Estate, 2000), p. 65.
30 Caroline Cook and Mary Sarre for the Youth Information Service, *Young People's Housing: A Study of Housing for Young People in the Borough of Milton Keynes* (Milton Keynes: Youth Information Service, 1992), pp. 2–3.
31 Cook and Sarre, *Young People's Housing*, p. 2.
32 MKBC, *Partnerships with People*, pp. 14–15.
33 Tom Richmond, 'Why in our back yard?', *Milton Keynes Citizen*, 15 April 1993.
34 Letters, *Milton Keynes Citizen*, 22 April 1993.
35 Robert Cook and Andrew Shouler, *Milton Keynes in the News* (Stroud: Sutton Publishing, 2001), p. 78.
36 M. S. Grieco, 'Corby: new town planning and imbalanced development', *Regional Studies*, 19, 1 (1985), pp. 9–18.
37 A. G. Champion and A. E. Green, *In Search of Britain's Booming Towns: An Index of Local Economic Performance for Britain* (Newcastle: Centre for Urban and Regional Development Studies, 1985), p. 33.
38 Table adapted from D. Middleton and S. Palmer, *Blacks Need Not Apply: A Report into the Problems of Unemployment among Ethnic Minorities* (Milton Keynes: Campaign Against Poverty, 1985), pp. 4–16, 25.
39 Middleton and Palmer, *Blacks Need Not Apply*, pp. 4–16.
40 Mrs Ferdous Rahman, *The Bangladeshi Community in Milton Keynes* (Milton Keynes: Milton Keynes Language Scheme, 1982).
41 Deakin and Ungerson, *Leaving London*, p. 158.
42 City Discovery Centre and Town and Country Planning Association, *Economic Development: The Milton Keynes Experience* (Milton Keynes: CDC/TCPA, 1988), p. 9.
43 Liddiard, *Felt Needs*, pp. 61–2.
44 MKDC, *Household Survey, 1976: Seven Years On, Technical Report 3: Employment* (Milton Keynes: MKDC, 1977), p. 43.
45 MKDC, *Employers' Survey Report, 1990* (Milton Keynes: MKDC, 1990) p. 23.
46 MKDC, *Employers' Survey Report, 1987* (Milton Keynes: MKDC, 1987), p. 9.
47 MKDC, *Employers' Survey Report, 1987*, p. 9; on retail occupations and the predominance of women in them, see Sophie Bowlby, 'From corner shop to hypermarket: women and food retailing', in Jo Little, Linda Peake and Pat Richardson (eds), *Women in Cities: Gender and the Urban Environment* (London: Macmillan, 1988), p. 74.
48 MKDC, *What's the Secret of Success in Milton Keynes?* (Milton Keynes: MKDC, not dated, c. 1990).
49 Anon., 'Unions face city test', *Milton Keynes Gazette*, 14 May 1987; Philip Bassett, 'The state of the (Milton Keynes) union', *Financial Times*, 9 May 1987.
50 Tom Richmond, 'Union city blues', *Milton Keynes Citizen*, 9 September 1993.
51 MKBC, *People and Housing in Milton Keynes: A Profile of Settlements from the 1991 Census*

(Milton Keynes: MKBC, 1993), *passim*. See also Anne Gray, *Social Exclusion: Inclusive New Town–North West Metropolitan Area* (http://www.forum.sozialarbeit.de/europa/2000-01de.shtml), p. 5.

52 Ruth Finnegan, *Tales of the City: A Study of Narrative and Urban Life* (Cambridge: Cambridge University Press, 1999), pp. 129–30.

53 Letter, 'It's like I'm living in a scrap yard', *Milton Keynes Citizen*, 27 August 1992; Anon., 'Problem estate was originally built with children in mind', *Milton Keynes on Sunday*, 28 September 1997; Anon., 'Our estate is neglected', *Sunday Citizen*, 20 June 1999.

54 J. H. Nicholson, New *Communities in Britain: Achievements and Problems* (London: National Council of Social Service, 1961), p. 133.

55 Roger Wilson, *Difficult Housing Estates* (London: Tavistock, 1963), p. 18.

56 Clive Lewis, '9.8%: Voters back council over tax increase', *Milton Keynes Citizen*, 25 February 1999.

57 Peter Hetherington, 'Town votes for 10 per cent rise in council tax to avoid cut in services', *Guardian*, 24 February 1999.

58 *Guardian* leader, 'The new Keynes', *Guardian*, 24 February 1999.

8

Sociability and Social Action in the Space Station City

After walking the city's soulless grid-designed streets, Gilbert and George yesterday declared they 'exuded sexuality': 'We very much like to expose ourselves in a new space. Our new work will be images of tears in a city, sweat in the city, blood in the city. This city exudes sexuality like all cities. Even the names are sexual.

> David Lister, 'Milton Keynes is one sexy city, say
> Gilbert and George', *Independent*, 23 June 1999

They met in 1967, roughly at the same time the new city was conceived, and there are incredible similarities between their work and the idealism of Milton Keynes.

> Steven Snoddy, Director of the Milton Keynes
> Art Gallery and Theatre, on Gilbert and
> George, and quoted in Lee Scriven, 'Wow!
> It's a city artists adore', *Milton Keynes Citizen*,
> 24 June 1999

The opening of the new art gallery in the summer of 1999 was special in itself as a long-overdue high-profile cultural facility for the new city. But it was also notable for the exhibition by Gilbert and George. And both artists said that they 'were pleased to be part of it':

> The mere mention of the name Milton Keynes brings a smile of enthusiasm to the faces of our younger friends. It is very important that this young 'Space Station' of a city now has a building devoted to contemporary culture.[1]

Their exhibition, entitled 'The Rudimentary Pictures', was not actually about Milton Keynes. It depicted London, where so many Milton Keynes migrants have come from, and Gilbert and George had themselves come up from London to open their exhibition. They had also picked up on the point that Milton Keynes was a young city, new and shiny, like a space station. Perhaps they were also implying that it was some sort of new satellite, which like any self-respecting edge city was developing its own internal orbital velocities rather than being a mere static satellite of the capital city.

It was obvious from their exhibits, and implicit within the quotes at the top of the chapter, that bodily excretions are an important building material in the making of a city. This is a fact that nobody who has written about Milton Keynes has really acknowledged before. Beyond the roads and the redways, the houses and the buildings, and the parks and the lakes, other, deeper and more human levels of construction have brought the city into existence. A huge and copious quantity of bodily fluids has gone into the making of the new city. Sweat is an obvious one: the sweat of construction workers, of competitors on the sports fields, of people barbecuing burgers or sausages on a hot summer's evening, or of a million and one home and garden improvements brought to fruition. Blood and tears have been shed in these activities, too. And there is of course another more intimate sexual realm. It is obvious that an unimaginable volume of fluids have been mingled over the years in the conception, gestation and birth of the new city and its citizens. And beyond that, back in the public sphere, millions of friendly feelings and public-spirited gestures have transferred the new city into a socially living entity. An utterly unquantifiable amount of calories has been burnt in all of these activities.

While this writer is disinclined to delve into the sexual realms of Milton Keynes, this chapter explores those other more visible aspects of community and association that have produced this living, sociable city. One aim of the chapter is to test the views of Melvin Webber, who predicted that social interaction within the urban society of the future would be based increasingly upon a more diverse and wide-ranging system of interests. We can see this in the ways in which people in Milton Keynes have used their spare time, whether for leisure or for more serious aims and activities.

LEISURE IN THE CITY DESIGNED FOR EASY LIVING

As a student of leisure in Milton Keynes argued during the later 1980s, the planners of Milton Keynes worked with an expansive notion of the social life of future urban society which 'envisaged social interaction, neighbourliness and a sense of community governed not so much by proximity and physical density [but by] common interests and voluntary association, determined not by neighbours and residential location, but by the circle of people one knows'.[2]

A belief in a fast-growing realm of choices within a situation of 'changing fashions in demand' underpinned the Milton Keynes Development Corporation's view that 'a high degree of *flexibility* should be built into the great part of the provision' to meet both the 'majority of demand' and in addition the aspirations and requirements of special interest groups.[3] MKDC recognised that the wider context for all this was increasing affluence and an expectation of more free time, a growing range of choices and greater mobility. The development corporation emphasised that both public and private leisure providers would be obliged to respond to these profound trends in society. MKDC was in agreement with the Central Council for Physical Recreation (CCPR) whose recent report had stated that 'increased affluence and car ownership have enabled more people to choose from a wider range of activities'.[4]

As a strategic planning and development authority, invested with considerable powers, MKDC's leisure provision deserves to be viewed as a key aspect of interventionist social development that aimed not merely to encourage Milton Keynes to come together socially, but also to encourage forms of recreation that were considered culturally improving and healthy for the individual. In other words, leisure provision in this as in other new towns was one level of the Labour-instigated postwar welfare state. The Arts Council, for example, was born in 1946, the same year that the New Towns Act was passed. Yet sports were relatively neglected until the 1960s, when local government was given 'progressively more direction in the use of the local rate to provide leisure activity', and the Sports Council was established by the new Labour government to promote sport and physical forms of leisure as part of a drive not simply to get rid of Britain's battered sporting reputation, but also to improve the physical well-being of the British people.[5] As the CCPR argued, many

British towns and cities showed a strong demand for more and better indoor and outdoor sports and leisure facilities.[6] Thus as a city largely creating its facilities anew within an under-provided region, the planned provision for leisure obviously had to meet this new demand and be flexible enough to accommodate changing trends. The sections on leisure in the *Plan for Milton Keynes* thus recommended the types of facilities required, but did not phase every one of these in from the very beginning. Local authorities, along with other statutory and voluntary agencies, were also expected to be providers.[7]

MKDC's strategy for recreation and sports provision may be viewed as threefold. One level was institutional: to enhance existing facilities in the established towns, and to provide new apparatus which would be available to all, in local activity centres, and in the campus schools, across the city.

The second but closely connected level was the encouragement of more informal leisure in the pubs, parks, redways and meeting places. And thirdly, it was also expected that commercial providers of leisure would play, as they certainly were to do, a major role.

A major leisure centre complete with swimming pool was planned and built in Bletchley, and the campus schools at Stantonbury and Woughton were also provided with swimming pools and a range of gymnasia and sports fields. In relation to schools, specifically, this reflected the aims of the plan to provide schools that would serve not only educational requirements, but which would furthermore become activity centres for people other than students and pupils. Some of the largest schools have long been used for adult education classes.

Most gridsquares had playing spaces for children allocated, and were to contain parks or playing fields for football, rugby and cricket. A number of small-fee public golf courses were built. During the mid-1990s, moreover, the National Hockey Stadium was constructed, and the smart new cricket pavilion and green was opened in Campbell Park. Outdoor water sports, especially fishing, were generously catered for, and other outdoor pursuits such as bowls, rambling, cycling, camping and caravanning made up 'the miscellaneous provision' that, according to the Sports Council, was necessary lest some areas of sporting and recreational provision be discriminated against.[8]

The provision for outdoor and indoor sports was generally good, and it evolved and grew with the size and diversity of the city's population. But if sports were generally well served, the arts and cultural facilities fared more poorly. The city centre, for example, developed a bad reputation for its limited leisure activities at night. Until The Point, Britain's first multiplex cinema, opened in 1985, there was little to do in the city centre once the shops had shut, bar a narrow range of new pubs, a few restaurants and a nightclub. Yet within three years of the cinema's opening, the development corporation could still admit to 'the woeful lack of nightlife' in the city centre.[9] This state of affairs was worsened by the decision of the new owners of the shopping building, POSTEL, in 1990, to close down the shopping mall at night. That amounted to a privatisation of public space that killed off the scope for developing any regular evening and night-time recreational and cultural facilities within the mall. Many people living in Milton Keynes reacted with anger to this loss of public space.[10]

As late as 1993, 26 years after designation, one of the more erudite and objective visitors to Milton Keynes could rightly complain that 'Sadly, if you want to see a play or hear a classical music concert [in Central Milton Keynes] you'll have to go elsewhere.'[11] Just one year previously, a reporter for *The Times*, describing young people in Milton Keynes as 'all revved up with nowhere to go', asked Melanie, a 20-year-old in a nightclub, what she found to do in Milton Keynes. 'You mean Legoland', came the reply: 'Well there's this and there's The Point, and that's it.'[12]

The opening of the Theatre District in Central Milton Keynes in 1999 was, as noted, an important landmark in the cultural history of Milton Keynes. Only a year later an indoor ski slope, another multiplex cinema and a new mall were up and running in a huge building nearby. Elsewhere in the city, furthermore, the expansion throughout the 1990s of commercial leisure outlets, whether restaurants, pubs and clubs, leisure centres and keep fit clubs, created a recreational culture that dramatically improved the range of opportunities both within the city centre and beyond it. Even critics of suburban towns could finally admit that, perhaps at long last, Milton Keynes was a hip and happening place.[13]

Implicit within that point was the unfortunately long-held view that, before the late 1990s, Milton Keynes really was the soulless and desolate place that its critics liked to think it was. Yet any such view was, frankly, based upon a lack of empirical evidence about the social life of the new city, for it ignored the contribution of people in Milton Keynes who actively made their own leisure and often provided the opportunities for others to take part in a wide variety of entertainments and get-togethers.

By 1980, for example, some 19 years before the opening of the new theatre, there were 'four formal theatre venues in Milton Keynes', namely the Jennie Lee Theatre at Bletchley Leisure Centre, the Lecture Theatre at the Open University, and one each on both Woughton and Stantonbury campuses. Professional theatre companies had toured to the city, but more importantly local groups of players had formed 'The Milton Keynes Theatre Consortium', to finance and promote plays. MKDC assisted with some costs, and publicity.[14]

Unfortunately, powerful opinion formers failed to acknowledge such 'bottom-up' social and cultural activity. Leader columns in newspapers are major influences on public opinion, or at least they purport to be, so it is a shame that they so often relied upon impressionism, the basis of weak journalism, when discussing Milton Keynes. Impressionism and ignorance were both clearly in evidence in the *Guardian* and *The Times* during the 25th anniversary of Milton Keynes in 1992. They argued that the city had no organic culture. The *Guardian*, for example, derided Milton Keynes' 'desolation and soulless atmosphere'.[15]

Writers on new towns and on town planning more generally, such as David Lock and Colin Ward, both of whom have been involved in the development of Milton Keynes, reacted angrily to such views. Lock and Ward pointed to Ruth Finnegan's findings in her book *The Hidden Musicians: Music Making in an English Town* (1989) which detailed the great diversity and enthusiasm of the musicians who made up the vibrant culture of music making in Milton Keynes. Finnegan, a social anthropologist at the Open University, found that classical musicians, brass bands, folk music, country and western, church and religious music, and popular music, especially rock, were being practised, played, listened to and enjoyed or derided in a wide variety of locations all across the city. Finnegan was particularly impressed by the number of rock bands, for example, who played in front rooms, garages, pubs and clubs to teenage or young audiences. This rock culture was subdivided into punk, new wave, heavy metal, new romantic, funk, soul, reggae, futurist and 60s sounds, 'to quote just a few'. The culture was mostly, but by no means exclusively, male.[16]

And it continued to thrive. At the gig venue, The Pitz, for example, based on Woughton Campus, a 'Band Blitz' competition was established in 1998. At the fourth annual Band Blitz in September 2001, the diversity of local rock music was strongly in evidence. Various singers or guitarists described their sound as 'hard metal' or 'grungy-type punk' or 'emo metal' as in emotional metal or 'mod, but not as you know it' or even as 'just a rock band, and we do what we want'. And if these bands were not to every-one's taste, Woughton Campus also hosted a tribute night to the music and career of Garth Brooks, a line dancing session, another 'local band showcase' and a variety of other acts, all in September. And a male voice choir was also appearing at Stantonbury Campus in that month.[17] So, both before and after the city centre became a fully established place of entertainment, music was flourishing in the city.

Music and those who made it represented perhaps the most sig-nificant element in the social formation of the new city, a city that was in fact about a generation old by the time Ruth Finnegan was making her observations. This was the element of self-help or, more precisely, collective self-help. This consisted in the voluntary grouping together of people with shared interests and tastes, and the making of their own entertainment, events and in some cases money. The contemporary social history of music making in Milton Keynes lends strong support to the views of Melvin Webber, discussed in a previous chapter, about the increasing primacy of voluntary and interest-based forms of association and participation. Equally significantly, this was grass roots creation and conviviality: people were doing it for themselves rather than merely being the pacified and obedient receivers of commercially driven youth cultural products.[18]

Yet as Pete Frame's *Rockin' Around Britain* documents, Milton Keynes developed still more fascinating and varied relationships to music making. The Bowl, of course, has been a major events stadium since The Police played there in the opening gig in 1980. Streets and roads in the 1980s gridsquare of Crown Hill were named after dead rock stars and singers: Presley Way, Lennon Drive, Bolan Court, Redding Grove and Orbison Court are just a few examples. The Stables venue at Wavendon, owned and run by the jazz couple Cleo Laine and Johnny Dankworth, has played host to a great variety of different music acts on the fringes of the designated area of Milton Keynes since the beginnings of the new city. A local resident also twinned up with long-haired guitarist Wild Willy Barrett to record the song 'Milton Keynes we love you'. In addition, the Concrete Cowboys got together in 1993 in order to perform their distinctive version of bluegrass music. They played at the Stables at Wavendon and in a number of pubs in Milton

Keynes.[19] Other bands whose members have been associated with Milton Keynes in terms of business or place of residence include Acid House, Blodwyn Pig and Jethro Tull.[20] Linford Manor, in the heart of Milton Keynes, became an internationally renowned recording studio during the latter 1990s, with artists such as Victoria Beckham and the cult female vocalist Polly Jean Harvey cutting tracks there. And Big George Webley, a recording artist who has written a number of famous television theme tunes – including those to Ricky Gervais's BBC series *The Office* and *Have I Got News For You* – lived in Stony Stratford at the time of writing.

Music was, of course, also listened to at home. It was one major activity in a home-based culture of leisure and entertainments that is also essential to any understanding of both social and personal life in the new city, and in contemporary England more generally. The home was the most common site of leisure and relaxation. By 1988, in fact, almost 100 per cent of people in Milton Keynes regularly watched television, a statistic that was slightly higher than the national average, but which probably reflects the greater penetration of Milton Keynes homes by cable. This was supplied to 55 per cent of homes in the new city. By 1988, over 65 per cent of households possessed a video recorder, 35 per cent had a home computer and 20 per cent a compact disc player, statistics which were again slightly above the national average, but similar to South Eastern levels of consumption.[21] These items would become increasingly popular during the 1990s. Other sources, furthermore, indicate the popularity of other home-based activities. Do-it-yourself and home improvements were well served by the superstores and garden centres that had opened in or near the new city, whilst gardening, which became something of a national passion during the 1990s, went from strength to strength. The majority of people in Milton Keynes have wanted a garden, and of those a majority have used and enjoyed the garden either for the aesthetic and expressive aspects of gardening, or as a site for outdoor recreation at home, or both.[22]

People enjoyed relaxing and entertaining at home. But although the people of Milton Keynes increasingly purchased video recorders and home computers and were wired up to the cable for television, there is little evidence that leisure became more private and home-based to the exclusion or reduction of leisure elsewhere. Drinking, going out to eat and going to the cinema were still popular activities. The Point cinema, which had opened in 1985, was visited at least once within a 12-month period by at least 55 per cent of the population.[23]

Interestingly, leisure trends in Milton Keynes during and since the 1980s bore a close resemblance to those of another contemporaneous new town, Telford in Shropshire. There, the 'rank order' of leisure activities in 1980 was characterised by watching television, listening to music, drinking, visiting friends, making local car trips to various destinations, and a variety of sociable pursuits at home.[24]

Yet the sort of leisure that people enjoyed often depended on a number of major influences and defining characteristics. Gender is a very important one, but, although gender differences in participation rates in various activities were only occasionally referred to in MKDC and council surveys, there was no systematic exploration of the differences between women's and men's leisure. However, we know from work undertaken at the Open University that women probably had less leisure time than men. Hence Rosemary Deem's book, *All Work and No Play*, a study of women's leisure in Milton Keynes during the early 1980s, found that female participation rates in leisure outside the home were generally lower than those of males.[25] As the development corporation noted in 1989, 'males were more likely to use leisure centres for dry sports than females; generally twice as many males participate in dry sports than women'. Women were 'more likely to escort others to facilities, i.e. children'.[26]

Another window onto the non-work life of Milton Keynes is provided by participation in the associations, societies and clubs that people have chosen to belong to in their spare time. Just over half of residents in the designated area were, by 1989, members of one or more clubs. Sports club membership was widespread. 'Members of places of worship' numbered 13 per cent, while 15 per cent of citizens belonged to at least one of a considerable variety of local social clubs. About 7 per cent of the population worked for voluntary and charitable groups. Of elderly people, 5 per cent participated in or belonged to senior citizens clubs, whilst 5 per cent of all women actively belonged to women's groups, notably mothers' clubs. The lowest rate of participation in any given strata of activity was within residents associations: 3 per cent, or 1 in every 33 of the population, were active in their estates residents association.[27]

On the surface, this may seem to be a paltry level of commitment at residential level, but it is not. In fact, it is not even historically a low level of commitment and local participation in associative activity. During the 1930s and 1940s, studies of the new Edgware estate in North London found that a small but committed band of local spirits could effectively form and mobilise local groups and associations. These studies, by the sociologist Ruth Durant (later Ruth Glass) and by the think-tank Political and Economic Planning (PEP), also highlighted the prominent role of women in local associative activity and organisation.[28] This continued into the new communities of the postwar period, and Milton Keynes was no exception.

ASSOCIATION, AGITATION AND LOCAL ISSUES IN MILTON KEYNES

The sociologist David C. Thorns has asserted the importance of non-workplace associations as local responses to broader social, economic and political processes. He argues that associative activity does not mean that all sorts of people from all walks of life are keen to get together to fight for a common end: class, gender and status group still influence the formation and membership of associations and action groups. And Thorns also notes that associative activity reflects a greater level of individualism, born of affluence, in the latter decades of the twentieth century. He further points to the demise of older local working-class communities, to the growing levels of home ownership that ostensibly separate owner-occupiers from a dwindling number of renters and council tenants, and the decline in large-scale manufacturing work. Taken together, and on the surface at least, these social and economic trends have eroded the local and collective basis of trades unions, and concerted political action. During the 1980s and 1990s it was fashionable for a number of sociologists, some of them based at the Open University in Milton Keynes, to argue that relatively wealthy groups of owner-occupiers would have less and less in common with poorer groups. In the pessimistic perspective of some sociologists, this is 'socio-tenurial polarisation'.[29]

Yet Thorns was more sophisticated than that, and he was not unduly pessimistic about present and future patterns of social organisation: in an era of growing consumption levels and of growing post-industrial employment, an eclectic range of associations emerges *beyond the workplace*, beyond trades unions, that confronts social, economic and political problems at the local level.[30] Milton Keynes was born in 1967, that year of the Summer of Love associated by many cultural commentators with a new and liberating individualism. It was also pitched, like a new baby born into a fast-changing world, into the era of de-industrialisation, a point noted in earlier chapters. Thus Milton Keynes has a strong relevance to debates about whether or not urban society has been fragmenting since 1970, and about the changing nature of associative or collective action in England. And there has been no shortage of meaningful collective action in the new city.

One of the earliest and longest-running campaigns, and certainly one of the most successful, was the agitation for a local hospital in the new city. The *Plan for Milton Keynes* had envisaged a new hospital for both the city and the region, but in 1973, as a consequence of the Conservative government's spending cuts, the Oxfordshire Regional Health Authority postponed plans to build a proposed hospital. In response, a teacher, Margaret Jones, formed the Hospital Action Group with a friend. Their tactics were simple and effective, and drew upon a time-honoured tradition of local agitation: a slogan was devised, 'Milton Keynes is dying for a hospital', and letters were written in droves to the local press. A delegation paid a visit to the Conservative Member of Parliament, William Benyon, and a number of small demonstrations in Westminster were arranged. The Health Minister Sir Keith Joseph and Geoffrey Rippon at the Department of the Environment received between them over 1,400 letters mobilised by the Hospital Action Group.

Despite these actions, the government and local health authorities failed to respond with any promise of a new hospital, so the campaign was stepped up during the mid-1970s, by which time the Labour Party was in government following the fall of the Conservative government in 1974. A huge orange question mark, made at Liz Leyh's studio at Stacey Hill Farm, was placed in one of the fields originally earmarked for the hospital,[31] and the Hospital Action Group symbolically asked the army to establish an emergency field hospital. Labour's Health Minister, Dr David Owen, was handed an 18,000-strong petition when he met with the protestors. The group also registered itself as a charity when, at last, it appeared that hospital plans were taking shape during the later 1970s, and it used its charitable status to win funding to keep the pressure on during 1979 and 1980. Once the hospital was announced, the action group even possessed a sum of money to help the hospital with any early minor financial difficulties it might have. Throughout the campaign, MKDC professed its strong support.

From 1980, as the first piece of turf was cut out of the earth to mark the construction of the new hospital, the local press paid tribute to the organisers of the hospital campaign in special 'Our hospital' editions, and gave expression to the view of Margaret Jones that with the beginnings of the new hospital would come different battles to be fought.[32] With some justification, the Milton Keynes Urban Studies Centre, based at the Open University, could argue that the action group was 'an extremely effective protest movement' that had been instrumental in reversing official health policy as it affected Milton Keynes.[33]

Significantly, the campaign was not limited to the middle-class women who initiated it. People from all classes, and home-owners as well as council tenants, were involved. The campaign proved that people could and did come together when major issues were involved.

Yet other campaigns were more specific in terms of their social composition, and also more locally based rather than town-wide. This became evident in the actions of the tenants of the gridsquares of Beanhill and Netherfield to get their architect-designed residences altered and improved in terms of appearance and performance. Milton Keynes Borough Council materials make clear that the majority of heads of households in these gridsquares were in manual work and, in terms of tenure, the great majority of dwellings were rented from the development corporation until 1992 and subsequently from the council.[34]

It was noted in a previous chapter that a writer for the *Architects' Journal* had lamented the 'indignity of pitched roofs' on the once flat-roofed and metal-clad dwellings of Norman Foster Associates-designed Beanhill. Here was an example of intellectuals and aesthetes judging by appearances before being availed of deeper facts about the modern housing that they held such a high regard for.

The first phase of Beanhill was completed by 1972. As early as spring 1977, the Beanhill Residents Association was holding meetings, some of them over 100 strong, to discuss with MKDC officials the condensation and general disrepair of their accommodation.[35] The problems persisted, despite expenditure on them, and tenants met regularly, often manifesting anger at the damp and mould and at the expense and inconvenience of fuel bills and repairs. There was even a rooftop prowler who worried or irritated residents by 'running along the flat single-storey roofs at 2 o'clock in the morning'.[36] The Beanhill Tenants Action Group (BTAG) was formed to get these problems solved. Its tactics over the coming years included meetings, letters to the local press, letters to the local MP and the petitioning of the development corporation.[37] BTAG demanded new pitched roofs, general repairs to exteriors and an upgrading of heating and insulation. By spring 1982 the new roofs and repairs had begun. There were, however, to be delays and further inconveniences about which the residents were keen to articulate their concerns, but by 1988 most of the roofs and repairs were complete. Furthermore, the popularity of the pitched roofs encouraged MKDC to remove flat roofs and introduce the pointed variety in public housing areas across the city. This was a triumph for 'bottom-up' traditionalism over the 'top-down', like-it-or-lump-it purveyors of rational modern architecture.[38] Nonetheless, there was no complacency on the part of residents. In 1989 a reporter for the national newspaper the *Guardian* found that 'in Beanhill, Norman Foster's putative paradise, they liked the inside of their bungalows but hated the dark corrugated cladding: "very noisy when it rains"'.[39]

During the 1990s, the residents of Beanhill faced further problems. Before Milton Keynes gained a unitary authority in 1997, the city was run by the borough council and Buckinghamshire County Council. The decision of the county council to close the Moorlands Community Centre in 1993, as part of a package of proposed £2 million cuts, induced a strong reaction from some local people.[40] They argued that the centre was a meeting place for a wide variety of groups, including job search, money advice, a child abuse clinic, a 'budget lunch' club, holiday play schemes, youth and senior citizens clubs, and other local groups that met there morning, afternoon and evening. The users group organised a petition, and a coachload of protestors was mobilised. The leader of the users group told the local newspapers that the centre was the 'heartbeat' not only of Beanhill but of other nearby estates: 'it caters from everyone from the cradle to the zimmer frame!'[41]

The majority of protestors against the closure of the Moorlands Centre were women.[42] The contribution of women to associative action in other estates with different social compositions to Beanhill is evident in the following examples. During the early 1980s the appearance of barriers and shrubbery at the ends of redways, where they met roads, was in no small part the result of local councillors reacting to action by mothers on Fishermead. Their children had suffered accidents and sometimes near-fatal collisions with cars.[43] Fishermead was less of a rental and manual working-class estate than Beanhill. During the 1980s it was developing a mixed tenure profile, so that by 1991 there was a mixture of home ownership, rental housing from the development corporation and shared ownership arrangements with housing associations. Half of the people in work were in manual employment, whilst about 15 per cent were professional and managerial.[44]

During the mid-1980s women in Fishermead and in the adjacent estate of Oldbrook were instrumental in the successful campaign to gain a chemist's shop and a general practitioners' surgery for the estates. Oldbrook's tenure was weighted more towards owner-occupation, with a figure developing towards 60 per cent home ownership and 22 per cent public rental by the end of the decade. Oldbrook was more middle-class than Fishermead, with 43 per cent employed in 'intermediate/clerical and administrative' jobs, 23 per cent within professional and managerial categories and 34 per cent doing manual work.[45] In the October 1985 issue of *Oggie Post*, the residents' newspaper for the Fishermead and Oldbrook estates, the Fishermead and Oldbrook residents association complained at the lack of health facilities on the estates. Hence a 'Doctor and Chemist Action Group' was formed by four women, one of whom also pointed out to the local press the continuing interface between the city's inadequate public transport and the inconvenience of having to travel across the city to get to a doctor or a chemist. Many pensioners, for example, who had no car were particularly inconvenienced by this state of affairs.[46] A door-to-door survey of people's requirements for a surgery and chemist's was carried out by the group in 1986, and a petition of over 400 signatures was presented to the Family Practitioners Committee in that year. The organisers of the petition had solicited the support of the Community Health Council to lend weight to it, and in early 1987 the outcome was declared:

> The Family Practitioners Committee, who had previously stated that there were not enough patients for a new surgery, finally wilted on seeing the results of the survey, and agreed to advertise the new post.[47]

Here were some successful campaigns, headed largely by women, located firmly within the city or within areas of the city. Some campaigns were heterogeneous in their social composition; others were quite homogeneous. Yet they all required collective determination over time. They also demonstrated that people understood the need to petition and mobilise the relevant local and national agencies. If we adopt Melvin Webber's terminology, this was social action within two inter-connected realms: the local realm and the realm of informal politics.

Some wider points are relevant to all this. It is notoriously difficult to calibrate women's involvement in local and informal political and practical action, but their predominance within it is undoubted. We should also be reminded of Milton Keynes' developing employment structure and the growing number of women going out to paid employment, both part and full time, during the 1980s and since, work that was and remains on average less well-paid than men's employment. Yet whilst there has been growing participation of women in the workplace, many sociologists argue that the very existence of such local campaigns, and the local women's networks that underpin them, reflects the still primary role of women as unpaid houseworkers and carers. In combination, then, 'women tend to be more concerned than men with their local residential environment':

> and therefore more likely to be provoked to campaign in their communities for better and more equitably located services, for better home and estate maintenance, for housing construction and design that meets their needs.[48]

Associative action was also evident in other locally famous examples of collective action, both of which may be viewed as environmental. We can see this in the attempts to establish a 'Greentown' in Milton Keynes, and in the campaign to 'Keep Willen Ever Tranquil'. To take Greentown first, this was a project, established during the early 1980s, to build 'a cooperatively run and ecologically sound village community in Milton Keynes', to wit, in the Crown Hill gridsquare.[49] Over 100 people were members of the Greentown Group, many of them professionals, and some associated with MKDC. They were sympathetic to the ideas of the Green movement, notably in the design of homes that were environmentally friendly because they used natural resources such as solar energy as cheaply and effectively as possible. Many in the group also favoured the application of such homes to low-rent public sector housing, where energy-efficient housing would be particularly useful for those with less money to spend on fuel and running costs.

In common with other locally committed organisations, members of the Greentown Group negotiated with MKDC, which it subsequently blamed for the demise of the project. MKDC wanted strong assurances about the financial backing and security of the Greentown venture, and sought information about the impact of the scheme on the local area. Moreover, as we saw in a previous chapter, MKDC underwent some changes in key personnel during the early 1980s. Some new development corporation officials possessed a more market-orientated ideology. Consequently they were less enthusiastic about experimentation in housing than their earlier counterparts had been. MKDC itself refrained from giving any firm backing and significant monetary help to the project, the very gestures required to secure financial investment from banks or building societies. This, claimed the group, placed them in a 'catch 22' situation, and relations with MKDC grew increasingly hostile. Unfortunately, there were also internal divisions amongst its members, and it too suffered from changes and turnover in personnel. By the mid-1980s, the dream of a community of energy-efficient and self-built homes had all but gone up in smoke.

The historical significance of Greentown's demise is twofold. A reforming and original project failed to reach its goal due to what it felt was a lack of cooperation with the relevant authorities and institutions. As Thorns has argued, many green initiatives have grown more radical, 'as the aim of establishing a more participatory process became frustrated by the existing social and political structures'.[50] This often led to increasing levels of conflict and tension between the various groups and organisations, which worked against the interests of poorer and less-well-resourced groups. Furthermore, it is a shame that a new city missed the opportunity to take advantage of some of the more innovative eco-friendly developments in late-twentieth century housing. Milton Keynes could have been in the forefront of building not only model housing, but ecologically based new *communities*. And this was at a time of greater experimentation with social housing following the Housing Act of 1980, and during a decade when environmentally friendly housing came onto the town planning agenda. Unfortunately, Greentown now lies, probably forever, in what Melvin Webber might have termed 'the counterfactual realm'.

The campaign to 'Keep Willen Ever Tranquil' was another environmentally orientated movement, but it was primarily a protest movement with more limited intentions. It came into existence during 1986 in order to prevent the construction of a road bridge

over nearby Willen Lake. Willen's socio-economic profile was a relatively wealthy one: 89 per cent of dwellings were owner-occupied
by the time of the 1991 Census, for example. Its occupational
profile included of 25 per cent professional/managerial workers,
and 48 per cent were in clerical and various types of white-collar
work. Less than a quarter of those in employment were involved
in manual work. However, support for KWIET transcended the
Willen estate, and probably involved people from a wide range of
occupations. A petition of over 9,000 signatures was got up and,
significantly, the group sought and gained the support of Milton
Keynes Borough Council to face up to both MKDC and the
Department of the Environment (DoE) in Whitehall. There was no
simple power bloc involved, no simple 'them' against 'us' in this
protest. Local councillors were also called upon to speak out
against the bridge, and the visual and sonic intrusion it would
create, but the combined might of the development corporation
and the DoE was enough to prevail. MKDC could and did point to
the rising levels of car ownership and usage nationally, and it also
emphasised the need for a new picturesque route up to the city
centre from the M1 to cope with growing traffic.[51]

The development corporation prevailed, and KWIET was dis-
banded during 1988. A road bridge carrying 'Portway' now
stands above the centre of Willen Lake. Yet the campaign to
prevent the construction of that bridge was significant as one of
myriad sporadic local groups that come into existence for a specific purpose and either achieve or fail to achieve their ends. It was
further proof that Milton Keynes was developing an associative
culture, one in which both common interests and a measure of
proximity could unite people, and proof that Webber was also
right to argue that localism might be becoming less significant as
a basis of community, but it was still, nonetheless, a key influence
on community.

CONCLUSION

This chapter has demonstrated that a city so often viewed as soulless because it was lacking in community was neither soulless nor
lacking in community. For the evolving social life of Milton Keynes
embraced 'interest communities' of people who came together
from different parts of the city to share a musical, sporting or other
recreational enthusiasm. People also came together, both within

housing estates and beyond them, to fight or petition for specific ends. Some groups were quite socially specific, whilst others were heterogeneous. And we also saw in previous chapters that making friends and neighbours was a continuing activity for newcomers to the new city. The home remained a bastion of relaxation and entertainments, and was augmented by the growing range of choice in television viewing and by the increasing purchase and use of computers at home, at work and at school and college.[52] It is not inaccurate to argue that both privacy and sociability were sought after by the vast majority of people, and that they wished to establish their own balance between these two ostensible opposites. The new city made this balance possible.

Milton Keynes, furthermore, mirrored both the changes and continuities that were occurring in the social life of England since 1970, a point made by the journalist Jeremy Seabrook when he visited the estate of Beanhill in the later 1970s. Unfortunately, Seabrook felt that the mirror of Milton Keynes reflected a national decline in communal gregariousness that he identified in his other, usually deeply pessimistic, writings. And this weakening of gregariousness was most fully in evidence among the working classes who had moved to Milton Keynes. For Seabrook, moving away from an older working-class area to a new home in Milton Keynes was, basically, a cultural mistake. People were becoming more home-based and materialistic, and that was having a negative effect on their group spontaneity. Of newly settled tenants in Beanhill, Seabrook wrote that 'The discipline to conform reaches deep into people's lives':

> The houses are new, they cry out for new curtains, new furniture, new appliances, almost for a new type of people . . . You would have to be very brave not to comply with the paradox of living privately in a profoundly conforming way . . . everybody is living a spectacle, trying to accommodate themselves to deeply imprisoning images of the better life.

So moving to Milton Keynes was a sort of imprisoning experience? For Seabrook, this perspective became so all-consuming that it led him to make miserable value judgements which contradicted the very testimony of the people he claimed to speak for. After one woman told him that living in Beanhill 'is like paradise compared to where I used to live' he interpreted this as evidence of 'a loss of any sense of communal belonging'. It revealed 'an air of the secularised afterlife'.[53]

The evidence in this chapter does not support Seabrook's impressionistic take on life in Beanhill. He was wrong about Beanhill, about Milton Keynes and, more widely, about England. For instance, his short visit to Milton Keynes did not acknowledge BTAG and its dual role: it was certainly an attempt to improve the material conditions of the home, but it was a critical and prolonged *collective* response to inadequacy from above.

We must also question the historical naïvety implicit in such terms as 'loss of any sense of communal belonging' and the rather pretentious 'air of the secularised afterlife'. For these terms reveal that Seabrook was driven by a view that there was more community back there in the terraced houses of the working-class heartlands, and back then, in the years before about 1950. Since the 1950s, Seabrook has argued in a number of passionate and worrisome books, society went into some sort of demise as people became more affluent, more used to choice and more independent of others.[54]

As a number of social historians have argued, however, from highly researched viewpoints, the notion that strong and tightly knit working-class communities once lived in straitened but happier circumstances in the older town and city centres has been greatly exaggerated. Many of the patterns which have increasingly characterised social relations in the years since 1970 were in existence, within admittedly different contexts, long before more recent years. As Joanna Bourke has argued, for example, the tensions and difficulties in earlier postwar urban communities have often been overlooked by social historians. There was, to take some important indicators, often conflict between different ethnic groups, and between 'rough' and 'respectable' people. Bourke has also pointed out that for many people there were tensions between the maintenance of privacy and the need for collective obligations. Hence, rather than living an intensely sociable life, people's relationships were more akin 'to a series of negotiations whereby individuals combined over one issue and dispersed over others'.[55]

This assessment bore a strong similarity with the social thinking of MKDC during the formulation of the Plan. The 1968 *Interim Report to Milton Keynes Development Corporation*, produced by the consultants Llewelyn-Davies, Weeks, Forestier-Walker and Bor, had made the following statement and prediction about the nature of associative activity. 'All towns generate interest groups', it argued, 'which grow, coalesce, fade away or redirect themselves over time. Milton Keynes will be no exception, and such groups will do much [to] provide focuses of activity, amusements and interaction.'[56]

NOTES

1 David Lister, 'Milton Keynes is one sexy city, say Gilbert and George', *Independent*, 23 June 1999.
2 Simon Cox, 'Changing concepts and attitudes to the provision of leisure in a new town' (London: Ealing College of Higher Education, BA (Hons) Humanities unpublished dissertation, not dated), p. 79.
3 Llewelyn-Davies, Weeks, Forestier-Walker and Bor, *Milton Keynes Plan: Interim Report to the MKDC* (London: Llewelyn Davies *et al.*, 1968), p. 9.
4 MKDC, *Recreation: Recreation Plan for Milton Keynes* (Milton Keynes: MKDC, 1970), p. 1.
5 John Clarke and Chas Critcher, *The Devil Makes Work: Leisure in Capitalist Britain* (London: Macmillan, 1985), p. 87; Tony Mason, *Sport in Britain* (London: Faber & Faber, 1988), pp. 81–3.
6 MKDC, *Recreation Plan for Milton Keynes*, p. 1.
7 MKDC, *Plan for Milton Keynes*, vol. 2, pp. 121–4.
8 MKDC, *Recreation Plan for Milton Keynes*, pp. 11–21.
9 David White, 'What's so bad about Milton Keynes?', *New Society*, 17 April 1988, p. 97.
10 Colin Ward, *New Town, Home Town* (London: Calouste Gulbenkian Foundation, 1993), pp. 99–102.
11 Susan Marling, *American Affair: The Americanisation of Britain* (London: Boxtree, 1993), p. 66.
12 Peter Barnard, 'All revved up and no place to go', *The Times Saturday Review*, 18 January 1992.
13 Jonathan Glancey, 'It's got plenty of roads. Now it's on the map', *Guardian*, 4 October 1999.
14 MKDC, *Theatre Audience Survey: Woughton Centre Theatre, 21–23 February, 1980* (Milton Keynes: MKDC, 1980), p. 1.
15 David Lock, 'Milton Keynes, new towns, and the British spirit', *Town and Country Planning*, April 1992, p. 108. See also 'Letters to the Editor' in *The Times*, 30 January 1992, for some responses to the article in the newspaper.
16 Ruth Finnegan, The *Hidden Musicians: Music Making in an English Town* (Cambridge: Cambridge University Press, 1989), pp. 104–6.
17 *Go*, 6 September 2001, a weekly free supplement with the *Milton Keynes Citizen*. See also www.milton.keynes.co.uk.
18 Finnegan, *Hidden Musicians*, p. 123.
19 Robert Cook, *Britain in Old Photographs: Milton Keynes* (Stroud: Sutton, 1995), pp. 63, 77.
20 Pete Frame, *Rockin' Around Britain* (London: Omnibus, 1999), p. 14.
21 MKDC, *Milton Keynes Insight* (Milton Keynes: MKDC, 1989), p. 4.
22 Commerce Business Directories, *Milton Keynes Business Directory, 1995–96* (Newport Pagnell: Commerce Public, 1995), p. 154. See also *Milton Keynes Business Directory* and *Milton Keynes Business File* for DIY and gardening centres. These are held at the City Discovery Centre, Bradwell Abbey, Milton Keynes.
23 MKDC, *Household Survey, 1988: Leisure and Recreation Technical Report* (Milton Keynes: MKDC, 1989), pp. 1–19; MKBC, *Household Survey, 1990* (Milton Keynes: MKBC, 1990), pp. 178–9; see also *Milton Keynes Citizen* on a weekly basis.
24 John R. Kelly, *Leisure Identities and Interactions* (London: George Allen & Unwin, 1983), pp. 16–17.
25 Rosemary Deem, *All Work and No Play: The Sociology of Women and Leisure* (Milton Keynes: Open University Press, 1986), *passim*.
26 MKDC, *Household Survey, 1988: Leisure and Recreation Technical Report*, p. 15.
27 MKBC, *Household Survey, 1990* (Milton Keynes: MKBC, 1990), p. 46; MKDC, *Milton Keynes Insight* (Milton Keynes: MKDC, March 1989).

28 Ruth Durant, *Watling: A Survey of Social Life on a New Housing Estate* (London: P. S. King, 1939), pp. 22–45; Political and Economic Planning, 'Watling revisited', *Planning*, 14, 270 (1947), p. 68.

29 Chris Hamnett, 'Consumption and class in contemporary Britain', in Chris Hamnett, Linda McDowell and Philip Sarre, *The Changing Social Structure* (London: Sage, 1993), pp. 199–243.

30 David Thorns, *Fragmenting Societies: A Comparative Analysis of Regional and Urban Development* (London: Routledge, 1992).

31 *City Limits*, 6, February–March 1977. I am grateful to Jackie Burton for this reference.

32 Elaine Scott, 'Work starts on general hospital', *Milton Keynes Gazette*, 13 June 1980; Viv Hardwick, 'Why no outpatients' department?', *Milton Keynes Gazette*, 20 June 1980; *Milton Keynes Gazette*, 30 March 1984, 'Our hospital', a 12-page special.

33 Milton Keynes Urban Studies Centre, *Notes on Milton Keynes* (Milton Keynes: MKUSC, 1981), p. 24.

34 For Beanhill, see MKBC, *People and Work in Milton Keynes: A Profile of Settlements from the 1991 Census, 10% Sample, Part 2* (Milton Keynes: MKBC, 1993), p. 14; MKBC, *People and Housing in Milton Keynes: A Profile of Settlements from the 1991 Census* (Milton Keynes: MKBC, 1993), p. 27. For Netherfield, see MKBC, *People and Work in Milton Keynes: A Profile of Settlements from the 1991 Census, 10% Sample, Part 2*, p. 98; MKBC, *People and Housing in Milton Keynes: A Profile of Settlements from the 1991 Census*, p. 155.

35 Anon., 'Tenants let off steam about complaints', *Milton Keynes Express*, 22 April 1977.

36 Viv Hardwick, 'Rooftop prowler target for Beanhill vigilantes', *Milton Keynes Gazette*, 5 December, 1975.

37 Will Bull, 'We want a decent roof over our heads, Beanhill tenants tell corporation', *Milton Keynes Express*, 22 October 1981.

38 Debbie Walshaw, 'Residents warm to flat roof victory', *Milton Keynes Mirror*, 26 May 1988; Corinna O'Neill, 'Three year plan to raise local roofs', *Milton Keynes Citizen*, 26 May 1988.

39 Charles Nevin, 'Myth and Milton Keynes', *Guardian*, 29–30 July 1989.

40 Alan Francis, Milton Keynes Green Party, letter, *Milton Keynes Gazette*, 21 January 1993; Anon., 'Campaign to preserve child abuse centre', *Milton Keynes Herald and Post*, 7 January 1993.

41 Sally Murrer, 'Residents rally to save "heartbeat" of Beanhill', *Milton Keynes Gazette*, 7 January 1993.

42 See photograph in *Milton Keynes Herald*, 7 January 1993.

43 Nicola Jarvis, 'Estate mums bid to improve safety', *Milton Keynes Gazette*, 13 November 1981.

44 MKBC, *People and Housing in Milton Keynes: A Profile of Settlements from the 1991 Census*, p. 99; MKBC, *People and Work in Milton Keynes: A Profile of Settlements from the 1991 Census; 10% Sample*, p. 65.

45 MKBC, *People and Housing in Milton Keynes: A Profile of Settlements from the 1991 Census*, p. 163; MKBC, *People and Work in Milton Keynes: A Profile of Settlements from the 1991 Census; 10% Sample, Part 2*, p. 104.

46 Anon., 'Battle stepped up for local chemist', *Standard*, 18 April 1986; Anon., 'Committee comes up with right diagnosis', *Milton Keynes Citizen*, 19 February 1987; Anon., 'Delight over victory in surgery campaign', *Milton Keynes Citizen*, 3 December 1986.

47 Dave Evans, 'Survey reveals massive demand for new GP', *Milton Keynes Herald*, 20 February 1987.

48 S. McKenzie and D. Rose, 'Industrial change, the domestic economy and home life', in Jo Little, Linda Peake and Pat Richardson (eds), *Women in Cities: Gender and the Urban Environment* (London: Macmillan, 1988), p. 35.

49 This discussion of Greentown is based upon 'Greentown: David Lock's papers', held at the City Discovery Centre, Bradwell Abbey, Milton Keynes. See also Godfrey Boyle, 'Whatever happened to Greentown?,' *Town and Country Planning*, June 1987, pp. 176–8.

50 Thorns, *Fragmenting Societies*, p. 263.

51 This account is based upon articles and letters in the following newspapers: *The Milton Keynes Citizen*, 23 July 1987; *Milton Keynes Gazette*, 13 August 1987; 27 August 1987, 7 January 1988, 21 January 1988; *Milton Keynes Herald*, 12 February 1988. On Willen's socio-economic profile, see MKBC, *People and Housing in Milton Keynes: A Profile of*

Settlements from the 1991 Census, p. 227, and MKBC, *People and Work in Milton Keynes: A Profile of Settlements from the 1991 Census; 10% Sample*, p. 137.

52   David Firnberg and David West, 'Milton Keynes: creating an information technology environment', in William H. Dutton, J. G. Blumler and Kenneth L. Kraemer (eds), *Wired Cities: Shaping the Future of Communications* (London: Cassell, 1987), pp. 392–408.

53   Jeremy Seabrook, 'Milton Keynes: a mirror of England', *Observer Magazine*, 5 February 1978.

54   Trevor Blackwell and Jeremy Seabrook, *A World Still to Win: The Reconstruction of the Postwar Working Class* (London: Faber & Faber, 1985). A strong critical appraisal of Seabrook's historicism as opposed to his historical understanding is provided by Huw Beynon, 'Jeremy Seabrook and the British working class', *The Socialist Register, 1982* (London: Merlin, 1982), pp. 285–301.

55   Joanna Bourke, *Working Class Cultures in Britain, 1890–1960: Gender, Class and Ethnicity* (London: Routledge, 1994), p. 159.

56   Llewelyn-Davies, Weeks, Forestier-Walker and Bor, *Milton Keynes Plan: Interim Report to MKDC* (London: Llewelyn-Davies *et al.*, 1968), p. 141.

9

Conclusion

At the end, some specificities of Milton Keynes emerge. Most interesting is the view that in this city the apparent paradox between nature and artificiality has been resolved; the concrete cows have become real and Milton Keynes is both town and country.
Sebastian Loew, 'Concrete facts and urban myths', *Times Higher Education Supplement*, 8 January 1999

The city has a growing number of radical supporters, among them Mr. Tim Mars, popularly known as 'the guru of Milton Keynes' and the author of a privately-produced tour brochure on the region. 'I liked the city so much I lived there', says Mr. Mars. [He] believes the city's lifestyle is closest to that of California, but with parks and lakes replacing the beach. [In] Milton Keynes he finds a definition of the aspirations of many of its residents: life is private, mobile, rural, and close to the city. It is certainly true for the people who live in this gentle garden suburb, life is less stressful, healthier and more efficient than for the vast majority of Britain's citizens.
Jim Kelly, 'Residents determined to have the last laugh', *Financial Times*, 3 April 1992

Aha! Cult TV comedy character Alan Partridge was originally intended to come from Milton Keynes. Steve Coogan's Norwich-based gormless sports reporter and chat show host has recently hit the national headlines, accused of making Norwich a national joke. But *mknews* can today reveal that Partridge was originally earmarked to come not from Norwich, but from MK. A Coogan source said: 'The natural choice was Milton Keynes. But it was rejected because it was too much of a cliché, what with the concrete cows, roundabouts, etc.'
Anon., 'Partridge originally planned as MK man', *mknews*, 11 December 2002

ACHIEVEMENTS AND SHORTCOMINGS

During the 1940s the popular historian Sir Arthur Mee described the village of Milton Keynes and its rustic location. 'It lies among meadows', wrote Mee, 'through which wind the Ouzel and its tributary brooks, and has thatched cottages which must have looked for centuries much as they look today.'[1]

Many of the housing areas of Milton Keynes still lie among meadows, and the rivers still flow through the new city. It could have been a more concretised place, but instead MK became a suburban garden city. This city also transcended the usual blandness and lack-of-things-to-do of which new suburbs are so often accused. Yet like so many suburban areas, it is a low-density environment. As noted in an earlier chapter, it was not deliberately planned to become what it has become, but that is what happened.

The origins and the major intentions of the *Plan for Milton Keynes* were discussed in Chapter 2. When we relate those intentions to the subsequent development of the new city, it is reasonable to conclude, and two planning historians based in Canada, Robert Shipley and Steven Gammon, have recently done so, that the Plan, and the implementation of the Plan, was broadly if not completely successful in fulfilling most of its goals.[2] These are as follows.

One main intention was to build a city that offered opportunity and freedom of choice in housing, education and work. There has been a considerable variety in housing, as noted in earlier chapters. Furthermore, the popularity of and satisfaction with much vernacular housing cannot be denied. It explains to a large degree why Milton Keynes has been generally, and genuinely, well liked by the majority of its residents.

Education has also been a major arena of increased opportunity. Milton Keynes has embraced the world-famous Open University, and many new, and some very large, schools and colleges. As we saw in Chapter 8, those schools were often locales for sociability as well as education. The number and variety of jobs in Milton Keynes also multiplied rapidly, and the new city was a growth area when other regions were in economic difficulty. And in terms of easy movement, easy access and good communications, the roads and the cars upon them describe a population able to achieve most or all of their choices. Public transport has, however, been a relative failure.

The Plan had also set out to provide an attractive city, which most people in Milton Keynes agree has occurred, as was noted in Chapters 3 and 6. And as Shipley and Gammon note, the parklands of the new city have been an undoubted success. Buildings, of course, are essential to the urban environment, and here the findings are more mixed. The architectural quality of many buildings is high, but in some it is low. Hence the attractiveness of many public and commercial buildings, and some rational housing, is 'debated', a point borne out by findings in Chapters 3 and 6.

Furthermore, the aim of the Plan to produce a socially active and participatory city has also been acknowledged by Shipley and Gammon, and Chapter 8 in this book strongly supports them. In addition, social balance, in terms of occupational class, was also emphasised by the plan. Certainly the number and range of jobs in the new city provided the structural basis for a population that closely, if not exactly, fitted the occupational profile of the South East of England. But social balance also incorporates age and ethnicity. Milton Keynes manifested considerable and growing ethnic diversity, although some groups appeared to be as disadvantaged as in older cities, a point discussed in Chapter 7. As for age, however, Milton Keynes was increasingly an 'older' city by the year 2000, albeit one with a younger population profile than the national average.

Certainly there have been problems, but the flexibility of the plan was proven to be its chief strength:

> From the standpoint of planning history, it can be argued that the case of Milton Keynes is an example of the efficacy of long range comprehensive planning, where fairly specific goals are set out and adhered to in the implementation of the plan. Since a great deal of long range planning today begins with 'visioning', which at least in part is supposed to involve goal setting, the lessons from Milton Keynes can be useful. In the final analysis, however, it is the close to 200,000 people who have 'voted with their feet' to live in Milton Keynes who are the best judges of the plan's success.[3]

THE NEGATIVE IMAGE PERSISTS

Why emphasise these aspects of Milton Keynes in the conclusion? The reason for this is twofold. First, as the initial chapter emphasised, Milton Keynes still has an image problem. In some cases this can be quite amusing. On its 'Map of the Shittish Isles', a free supplement with *Viz* comic's *Summer Special* in 2001, Milton Keynes appeared to summarise all that was smelly and rotten about Britain: the new city alone was represented by a singular steaming turd. Other towns, however, were represented by a famous local landmark and a steaming turd. Perhaps a steaming concrete cow pat would have been the most effective signifier, next to the shopping building or The Point or the new theatre.

The television comedian Steve Coogan may think the image of Milton Keynes is a cliché,[4] but that cliché unfortunately still continues to be evident in contemporary English literature. On 23 November 2001, BBC Radio 4 broadcasted Arnold Wesker's first play for over 20 years. In *Groupie*, the main characters were an artist, who lives in London, a man in constant engagement with the ups and downs of life. The other character, played by the well-known actress Barbara Windsor, was a rather sad woman, lacking in self-esteem. She lived a vicarious twilight existence, and she lived it in Milton Keynes. It was only when she read the autobiography of the artist that she realised they had shared a childhood in the East End of London. In corresponding with and eventually meeting with this awkward but fun-loving painter in London, she began to live life more fully. They both went for walks in London, and reminisced about life in the old East End, reviving their memories of Brick Lane, the old market, the local characters and so on. These were the location of Wesker's earlier works. What the play unwittingly transmitted was an impression that, in 20 years, Wesker had not really moved on in the way that both London and Milton Keynes have moved on.

The following quote comes from Tim Lott, 'a West London-based writer' whose novel *Rumours of a Hurricane* is set in Fulham, West London, and Milton Keynes. The novel portrays the life of a skilled printer – 'Charlie' – who thought he had 'a job for life' until Mrs Thatcher, and her ideology, was elected to power in 1979. With his wife, Charlie moves from London to Milton Keynes in 1980, after he has seen the television advertisements of Milton Keynes Development Corporation. The wide open spaces, clean streets and nice new housing appeal greatly to him. Subsequently, however, he suffers a broken marriage, loneliness, unemployment, a failed retail business, and death resulting from a horrific road accident.[5] 'The book starts off in a Fulham council estate', writes Lott:

And it's really a look at the Eighties from the perspective of a normal guy, a kind of worm's eye view of a decade when there was huge social change taking place. I chose Milton Keynes because anonymous soulless places like that represent that time for me. It was the first time when mobility became huge and people were moving around a lot. A huge number of people moved from London to places like Milton Keynes in an attempt to leave the inner cities, only to discover they were now living somewhere that was even grimmer.[6]

These are unoriginal and inaccurate views about Milton Keynes masquerading as meaningful literary insights. For one thing, increased mobility did not begin anew during the 1980s; it went back decades. And such terms as 'anonymous' and 'soulless' might be applied to anywhere new where one does not live. Surface readings of Milton Keynes are still made too readily.

THE RELEVANCE OF MILTON KEYNES TO CONTEMPORARY DEBATES ABOUT THE FUTURE OF ENGLISH TOWNS AND CITIES

There is, however, a further and more important reason to draw attention to what is generally popular and successful about Milton Keynes: this is because Milton Keynes is ignored or woefully misunderstood in current professional and political debates about England's so-called 'urban renaissance'. Within these debates, the fashionable movement among famous architects and some town planners called 'new urbanism' defines itself against suburbanism. New urbanism privileges high-density housing and public transport, and likes to 'cram' people into living spaces. 'Cramming' is one of the favourite words in the new urbanist lexicon.

Architects with new urbanist credentials, and also with considerable international reputations, have not really been favourable in their judgements of the new city. Harley Sherlock, for example, whilst acknowledging the careful and attractive planting and the successful road system, is nonetheless dismissive of the idea that Milton Keynes can be any sort of model for future urbanisation. 'By no stretch of the imagination', writes Sherlock, 'is it a city in any usual sense of the word':

> Spread out as it is, it is not only extravagant of land, it is also extravagant of fuel, because every 'local' journey is a comparatively long one. Therefore, although it is an interesting experiment and liked by

many of its inhabitants, Milton Keynes cannot be seen as a proto-type for the cities of an environmentally-conscious twenty-first century.[7]

And he goes on to mention the 'scattered communities' of Milton Keynes, as if they existed away and in isolation from each other, and beyond the networks that make up urban living. In a book with a picture of London's Soho on the cover, Sherlock simply never expresses approval of low-density cities. Real cities, by implication, are not like Milton Keynes at all: they are busy and crowded, vibrant with density, and more compact, like Berlin or Bologna. The fact that Milton Keynes is 'different' is taken as an excuse to side-step its achievements rather than to fully acknowl-edge them, although Sherlock did at least admit to its popularity with its residents. Yet despite this important point, there is no real sense in which the lessons of Milton Keynes are being objectively assessed in current debates about urban renewal. Richard Rogers, otherwise known as Lord Rogers of Riverside, and the Head of the Labour government's so-called 'Urban Task Force', has declared himself an enemy of low-density English suburbs and new towns. It is perhaps unsurprising, then, that the Urban Task Force's 1998 Report, *Towards an Urban Renaissance*, with its preface by a former Mayor of Barcelona, ignores Milton Keynes.[8]

As David Lock has argued, however, the issue about densities in general and about densities in Milton Keynes in particular, is a complex one. Lock is a town planner, who worked for Milton Keynes Development Corporation from 1978 to 1981. He is one of the few ex-members of MKDC who has actually lived in Milton Keynes; he has been there since 1977. Lock has argued passion-ately against the view that people in English towns and cities deserve to live in increasingly crammed environments, something that Lord Rogers and others have repeatedly called for.[9] Lock is also nuanced and realistic about the issue of densities in Milton Keynes, for, as he observes, taken as a whole Milton Keynes is a low-density city, but the housing estates are not necessarily thinly spread with people and accommodation. 'There is a myth in England', argues Lock:

> that the densities of MK are very low, that it's a sprawling spread-out place, and everybody from the Secretary of State to one's aunt in Stoke on Trent has the same prejudice about MK. And this does intrigue me, because we spent a lot of time in the corporation on the issue of density. It mattered very much to us because of the rate [at]

which we had to work out how much land we needed each year to meet our goals. So density was an issue [because] you couldn't find a common agreement about how you measured it. Is it net density? Is it gross density? Is it town density? Is it gridsquare density? Is it people per hectare? [Taken] as a whole, the city is generously endowed with parks and playing fields and woodlands and so on, so the density of the town [may] be relatively low. But the actual density of the living areas is relatively high.[10]

Average densities in Milton Keynes have grown at about 18 to 24 houses or dwellings per acre. These are high by American standards, but low in comparison with European cities or with Tokyo, for example.[11] Ultimately, however, most English people do not want to be crammed in, but they do want to live in sociable towns and cities. Most people do not mind high-ish densities, even if they prefer lower ones, but they do not wish to inhabit high-density areas that are mixed-use and avowedly urban environments. They like the city-in-the-country ethos of Milton Keynes: findings in previous chapters demonstrate that most people want space and light and air, houses with gardens, nice parks, fast roads and they also want the attractions of a vibrant city centre. But they want these attractions at a convenient distance, not in the same street.

Does that make MK any less of a city than 'traditional' cities? The answer to that question is a resounding 'no'. It is not at all difficult to counteract any argument that Milton Keynes somehow lacks what 'real' cities possess. The eminent Danish architect and writer Steen Eiler Rasmussen was both an Anglophile and a London-phile. He revelled in the liveliness and architectural diversity of England's great cities. He was also deeply interested in Milton Keynes, which he viewed as an original heir to Ebenezer Howard's garden city movement and to a number of other influences in English life: the love of villagey residential areas, and the penchant for neat, square buildings and houses. Furthermore, when it came to the relationship of town planning to social evolution, he warned against any attempt to remove the flexibility that had informed the original *Plan for Milton Keynes* by opting for more radical new directions. He also emphasised the fact that, in addition to the newness, there were, and remain, some attractive old parts, and that the designated area as a whole contained a huge level of diversity. 'If the building of Milton Keynes is not disturbed too much by pre-conceived ideas of what a city should be like', he wrote in the early 1990s:

but implemented with consistency, it should be a city that could satisfy all the needs of the town dwellers and have a greater variety of things to offer than most cities in the world. From the city centre, the great mart, which is the core of city life, you can go down to the residential squares. Each is a neat, little local town with all its little houses and gardens, but with a protecting backdrop of great trees, full of bird life. You can come to working places, to the Open University, to all sorts of social activities. You can also drop into real provincial towns like Stony Stratford, or into the old villages which, with their churches, pubs and greens, adapt themselves to the city as has, for instance, Bethnal Green to London. And you can feel at ease in the linear parks.

Rasmussen also went on to argue that all social strata have been attracted to Milton Keynes, that a social mix had been established in just a few decades: 'the city is, after all, not the roads, trees and houses, but the people'.[12]

Professor Sir Peter Hall, Chairman of the Town and Country Planning Association, argued forcefully in 1999 in favour of Rasmussen. Hall emphasised Rasmussen's awareness of the popularity of suburban living in the capital, and by implication in England more generally. For Hall, the careful preservation of adequate as opposed to high densities should be a paramount consideration in current planning debates. And the new towns and the suburbs should be central to the wider discussion about urban regeneration, not marginal to it.[13]

These debates will affect how Milton Keynes, this aesthetically unique city, will shape up in the short to medium term. For it is clear that Milton Keynes cannot escape them. Demographic change alone ensures this. As a consequence of government rethinking about population growth and population change during the 1990s, there is to be more building of higher-density homes in new housing areas in Milton Keynes and also in the central areas. The new city will also expand spatially beyond its original borders. This change of approach was engendered not only by population growth estimates, but also by changes in household composition. For a growing percentage of single-only or couple-only homes has been forecast to continue into the twenty-first century, as a consequence of divorce, of an ageing of the population and of many people increasingly choosing not to marry and not to have children. The statistics for Milton Keynes for the year 2000 illustrated that household composition in the new city was quite close to the national picture. Moreover, the earlier pattern of a predominance of couples with children, a pattern that had characterised so much suburban and new town housing during the twentieth century, was no longer the case in this suburban city. For example, 'single people households' made up 24 per cent, or one-quarter, of all household types in Milton Keynes by 2000. And 30 per cent of homes contained 'people under 65 without children', and that mostly meant couples. That was the largest group of household types in Milton Keynes after 30 years of growth. The second largest was 'people under 65 with children', which really meant a couple with one or more offspring. They amounted to 28.5 per cent. Single people with children were still a small percentage of the city's households, at less than 7 per cent. What was clear from these statistics was the variety of housing required for such groups, most of which were set to increase in large numbers. By the year 2011, the city council predicted, the city's population would rise to 209,000, and that would require a further 18,000 dwellings to be built.[14]

Milton Keynes will need to continue to build a variety of housing types to accommodate this growing and changing population profile, and also to keep the city looking interesting. Hence a new development plan is currently being debated. It will increase densities across the city, especially in the city centre, which will be quite markedly redesigned and redeveloped.[15]

Any assessment of how far the future of Milton Keynes may be understood from its early and recent past is not really an exercise for historians. There do appear, however, to be clear, almost unambiguous lessons in the brief but profound history of the city. Those who seek to alter the future of Milton Keynes should not ignore them, because thus far, and as a consequence of both contingency and design, Milton Keynes has worked, and this was in no small part because the plans laid by MKDC between 1967 and 1970 were flexible. Flexibility was a major force for mitigating unforeseen or difficult problems that might arise. Unfortunately the new orthodoxy of assumption against the motor car and against low densities appears to be inflexible.

All of this raises some interesting questions for the future of Milton Keynes. Walking is a popular form of exercise, for example, and economically sustainable. And most people in Milton Keynes can walk freely about the city, on paths or redways. So why should motor cars be viewed as enemies of walking cities, when the experience of Milton Keynes, and of most other cities for that matter, suggests two important things? First, most people cannot or will not do without their cars. And second, with careful design, fast roads can be incorporated into cities to facilitate uncluttered motorised transportation.

Ultimately, the preferences of people in Milton Keynes suggest that people want to drive cars, walk and take buses and trains when it suits them. Failure to acknowledge this flexibility and diversity counteracts not simply some of the principles of the original plan, but the expansive and mobile lifestyles that emerged in Milton Keynes and which are shared by most people in other urban areas.[16] This is a reminder of the 'edge city' living that Milton Keynes satisfies.

And it is right here that the experience of Milton Keynes should be central, not marginal, to current debates about urban regeneration. For in a city with an aggregate low density, and because that low density is popular, great care will have to be taken not to spoil this fragile ecology. Milton Keynes thus poses a key question for the merchants of high-density new urbanism.

Conversely, however, this is a city where public transport may require higher densities to make it viable. Hence new urbanism in fact raises a challenge for Milton Keynes. Consequently, this city is on the edge in another key sense: it is on the knife-edge of an apparent contradictory pull between more-of-the-same and something quite different. Perhaps a carefully plotted and planned middle way is the most sensitive solution, where flexibility and information-for-policy to guide future development remain leading principles in the future evolution of the new city. Perhaps even a rejection of new urbanism is required? As a student of architecture from Cambridge University has argued, 'each town has to be considered individually', and Milton Keynes especially so: 'In MK we need to reinforce local optimism by discarding new urbanism values and encouraging it to become the best of what it was meant to be.'[17] It is a compelling point for consideration because, as noted above, low densities, flexibility and car usage do not sit easily with the defining principles of new urbanism.

So, are the planning lessons from Milton Keynes really to be ignored or denigrated by architects and urban design experts? After all, Milton Keynes was and remains a predominantly suburban city, in a country whose inhabitants are predominantly suburbanites and who, in the face of official or intellectual dismay, continue to flock to the suburbs and to new housing estates.[18] Hence Milton Keynes crystallises new suburban living in multicultural England. But Richard Rogers and other urban mould makers fail to adequately explain and provide for this popular phenomenon. Reports by a number of researchers and experts on urban affairs have emphasised that contempt for suburbia at the heart of Rogers's 'vision' evidences an elitist disdain for people's residential preferences.[19]

And here, we can see the myopia of Rogers and others who ignore Milton Keynes, and we can see this myopia in two connected ways. If Milton Keynes is to have a sustainable future it seems crazy to ignore the lessons of its past. And if English cities are to be popular and happy places, it is unwise to ignore the lessons from Milton Keynes.

A CITY OF OUR TIME

An earlier chapter noted the references to the Minoan double-headed axe and the implicit similarities between the laid-back Minoan palace cities and Milton Keynes. Some of the planners who suggested this Minoan symbolism were at the height of their powers during the 1950s and 1960s, decades when there was considerable intellectual discovery about Minoan civilisation. These discoveries resulted from both archaeology in Crete and from the cracking of Linear B, the hitherto untranslated script of the Minoans. Michael Ventris, the Englishman who achieved this feat during the early 1950s, used a grid of characters to assist their syllabic decoding. By repeatedly placing and rearranging characters on the grid, he hoped to expose the phonetic meaning of Linear B. Ultimately, however, although the grid was a useful tool, it took both intuition and cultural understanding to crack the enigma.[20]

The grid in Milton Keynes has been used by many a writer to make only a superficial de-coding of the city and its apparent soullessness. But what those writers wilfully or unwittingly misinterpreted was the point that the motorised movement and access encouraged by the grid was the key to community and connection, not its antithesis. The continuing criticisms of public transport in Milton Keynes, therefore, reveal no desire to be based continuously at home in the gridsquare. Rather, they show that, in a low-density city, those without a car or with mobility problems want to be able to get about as easily as possible. The grid thus reveals an aspiration for movement and for meaningful connection with the social, cultural and economic life of the city. And within the grid itself, an informed understanding of the new city's culture reveals why people continue to migrate to Milton Keynes, and why they chose to stay there. Housing, environment and opportunity, and the desire to live in meaningful networks of people, remained at the heart of this mass resettlement in Milton Keynes. And they remained the major reasons why most people changed their home in late-twentieth-century England.

England has moved away from the industrial era. The offices, shops, employment parks and suburban housing of Milton Keynes reveal the dominant forces sweeping through the social, economic and urban landscapes of England since the 1960s. Milton Keynes is thus at the heart of the new suburban landscapes of England. Hence, in addition to its relevance to town planning debates about our immediate future, it can also tell us much about the changes and developments of our recent history. For this reason, too, it will be the subject of further historical analysis and evaluation in years to come.

NOTES

1 Arthur Mee, *Buckinghamshire: Country of the Chiltern Hills* (London: Hodder & Stoughton, 1947), p. 191.
2 Robert Shipley and Steven Gammon, 'The six planning goals of Milton Keynes: a third decade report card', *Planning History*, 24, 1 (2002), pp. 36–45.
3 Shipley and Gammon, 'The six', p. 43.
4 However, the issue of *mknews* for 11 December 2002 also states that 'Ironically, as revealed in *mknews* recently, Coogan's next major TV project is Milton Keynes-based.'
5 Tim Lott, *Rumours of a Hurricane* (London: Penguin, 2002).
6 Tim Lott, *Interview*, 5 January 2001, www.mychelsea.net/chelsea/arts-timlott.html.
7 Harley Sherlock, *Cities Are Good For Us* (London: Paladin, 1991), pp. 93, 247.
8 Urban Task Force, *Towards an Urban Renaissance* (London: Spon, 1998).
9 David Lister, 'Labour peer Rogers sets out his vision for an urban revolution', *Independent*, 21 May 1997; Richard Rogers, 'Save our cities', *Observer*, 13 February 2000; Richard Rogers and Richard Burdett, 'Let's cram more into the city', *New Statesman*, 22 May 2000, p. 25; Richard Rogers and Richard Burdett, 'Let's cram more into the city', in Marcial Echenique and Andrew Saint (eds), *Cities for the New Millennium* (London: Span, 2001) pp. 9–14.
10 Mark Clapson, Mervyn Dobbin and Peter Waterman, *The Best Laid Plans: Milton Keynes since 1967* (Luton: Luton University Press, 1998), pp. 45–6.
11 Clapson, Dobbin and Waterman, *Best Laid Plans*, p. 46. Ralph Rugoff, 'Inside the virtual city', *The Business, Financial Times Weekend Magazine*, 22 January 2000.
12 Steen Eiler Rasmussen, 'Reflections on Milton Keynes', in Derek Walker (ed.), *Architectural Design Profile No. 111: New Towns* (London: Architectural Design, 1994), p. 13.
13 Peter Hall, *Sustainable Cities or Town Cramming?* (London: Town and Country Planning Association, 1999), *passim*.
14 Milton Keynes Council, *Population Bulletin, 2000/2001* (Milton Keynes: Milton Keynes Council, 2000), pp. 4, 8, 23; these figures will be revised upwards.
15 The main agencies for this are EDAW Planning, English Partnerships, Milton Keynes Council and Central Milton Keynes Partnerships. See www.mkweb.co.uk.

16 See Deyan Sudjic, *The Hundred Mile City* (London: Andre Deutsch, 1992). The local newspapers have touched upon this theme: Anon., 'Is MK now just a London suburb?', *Citizen*, 4 January 2001.

17 Simon James Gould, 'The evolution of the public realm in Milton Keynes: from a decentralised to a centralised urbanism' (Cambridge: unpublished dissertation for the Diploma in Architecture, Cambridge Universtiy, 2002), p. 38.

18 Brian Groom, 'Suburbs face population boom', *Financial Times*, 5–6 December 1998.

19 Michael Gwilliam, Caroline Bourne, Corinne Swain and Anna Prat, *Sustainable Renewal of Suburban Areas* (York: Joseph Rowntree Foundation, 1998); Katie Williams, 'The wrong starting point', *Town and Country Planning*, September 1999, p. 263.

20 Andrew Robinson, *The Man Who Deciphered Linear B* (London: Thames and Hudson, 2002).

References

Aaronovitch, David, *Paddling to Jerusalem: An Aquatic Tour of Our Small Country* (London: Fourth Estate, 2000).

Anon., 'A "pop" interim report to everyone', *North Bucks Times*, 22 January 1969.

Anon., 'Anxiety about new city sprawl', *North Bucks Times*, 18 December, 1968. Anon.,

'Anxiety about new city sprawl', *Bletchley Gazette*, 20 December 1968.

Anon., 'Battle in Bucks', *The Times*, 1 July 1966.

Anon., 'Battle stepped up for local chemist', *Milton Keynes Standard*, 18 April 1986.

Anon., 'Bitter blow to many farmers', *North Bucks Times*, 18 January 1967.

Anon., 'Campaign to preserve child abuse centre', *Milton Keynes Herald and Post*, 7 January 1993.

Anon., 'City's assurances to the villages', *North Bucks Times*, 15 April 1970.

Anon., 'Committee comes up with right diagnosis', *Milton Keynes Citizen*, 19 February 1987.

Anon., 'Council's growing problem', *Milton Keynes Citizen*, 2 November 2002.

Anon., 'Delight over victory in surgery campaign', *Milton Keynes Citizen*, 3 December 1986.

Anon., 'Farmer will emigrate', *The Times*, 13 January 1967.

Anon., 'Farmers protest at new city plans', *Slough Express*, 4 December 1964.

Anon., 'Farmers ready to go to jail', *Bletchley Gazette*, 26 January 1967.

Anon., 'Farmers to fight new town plan', *The Times*, 15 April 1966.

Anon., 'Farmers worried by new city', *The Times*, 20 January 1969.

Anon., 'Fight is still on, says NFU', *North Bucks Times*, 1 February 1967.

Anon., 'Is MK now just a London suburb?', *Milton Keynes Citizen*, 4 January 2001.

Anon., 'Milton Keynes is her name', *North Bucks Times*, 1 February 1967.

Anon., 'Milton Keynes: a dreadful warning', *Time Out*, 22–29 October 1972.

Anon., 'New city plan', *North Bucks Times*, 12 February 1969.

Anon., 'Our estate is neglected', *Milton Keynes Sunday Citizen*, 20 June 1999.

Anon., 'Planners quizzed on new city proposals', *North Bucks Times*, 12 February 1969.

Anon., 'Planning: North Bucks Monster', *New Society*, 19 January 1967, p. 95.

Anon., 'Problem estate was originally built with children in mind', *Milton Keynes on Sunday*, 28 September 1997.

Anon., '"Sit tight" advice to city farmers', *North Bucks Times*, 10 July 1968.

Anon., 'Storyteller: Jack's view of city goes on TV – nationwide', *Milton Keynes Mirror*, 10 August 1977.

Anon., 'Tenant farmers: at least five years compensation', *Bletchley Gazette*, 24 February 1967.

Anon., 'Tenants let off steam about complaints', *Milton Keynes Express*, 22 April 1977.

Anon., 'They look before they come', *North Bucks Times*, 12 June 1968.

Anon., 'Unions face city test', *Milton Keynes Gazette*, 14 May 1987.

Anon., 'We deplore land loss but will pull together', *North Bucks Times*, 18 January 1967.

Bainbridge, Beryl, *English Journey, or, The Road to Milton Keynes* (New York: Carroll and Graf, 1997).

Barker, Paul, 'Though un-English and much sneered at, Milton Keynes is a success' [etc.], *New Statesman*, 4 October 1996.

Barnard, Peter, 'All revved up and no place to go', *The Times Saturday Review*, 18 January 1992.

Bassett, Philip, 'The state of the (Milton Keynes) union', *Financial Times*, 9 May 1987.

Beauchamp, Suzanne, 'Social development' (1969) reprinted in Mark Clapson, Mervyn Dobbin and Peter Waterman (eds), *The Best Laid Plans: Milton Keynes since 1967* (Luton: Luton University Press, 1998).

Bell, Daniel, 'The coming of the post-industrial society', in Jencks, Charles (ed.), *The Post-Modern Reader* (London: Academy, 1992).

Bendixson, Terence and Platt, John, *Milton Keynes: Image and Reality* (Cambridge: Granta, 1992).

Best, John, 'Milton Keynes: maturing new town or regional adolescent', *Town and Country Planning*, February 2001.

Beynon, Huw, 'Jeremy Seabrook and the British working class', *The Socialist Register, 1982* (London: Merlin, 1982), pp. 285–301.

Bibby, Andrew, 'Milton Keynes is twenty something', *Independent*, 18 January 1992.

Binding, Chris, 'Angry farmers warn: we shoot to kill', *Milton Keynes Gazette*, 14 February 1975.

Bishop, Jeff, *Milton Keynes: The Best of Both Worlds? Public and Professional Views of a New City* (Bristol: School of Advanced Urban Studies, 1986).

Blackwell, Trevor and Seabrook, Jeremy, *A World Still to Win: The Reconstruction of the Postwar Working Class* (London: Faber & Faber, 1985).

Booker, Christopher, *The Seventies: Portrait of a Decade* (Harmondsworth: Penguin, 1980).

Bor, Walter, testimony in Mark Clapson, Mervyn Dobbin and Peter Waterman (eds), *The Best Laid Plans: Milton Keynes since 1967* (Luton: Luton University Press, 1998).

Bourke, Joanna, *Working Class Cultures in Britain, 1890–1960: Gender, Class and Ethnicity* (London: Routledge, 1994).

Bowlby, Sophie, 'From corner shop to hypermarket: women and food retailing', in Jo Little, Linda Peake and Pat Richardson (eds), *Women in Cities: Gender and the Urban Environment* (London: Macmillan, 1988).

Boyd, F. and Evans, L., *American Paintings* (London: Nicola Barker and Angela Flowers Gallery, 2000).

Boyle, Godfrey, 'Whatever happened to Greentown?' *Town and Country Planning*, June 1987.

Brace, Matthew, 'How Milton Keynes has become "Little Hong Kong"', *Independent*, 6 July 1998.

Brinig, Denise, 'What it's really like to live in Milton Keynes', *Over 21*, July 1978.

Brooks, Caroline, 'The Lakes Estate, Bletchley: a case study of a GLC overspill development built on Radburn principles' (Oxford: Oxford Brookes University, unpublished project, Diploma in Town Planning, 1991).

Bryson, Bill, *Notes From a Small Island* (London: Black Swan, 1996).

Buckinghamshire County Council, *North Bucks New City: CDA and Designation, 1 – Written Statement* (Aylesbury: Buckinghamshire County Council, not dated). Buckinghamshire County Council, *North Bucks New City: CDA and Designation, 2*

– *Report* (Aylesbury: Buckinghamshire County Council, not dated).

Bull, Will, 'We want a decent roof over our heads, Beanhill tenants tell corporation', *Milton Keynes Express*, 22 October 1981.

Burnett, John, *A Social History of Housing, 1815–1985* (London: Routledge, 1991).

Cadogan, Gerald, *Palaces of Minoan Crete* (London: Methuen and New York, 1980).

Campbell, Beatrix, *Wigan Pier Revisited: Poverty and Politics in the '80s* (London: Virago, 1984).

Cato, Muriel, '"I'm all right here" says Jack', *Milton Keynes Express*, 18 November 1977.

Champion, A. G. and Green, A. E., *In Search of Britain's Booming Towns: An Index of Local Economic Performance for Britain* (Newcastle: Centre for Urban and Regional Development Studies, 1985).

Chant, Colin, 'Greece: urbanisation in the Aegean region', in Colin Chant and David Goodman (eds), *Pre-industrial Cities and Technology* (London: Routledge, 1999).

Charlesworth, Julie and Cochrane, Allan, 'Tales of the suburbs: the local politics of growth in the South-East of England', *Urban Studies*, 31, 10 (1994).

Charlesworth, Julie and Cochrane, Allan, 'Anglicising the American Dream: tragedy, farce and the "post-modern" city', draft of conference paper presented to the British Sociological Association Conference 1995: 'Contested Cities', University of Leicester, 10–13 April 1995.

Charlesworth, Julie and Cochrane, Allan, 'American Dreams and English Utopias', in Mark Clapson, Mervyn Dobbin and Peter Waterman (eds), *The Best Laid Plans: Milton Keynes since 1967* (Luton: Luton University Press, 1998).

Chave, S. P. W., 'Mental health in Harlow new town', *Journal of Psychosomatic Research*, 10, 1966.

Cherry, Gordon, *Town Planning in Britain since 1900* (Oxford: Blackwell, 1996).

City Discovery Centre, *Milton Keynes: The Development of a New City* (Milton Keynes: City Discovery Centre, 1993)

City Discovery Centre and Town and Country Planning Association, *Economic Development: The Milton Keynes Experience* (Milton Keynes: CDC/TCPA, 1988).

Clapson, Mark, *Invincible Green Suburbs, Brave New Towns: Social Change and Urban Dispersal in Postwar England* (Manchester: Manchester University Press, 1998)

Clapson, Mark, 'Technology, social change, and the planning of a post-industrial city: a case study of Milton Keynes', in David Goodman and Colin Chant (eds), *European Cities and Technology: Industrial to Post-Industrial City* (London: Routledge, 1999).

Clapson, Mark, 'Suburbia and party politics', *History Today*, September 2001.

Clapson, Mark, Dobbin, Mervyn and Waterman, Peter (eds), *The Best Laid Plans: Milton Keynes since 1967* (Luton: University of Luton Press, 1998).

Clarke, John and Critcher, Chas, *The Devil Makes Work: Leisure in Capitalist Britain* (London: Macmillan, 1985)

Coles, Wayne, 'Now Bill loves the city', *Milton Keynes Citizen*, 19 October 2000.

Commerce Business Directories, *Milton Keynes Business Directory, 1995–96* (Newport Pagnell: Commerce Public, 1995).

Commission for New Towns, *Milton Keynes: 2001 Official City Atlas* (Reading: GEOProjects, 2001).

Cook, Caroline and Sarre, Mary, for the Youth Information Service, *Young People's Housing: A Study of Housing for Young People in the Borough of Milton Keynes* (Milton Keynes: Youth Information Service, 1992).

Cook, Robert, *Britain in Old Photographs: Milton Keynes* (Stroud: Sutton, 1995).

Cook, Robert, and Shouler, Andrew, *Milton Keynes in the News* (Stroud: Sutton Publishing, 2001).

Cooper, Richard, 'Blair set for city TV debate', *Milton Keynes Sunday Citizen*, 13 May 2001.

Cox, Simon, 'Changing concepts and attitudes to the provision of leisure in a new town' (London: Ealing College of Higher Education, BA (Hons) Humanities unpublished dissertation, not dated).

Crossman, Richard, *The Diaries of a Cabinet Minister*, vol. 1, *Minister of Housing, 1964–1966* (London: Hamish Hamilton and Jonathan Cape, 1975).

Cunningham, Sandy, 'From soap suds to soap box', *Architectural Design*, XLV (1975).

Davies, Hunter, *London to Loweswater: A Journey through England at the End of the Twentieth Century* (Edinburgh: Mainstream Publishing, 1999).

Deakin, Nicholas and Ungerson, Claire, *Leaving London: Planned Mobility and the Inner City* (London: Heinemann, 1977).

Deem, Rosemary, *All Work and No Play: The Sociology of Women and Leisure* (Milton Keynes: Open University Press, 1986).

Dennis, Norman, 'The popularity of the neighbourhood community idea', in R. E. Pahl, *Readings in Urban Sociology* (Oxford: Pergamon Press, 1968).

Detorakis, Theocaris E., *History of Crete* (Heraklion, Crete: Geronymaki, 1994).

Donnison, D. V., *The Government of Housing* (Harmondsworth: Penguin, 1967).

Durant, Ruth, *Watling: A Survey of Social Life on a New Housing Estate* (London: P. S. King, 1939).

Ellen, Barbara, 'Dire Rea', *Observer*, 1 February 1998.

Enever, Ted, *Britain's Best Kept Secret: Ultra's Base at Bletchley Park* (Trowbridge, Wiltshire: Sutton Publishing, 1999).

Evans, Dave, 'Survey reveals massive demand for new GP', *Milton Keynes Herald*, 20 February 1987.

Financial Times Regional Report, 'Milton Keynes', *Financial Times*, 21 October 1985.

Finnegan, Ruth, *The Hidden Musicians: Music Making in an English Town* (Cambridge: Cambridge University Press, 1989).

Finnegan, Ruth, *Tales of the City: A Study of Narrative and Urban Life* (Cambridge: Cambridge University Press, 1999).

Firnberg, David and West, David, 'Milton Keynes: creating an information technology environment', in William H. Dutton, J. G. Blumler and K. L. Kraemer (eds), *Wired Cities: Shaping the Future of Communications* (London: Cassell, 1997).

Fisk, Eugene, *People in their Place* (Milton Keynes: People's Press, 1985).

Fletcher, Ronald, *The Family and Marriage in Modern Britain* (Harmondsworth: Penguin, 1974).

Ford Foundation, New York, grant number 6700083, Centre of Environmental Studies: *Memorandum by the Minister of Housing and Local Government; Centre for Environmental Studies*.

Ford Foundation, New York, grant number 6700083: Memo from F. Champion Ward via Joseph Daniel to McGeorge Bundy, *Grant Request, International Affairs*, 14 July 1966.

Frame, Pete, *Rockin' Around Britain* (London: Omnibus, 1999), p. 14.

Francis, Alan, *Access to Housing in Milton Keynes* (Milton Keynes: Milton Keynes Forum Paper No. 11, 1990).

Francis, Alan, Milton Keynes Green Party, letter, *Milton Keynes Gazette*, 21 January 1993.

French, J., 'Wolverton: a magnet for migrants 1837–1861', *Records of Buckinghamshire*, 28 (1986).

Gans, Herbert J., 'Planning for people, not buildings', *Environment and Planning*, 1 (1969).

Garreau, Joel, *Edge City: Life on the New Frontier* (New York: Doubleday, 1992).

Giles, A. K., 'The impact of urban development on agriculture: a case study of Milton Keynes', in Ray Thomas, (ed.), *Perspectives on New Towns Development: Proceedings of a Conference Organised by the New Towns Study Unit, and the Regional Studies Association at Walton Hall, 15 November 1975* (Milton Keynes: New Towns Study Unit, Open University, 1976).

Gillilan, Lesley, 'Brave new town', *Observer Magazine*, 2 July 2000.

Glancey, Jonathan, 'It's got plenty of roads. Now it's on the map', *Guardian*, 4 October 1999.

Gould, Simon James, 'The evolution of the public realm in Milton Keynes: from a decentralised to a centralised urbanism' (Cambridge: unpublished dissertation for the Diploma in Architecture, Cambridge University, 2002).

Gray, Anne, *Social Exclusion: Inclusive New Town–North West Metropolitan Area* (http://www.forum.sozialarbeit.de/europa/2000-01de.shtml).

Grieco, M. S., 'Corby: new town planning and imbalanced development', *Regional Studies*, 19, 1 (1985).

Groom, Brian, 'Suburbs face population boom', *Financial Times*, 5–6 December 1998.

Guardian leader, 'The new Keynes', *Guardian*, 24 February 1999.

Gwilliam, Michael, Bourne, Caroline, Swain, Corinne and Prat, Anna, *Sustainable Renewal of Suburban Areas* (York: Joseph Rowntree Foundation, 1998).

Hall, Peter, *Sustainable Cities or Town Cramming?* (London: Town and Country Planning Association, 1999).

Hall, Peter and Ward, Colin, *Sociable Cities: The Legacy of Ebenezer Howard* (Chichester: John Wiley, 1998).

Hamnett, Chris, 'Consumption and class in contemporary Britain', in Chris Hamnett, Linda McDowell and Philip Sarre (eds), *The Changing Social Structure* (London: Sage, 1993).

Hardman, Robert, 'How the "truly classless society" of Milton Keynes learned to love life in themed grid squares', *Daily Telegraph*, 20 January 1992.

Hardwick, Viv, 'Rooftop prowler target for Beanhill vigilantes', *Milton Keynes Gazette*, 5 December 1975.

Hardwick, Viv, 'Why no outpatients' department?', *Milton Keynes Gazette*, 20 June 1980.

Harris, Robert, *Enigma* (London: Hutchinson, 1995).

Hedges, Alan for MKDC, *Report on Research into Shopping Attractions* (Milton Keynes: MKDC, 1976).

Heraud, B. J., 'The new towns and London's housing problem', *Urban Studies*, 3, 1 (1966).

Heraud, B. J., 'Social class and the new towns', *Urban Studies*, 5, 1 (1968).

Hetherington, Peter, 'Town votes for 10 per cent rise in council tax to avoid cut in services', *Guardian*, 24 February 1999.

Hill, Marion (ed.), *Bigger, Brighter, Better: The Story of Bletchley 1944–1966, As Told by its Residents* (Milton Keynes: Living Archive Project, 1996).

Hirst, Paul, 'Miracle or mirage? The Thatcher years', in Nick Tiratsoo (ed.), *From Blitz to Blair: A New History of Britain Since 1939* (London: Weidenfeld & Nicolson, 1997).

Hoggart, Simon, 'Forever England', *Observer Magazine*, 10 June 1990.

Homer, Andrew, 'Administration and social change in the postwar British new towns: a case study of Stevenage and Hemel Hempstead' (Luton: University of Luton, unpublished Ph.D. thesis, 1999).

Hyde, Francis E., 'The growth of a town, part 2: a study of the economic forces controlling the growth of Stony Stratford, Buckinghamshire', *Town Planning Review*, 20, 3 (1949).

Jarvis, Nicola, 'Estate mums bid to improve safety', *Milton Keynes Gazette*, 13 November 1981.

Johnstone, Helen, 'Villagers fear being engulfed as Milton Keynes expands', *The Times*, 8 March 2000.

Kahn, Alfred J., 'The social planner and the city: the task in perspective', in Alfred J. Kahn, *Studies in Social Policy and Planning* (New York: Russell Sage, 1969).

Kahn, Alfred J., *Theory and Practice of Social Planning* (New York: Russell Sage, 1969).

Kelly, John R., *Leisure Identities and Interactions* (London: George Allen & Unwin, 1983), pp. 16–17.

King, Anthony D., 'Reworlding the city', *Planning History*, 22, 3 (2000).

Kitchen, Roger, 'Moving to Milton Keynes', *New Society*, 22 August 1974.

Kitchen, Roger, 'Community newspapers', *Architectural Design*, XLV (1975), p. 762.

Kitchen, Roger, 'The silent majority speaks', *Architectural Design*, XLV (1975).

Kitchen, Roger, 'Doing a Moonlight' (Milton Keynes: Living Archive Project, 1975, Unpublished manuscript).

Krier, Leon, *Houses, Palaces, Cities* (London: Architectural Design Editions, 1984).

Larner, Steve and Hammond, Nick, 'D-Ream comes true', *Milton Keynes Citizen*, 8 May 1997.

Lawless, Paul, *Britain's Inner Cities: Problems and Policies* (London: Harper and Row, 1981).

Lewis, Clive, '9.8%: Voters back council over tax increase', *Milton Keynes Citizen*, 25 February 1999.

Liddiard, Penny, *Milton Keynes Felt Needs Project: A Preliminary Study of the Felt Needs of People Living in Relative Poverty on a Milton Keynes Housing Estate* (Milton Keynes: Department of Health and Social Welfare, Open University, 1988).

Lister, David, 'Labour peer Rogers sets out his vision for an urban revolution', *Independent*, 21 May 1997.

Lister, David, 'Milton Keynes is one sexy city, say Gilbert and George', *Independent*, 23 June 1999

Living Archive Project (Wolverton, Milton Keynes), selected tapes.

Llewelyn-Davies, Lord, *Centre for Environmental Studies: A Programme of Work for the Centre, Note by the Chairman for Discussion by the Governors* (New York: Ford Foundation, grant number 6700083, 1966).

Llewelyn-Davies, Richard, 'Town design', *Town Planning Review*, 37, 3 (1966).

Llewelyn-Davies, Weeks, Forestier-Walker and Bor, *Milton Keynes Plan: Interim Report to the MKDC* (London: Llewelyn-Davies *et al.*, 1968), Foreword by Lord Campbell.

Lock, David, 'Greentown: David Lock's papers', held at the City Discovery Centre, Bradwell Abbey, Milton Keynes.

Lock, David, 'Milton Keynes, new towns, and the British spirit', *Town and Country Planning*, April 1992.

Lock, David, testimony in Mark Clapson, Mervyn Dobbin and Peter Waterman (eds), *The Best Laid Plans: Milton Keynes since 1967* (Luton: Luton University Press, 1998).

Lott, Tim, Interview, 5 January 2001, www.mychelsea.net/chelsea/arts-timlott.html.

Lott, Tim, *Rumours of a Hurricane* (London: Penguin, 2002).

Mactaggart, Rowan, 'Newcomers to Milton Keynes: getting their housing priorities right', *Architectural Design*, XLV (1975).

Markham, Sir Frank, *History of Milton Keynes and District*, vol. 2, *from 1800 to about 1950* (Luton: White Crescent Press, 1986).

Marling, Susan, *American Affair: The Americanisation of Britain* (London: Boxtree, 1993).

Mars, Tim, 'Little Los Angeles in Bucks', *Architects' Journal*, 15 April 1992.

Mars, Tim, 'Milton Keynes: a view from exile', in Mark Clapson, Mervyn Dobbin and Peter Waterman (eds), *The Best Laid Plans: Milton Keynes since 1967* (Luton: Luton University Press, 1998).

Mars, Tim, 'The life in new towns', in Anthony Barnett and Roger Scruton (eds), *Town and Country* (London: Jonathan Cape, 1998).

Marwick, Arthur, *British Society since 1945* (Harmondsworth: Penguin, 1987).

Mason, Tony, *Sport in Britain* (London: Faber & Faber, 1988).

McKenzie S. and Rose, D. 'Industrial change, the domestic economy and home life', in Jo Little, Linda Peake and Pat Richardson (eds), *Women in Cities: Gender and the Urban Environment* (London: Macmillan, 1988).

McKie, David, *A Sadly Mismanaged Affair* (London: Croom Helm, 1973).

Mee, Arthur, *Buckinghamshire: Country of the Chiltern Hills* (London: Hodder & Stoughton, 1947).

Middleton, Dave and Palmer, Stewart, *Blacks Need Not Apply: A Report into the Problems of Unemployment among Ethnic Minorities* (Milton Keynes: Campaign Against Poverty, 1985).

Mills, A. D., *Oxford Dictionary of English Place Names* (Oxford: Oxford University Press, 1998).

Milton Keynes Borough Council, *Household Survey, 1990* (Milton Keynes: MKBC, 1990).

Milton Keynes Borough Council, Directorate of Housing Services, *Putting Progress into Practice: Housing Investment Programme 1992–94, Strategy Statement August, 1991* (Milton Keynes: MKBC, 1991).

Milton Keynes Borough Council, *People and Housing in Milton Keynes: A Profile of Settlements from the 1991 Census* (Milton Keynes: MKBC, 1993).

Milton Keynes Borough Council, *People and Housing in Milton Keynes: A Profile of Settlements from the 1991 Census, 10% Sample* (Milton Keynes: MKBC, 1993).

Milton Keynes Borough Council, *People and Work in Milton Keynes: A Profile of Settlements from the 1991 Census* (Milton Keynes: Milton Keynes Borough Council and the Commission for New Towns, 1993).

Milton Keynes Borough Council, *People and Work in Milton Keynes: A Profile of Settlements from the 1991 Census; 10% Sample, Part 2* (Milton Keynes: MKBC, 1993).

Milton Keynes Borough Council, *Partnerships with People: Housing Investment Programme Strategy Statement for 1993–94* (Milton Keynes: MKBC, 1994).

Milton Keynes Council, *Facts and Figures, 1999–2000* (Milton Keynes: Milton Keynes Council, 1999).

Milton Keynes Council, *Population Bulletin, 2000/2001* (Milton Keynes: Milton Keynes Council, 2000).

Milton Keynes Council, *Geographical Information Services, information dated 'Stock at 31/12/2001'*.

Milton Keynes Development Corporation, *Second Annual Report*: *Parliamentary Papers* 1968–69, Vol. 43.

Milton Keynes Development Corporation, *Northern Towns Study: Commercial Survey* (Milton Keynes: MKDC, 1970).

Milton Keynes Development Corporation, *Recreation: Recreation Plan for Milton Keynes* (Milton Keynes: MKDC, 1970).

Milton Keynes Development Corporation, *The Plan for Milton Keynes* (2 vols) (Milton Keynes: MKDC, 1970).

Milton Keynes Development Corporation, *The Plan for Milton Keynes: Technical Supplement No. 2: Household Survey* (Milton Keynes: MKDC, 1970).

Milton Keynes Development Corporation, *The Plan for Milton Keynes: Technical Supplement No. 3: Public Reaction to the Interim Plan* (Milton Keynes: MKDC, 1970).

Milton Keynes Development Corporation, *The Plan for Milton Keynes: Technical Supplement No. 4: Notes on Monitoring and Evaluation* (Milton Keynes: MKDC, 1970)

Milton Keynes Development Corporation, *Four Years On: The Milton Keynes Household Survey, 1973, Summary Report* (Milton Keynes: MKDC, 1974).

Milton Keynes Development Corporation, *New City, Milton Keynes* (Milton Keynes: MKDC, 1974).

Milton Keynes Development Corporation, *New City: Milton Keynes* (Milton Keynes: MKDC, 1975).

Milton Keynes Development Corporation, *Residential Design Feedback: Report of Studies* (Milton Keynes: MKDC, 1975).

Milton Keynes Development Corporation, *Milton Keynes Household Survey, 1976: Seven Years On, Technical Report 2* (Milton Keynes: MKDC, 1977).

Milton Keynes Development Corporation, *Milton Keynes*

Household Survey, 1976: Seven Years On, Technical Report 3: Employment (Milton Keynes: MKDC, 1977).

Milton Keynes Development Corporation, *Milton Keynes Seven Years On: The Summary Report of the 1976 Household and Employers' Surveys* (Milton Keynes: MKDC, 1977).

Milton Keynes Development Corporation, *Theatre Audience Survey: Woughton Centre Theatre, 21–23 February, 1980* (Milton Keynes: MKDC, 1980).

Milton Keynes Development Corporation, *Milton Keynes Household Survey, 1983: Demographic Report* (Milton Keynes: MKDC, 1984).

Milton Keynes Development Corporation, *Employers' Survey Report, 1987* (Milton Keynes: MKDC, 1987).

Milton Keynes Development Corporation, *Milton Keynes* (Milton Keynes: MKDC, 1988).

Milton Keynes Development Corporation, *Milton Keynes Household Survey, 1988: Demography Technical Report* (Milton Keynes: MKDC, 1989).

Milton Keynes Development Corporation, *Milton Keynes Household Survey, 1988: Employment Technical Report* (Milton Keynes: MKDC, 1989).

Milton Keynes Development Corporation, *Milton Keynes Household Survey, 1988: Food and Grocery Shopping Technical Report* (Milton Keynes: MKDC, 1989).

Milton Keynes Development Corporation, *Milton Keynes Household Survey, 1988: Leisure and Recreation Technical Report* (Milton Keynes: MKDC, 1989).

Milton Keynes Development Corporation, *Milton Keynes Insight* (Milton Keynes: MKDC, March 1989).

Milton Keynes Development Corporation, *Employer's Survey Report, 1990* (Milton Keynes: MKDC, 1990).

Milton Keynes Development Corporation, *Milton Keynes Employment Survey, 1990* (Milton Keynes: MKDC, 1990).

Milton Keynes Development Corporation, *Walnut Tree Neighbourhood Review, July through December, 1990: A Report on the Community Development Programme Undertaken by MKDC between 1987 and 1990* (Milton Keynes: MKDC, 1990).

Milton Keynes Development Corporation, *What's the Secret of Success in Milton Keynes?* (Milton Keynes: MKDC, not dated, *c.* 1990).

Milton Keynes Development Corporation, *Milton Keynes Population Bulletin, 1991* (Milton Keynes: MKDC and Chesterton Consulting, 1991).

Milton Keynes Development Corporation, *Milton Keynes Planning Manual* (Milton Keynes: MKDC, 1992).

Milton Keynes Development Corporation and Social and Community Planning Research, *Four Years On: The Milton Keynes Household Survey* (Milton Keynes: MKDC, 1974).

Milton Keynes Economic Partnership, *1998 Employment Survey* (Milton Keynes: Milton Keynes Economic Partnership, 1998).

Milton Keynes Economic Partnership, *Milton Keynes Insight*, 20 (2001).

Milton Keynes Gazette, 30 March 1984, 'Our hospital', a 12-page special.

Milton Keynes Urban Studies Centre, *Notes on Milton Keynes* (Milton Keynes: MKUSC, 1981).

Ministry of Housing and Local Government, *South East Study, 1964–1981* (London: HMSO, 1964)

Ministry of Housing and Local Government, *Northampton, Bedford and North Bucks Study: An Assessment of Inter-related Growth* (London: HMSO, 1965).

Ministry of Housing and Local Government, *The Needs of New Communities: A Report of Social Provision in New and Expanding Towns* (London: HMSO, 1967).

Morrison, Blake, 'How the other half lives', *Independent on Sunday Magazine*, 15 June 1997.

Mortimer, Pat, 'Urbanisation in North Buckinghamshire, 1930–1970' (Milton Keynes: unpublished M.Phil., Open University, 1986).

Mosscrop, Stuart, 'Making sense of the centre', *Architectural Design Profile 111: New Towns* (London: Architectural Design, 1994).

Mumford, Lewis, *The City in History* (Harmondsworth: Penguin, 1979).

Murrer, Sally, 'Residents rally to save "heartbeat" of Beanhill', *Milton Keynes Gazette*, 7 January 1993.

Nairn, Ian, 'The best in Britain', *Observer Weekend Review*, 22 November 1964.

National Farmers Union, *Annual Report, 1968* (London: NFU, 1968).

Nevin, Charles, 'Myth and Milton Keynes', *Guardian*, 29–30 July 1989.

Newby, Howard, *Green and Pleasant Land? Social Change in Rural England* (London: Hutchinson, 1985).

Nicholson, J. H., *New Communities in Britain: Achievements and Problems* (London: National Council of Social Service, 1961).

Nuttall, Nick, 'Prescott bids to cut urban sprawl', *The Times*, 8 March 2000.

O'Neill, Corinna, 'Three year plan to raise local roofs', *Milton Keynes Citizen*, 26 May 1988.

Owens, Ruth, 'The great experiment', *Architects' Journal*, 15 April 1992.

People's Press, The, *This Place Has its Ups and Downs, or Kids Could Have Done it Better etc.* (Milton Keynes: People's Press, 1977).

Pevsner, Professor Sir Nikolaus, *The Plan for Milton Keynes: Technical Supplement No. 8: Preservanda and Conservanda in Milton Keynes* (Milton Keynes: MKDC, 1970).

Pevsner, Nikolaus and Williamson, Elizabeth, *The Buildings of England: Buckinghamshire* (Harmondsworth: Penguin, 1994).

Planning Exchange, The, *The New Towns Record*: 'Residents Questionnaires: Milton Keynes' (Glasgow: The Planning Exchange, CD Rom, 1996).

Political and Economic Planning, 'Watling revisited', *Planning*, 14, 270 (1947).

Pooley, Fred, 'Buckinghamshire new city', *Ekistics*, 19, 114 (1965).

Pooley, Fred, *North Bucks North City* (Aylesbury: Departments of Architecture and Planning, Buckinghamshire County Council, 1966).

Priestley, J. B., *English Journey* (London: Heinemann, 1934).

Radio Times, 30 September 1965, 7 October 1965, 14 October 1965.

Rahman, Mrs Ferdous, *The Bangladeshi Community in Milton Keynes* (Milton Keynes: Milton Keynes Language Scheme, 1982).

Rasmussen, Steen Eiler, 'Reflections on Milton Keynes', in Derek Walker, (ed.), *Architectural Design Profile No. 111: New Towns* (London: Architectural Design, 1994).

Reisman, David, *The Lonely Crowd: A Study of the Changing American Character* (New Haven, CT and London: Yale University Press, 1950).

Richmond, Tom, 'Why in our back yard?', *Milton Keynes Citizen*, 15 April 1993

Richmond, Tom, 'Union city blues', *Citizen*, 9 September 1993.

Roberts, Elizabeth, *Women and Families: An Oral History, 1940–1970* (Oxford: Blackwell, 1995).

Robinson, Andrew, *The Man Who Deciphered Linear B* (London: Thames and Hudson, 2002).

Rogers, Richard, 'Save our cities', *Observer*, 13 February 2000.

Rogers, Richard and Burdett, Richard, 'Let's cram more into the city', *New Statesman*, 22 May 2000.

Rogers, Richard and Burdett, Richard, 'Let's cram more into the city', in Marcial Echenique and Andrew Saint (eds), *Cities for the New Millennium* (London: Spon, 2001).

Ross, George, *Basildon 1915–1986: From Country Life to the Brink of Despair: When the Bulldozers Take Over* (Basildon: George Ross, 1986).

Roy, Alexander, *The Impact of Japanese Investment on the New Town of Milton Keynes* (London: South Bank University Best Masters Dissertation in International Business, published by dissertation.com, 1998).

Rugoff, Ralph, 'Inside the virtual city', *The Business, Financial Times Weekend Magazine*, 22 January 2000.

Sainsbury, P. and Collins, Joyce, 'Some factors relating to mental illness in a new town', *Journal of Psychosomatic Research*, 10, 1966.

Saint, Andrew, '"Spread the people": the LCC's dispersal policy', in Andrew Saint, (ed.), *Politics and the People of London: The London County Council, 1889–1965* (London: Hambledon, 1989).

Schaffer, Frank, *The New Town Story* (London: Paladin, 1972), pp. 39–52.

Scott, Elaine, 'Work starts on general hospital', *Milton Keynes Gazette*, 13 June 1980.

Seabrook, Jeremy, 'Milton Keynes: a mirror of England', *Observer Magazine*, 5 February 1978.

Sherlock, Harley, *Cities Are Good For Us* (London: Paladin, 1991).

Shipley, Robert and Gammon, Steven, 'The six planning goals of Milton Keynes: a third decade report card', *Planning History*, 24, 1 (2002).

Shostak, Lee, testimony, in Mark Clapson, Mervyn Dobbin and Peter Waterman (eds), *The Best Laid Plans: Milton Keynes since 1967* (Luton: Luton University Press, 1998).

Smith, Michael, *Station X: The Codebreakers of Bletchley Park* (London: Channel 4 Books, 1998).

Smyth, Gareth (ed.), *Can the Tories Lose? The Battle for the Marginals* (London: Lawrence & Wishart, 1991).

Stevenson, John, 'The Jerusalem that failed? The rebuilding of postwar Britain', in Terence Gourvish and Alan O'Day (eds), *Britain since 1945* (London: Macmillan, 1991).

Story, Jack Trevor, *Dwarf Goes to Oxford* (Milton Keynes: Leveret Press, 1987).

Sudjic, Deyan, *The Hundred Mile City* (London: Andre Deutsch, 1992).

Thomas, Ray, 'Impressions from Milton Keynes', *Town and Country Planning*, 40, 1 (1972).

Thomas, Ray and Cresswell, Peter, *The New Town Idea* (Milton Keynes: Open University Press: DT201, Urban development unit 26, 1973).

Thompson, Damien, 'Churches unite to provide a central soul', *Daily Telegraph*, 23 January 1992.

Thorns, David C., *Fragmenting Societies: A Comparative Analysis of Regional and Urban Development* (London: Routledge, 1992).

Turner, Jane and Jardine, Bob, *Pioneer Tales: A New Life in Milton Keynes* (Milton Keynes: People's Press, 1985).

Underhill, William, 'A monument to approval by Japanese investors', *Daily Telegraph*, 23 January 1992.

Underhill, William, 'No place like it for Eastern promise', *Daily Telegraph*, 23 January 1992.

University of Reading, Department of Agricultural Economics and Management, *Milton Keynes 1967: An Agricultural Inventory* (Reading: University of Reading, 1968).

University of Reading, Department of Agricultural Economics and Management, *Milton Keynes Revisited* (Reading: University of Reading, 1972).

University of Reading, Department of Agricultural Economics and Management, *Milton Keynes Revisited: 1971* (Reading: University of Reading, miscellaneous study, no. 51, 1972).

University of Reading, Department of Agricultural Economics and Management, *Milton Keynes 1973: Case Studies in a Dwindling Agriculture* (Reading: University of Reading, miscellaneous study no. 57, 1974).

University of Reading, Department of Agricultural Economics and Management, *Milton Keynes 1967–1985: The Farming Story* (Reading: University of Reading, miscellaneous study no. 73, 1985).

Urban Task Force, *Towards an Urban Renaissance* (London: Spon, 1998).

Walker, Derek, *The Architecture and Planning of Milton Keynes* (London: Architectural Press, 1982).

Walker, Derek, 'Industrial and commercial buildings', *Architectural Design Profile 111: New Towns* (London: Architectural Design, 1994).

Walker, Derek, 'Introduction', *Architectural Design Profile 111: New Towns* (London: Architectural Design, 1994).

Walker, Derek, 'Unbuilt Milton Keynes', *Architectural Design Profile 111: New Towns* (London: Architectural Design, 1994).

Walshaw, Debbie, 'Residents warm to flat roof victory', *Milton Keynes Mirror*, 26 May, 1988.

Ward, Colin, *New Town, Home Town* (London: Caloutse Gulbenkian Foundation, 1993).

Waterman, Peter, 'Social development in action', in Mark Clapson, Mervyn Dobbin and Peter Waterman (eds), *The Best Laid Plans: Milton Keynes since 1967* (Luton: Luton University Press, 1998).

Webber, Melvin M., 'Planning in an environment of change, part 1: beyond the industrial age', *Town Planning Review*, 39 (1968–69).

Webber, Melvin M., 'Order in diversity: community without propinquity', in Lowdon Wingo (ed.), *Cities and Space: The Future Use of Urban Land* (Baltimore, MD: Johns Hopkins University Press, 1970).

Webber, Melvin M., 'The post-city age', in Larry S. Bourne (ed.), *Internal Structure of the City: Readings on Space and Environment* (New York: Oxford University Press, 1971).

White, David, 'What's so bad about Milton Keynes?', *New Society*, 17 April 1988.

Whitehand, J. W. R. and Carr, C. M. H., *Twentieth Century Suburbs: A Morphological Approach* (London: Routledge, 2001).

Williams, Katie, 'The wrong starting point', *Town and Country Planning*, September 1999.

Willmott, Peter, 'Housing density and town design in a new town: a pilot study at Stevenage', *Town Planning Review*, 33, 2 (1962).

Wilson, Roger, *Difficult Housing Estates* (London: Tavistock, 1963).

Wofle, Ivor de with Nairn, Ian, *Civilia: The End of Sub Urban Man* (London: Architectural Press, 1971).

Young, David, 'Urban revolution in full bloom after 25 years of growth', *The Times*, 26 April 1991.

Young, John, 'In the vanguard of social progress', *The Times*, 11 October 1996.

Young, Michael and Willmott, Peter, *Family and Kinship in East London* (London: Routledge & Kegan Paul, 1957).

Index